Mr. George P. Kendall
9019 Second St.
Mill Creek Manor
Levittown, Pa.
W164263
Hands off

Mr. George P. Kendall

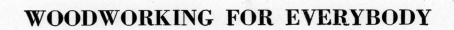

WOODWORKING FOR EVERYBODY

WOODWORKING

FOR

EVERYBODY

By JOHN GERALD SHEA
Author, Editor, and Designer

and PAUL NOLT WENGER, Ed.D.
*Chairman, Department of Industrial Arts
and Vocational Education,
Teachers College of Connecticut,
New Britain, Connecticut*

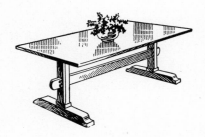

INTERNATIONAL TEXTBOOK COMPANY

Scranton   *Pennsylvania*

FIRST SCHOOL EDITION

First printing, September, 1944
Second printing, January, 1945
Third printing, August, 1945
Fourth printing, June, 1946
Fifth printing, July, 1947
Sixth printing, June, 1948
Seventh printing, July, 1949
Eighth printing, December, 1949

FIRST TRADE EDITION

First printing, August, 1945
Second printing, June, 1946
Third printing, July, 1947
Fourth printing, December, 1949

Total issue, 28,500

THE HADDON CRAFTSMEN, INC., SCRANTON, PENNSYLVANIA

FOREWORD

ANYONE who has watched a carpenter at work, shaping and fitting boards together, has undoubtedly been fascinated by the things he saw. The good, clean smell of fresh lumber and the skill of the craftsman in his use of saws, chisels, and planes is something which is bound to hold the interest and admiration of the average person.

Only those who have used woodworking tools and who have experienced the pleasure of making things out of wood, can fully describe the joys of woodworking. This holds true of both those who follow woodworking as a pleasant hobby, or as a means of livelihood.

Moreover, the urge to participate in this activity is not restricted to any particular age, group or gender. The child who has reached the toddling stage is eager to hold and use a hammer and saw—and the resultant destruction may be considerable! But, from infancy on, the desire to use tools continues. The little boy and the little girl progress year by year and their ability to make things with tools generally increases as they go along.

Nor does this urge and desire to build things diminish as the youngsters develop into adults. On the contrary, woodworking as a profitable adult hobby has developed to vast proportions. The professional man, the tradesman, the retired business man—and woman as well—have turned to this hobby for relaxation, for profit, and for pleasure.

This wide general interest in woodworking caused the compilation of this book. Herein is presented an informal, non-technical approach to the subject. It endeavors to explain the background, technique, and general practice of woodworking in terms understandable to both the student and interested layman. It was designed to serve all those who are interested in the subject and who desire a practical text and guide.

In preparing the manuscript, attention was focused on the particular needs of adult woodworking hobbyists, home craftsmen, and the average householder who is interested in woodworking from a practical standpoint. Wouldn't a book such as this be useful to each of these classifications? It seemed that it would.

Basic information regarding tools, techniques, and general practices of woodworking, as explained in this book, is of universal importance regardless of the particular group by whom this information is considered. Obviously, the book could not undertake to explain any special way in which any special group of students or laymen should proceed with the common practices of woodworking. However, the text does most definitely strive to take into full sympathetic consideration the student's and inexperienced layman's point of view regarding the subject.

WOODWORKING FOR EVERYBODY is not offered as a step-by-step sort of book. It is not necessary to read and understand page 12 before turning to page 77. But it will be found that a certain chapter or a certain page contains full information regarding the job in woodworking which you wish to perform. It will likewise be found that the various elements of woodworking practices are treated in natural sequence.

You will find that there is a best way to drive a nail, to use a saw, to handle a chisel, to plane a board, and to use the many other tools. Skill with tools increases with experiences and study of their uses. The book may be used freely for reference by the woodworking hobbyist, and the general reader, who may turn to these pages for the specific woodworking information which they desire to obtain.

It is the sincere hope and desire of those who prepared this book that all who use it may be successfully served.

John G. Shea
Paul N. Wenger

Greenwich, Connecticut

In acknowledgment, the authors wish to thank Captain John A. Bogart, the talented young man who completed his illustration assignment on this book just prior to enlistment in the Army Air Force. As a civilian artist, Captain Bogart brought a degree of talent and enthusiasm to his work prophetic of the many splendid citations which later distinguished his record as a combat officer. Miss May F. Shea, sister of one of the authors, assisted from the beginning in handling involved secretarial details, editing and indexing.

For photographs used in WOODWORKING FOR EVERYBODY special acknowledgment is made to the United States Forest Service, the American Walnut Manufacturers Association, the Southern Pine Association, the E. L. Bruce Company, the Insular Lumber Company, the Harbor Plywood Corporation, the E. I. DuPont De Nemours and Company, and the Nicholson File Company.

For making available illustrations and working drawings of designs by John G. Shea which previously appeared in their magazines, the authors wish to thank the editors of *House Beautiful, The Home Craftsman, Popular Homecraft, Popular Mechanics,* and *Woman's Home Companion.*

The following companies were most generous and cooperative in providing illustrations and information: Henry Disston and Sons, Incorporated, North Brothers Manufacturing Company, Progressive Manufacturing Company, Delta Manufacturing Company, Walker Turner Company, Irwin Augur Bit Company, Stanley Tools, Adjustable Clamp Company, L. S. Starrett Company, Millers Falls Company, the Cincinnati Tool Company, the De Walt Saw Company, and Brodhead Garrett Company.

CONTENTS

PROJECTS

THE STORY OF WOOD

Explanation of Illustrations

1 White pine forest. The healthy growth of well-spaced timber indicates the advantages of forest management. *Photo by U. S. Forest Service.*

2 Felling a large fir tree. These large trees as well as the giant redwoods, grow abundantly in the State of Washington. *Photo by U. S. Forest Service.*

3 Stacking enormous piles of pulpwood with a mechanical stacker. Later this pulpwood will be used in the manufacture of paper and other products. *Photo by U. S. Forest Service.*

4 Philippine mahogany stacked for air seasoning. Huge quantities of this lumber are used annually in the United States. *Courtesy, Insular Lumber Company.*

5 White pine logs in pond prior to delivery to sawmill. It is estimated that the pond contains thirty-five million board feet of white pine. *Photo by U. S. Forest Service.*

6 Cellophane, in its final stage of manufacture, being wrapped in huge rolls. It hardly seems possible that pulpwood forms the chief ingredient of this glistening, transparent material. *Courtesy, E. I. DuPont De Nemours and Company.*

7 Sawing synthetic sponge to convenient size. Wood pulp, chemically treated, is the chief ingredient of this modern, man-made sponge. *Courtesy, E. I. DuPont De Nemours and Company.*

8 This remarkable photograph shows for the first time the *actual* chemical transformation of viscose liquid into a rayon thread. The blur in the photograph indicates the change of the liquid into cellulose filaments, which, of course, cannot be seen by the naked eye.

THE STORY OF WOOD

1

2

3

4

5

6

7

8

WHEN making things of wood it is a very good idea to know something about wood itself. We all know that wood comes from trees and that trees grow mostly in forests. We also know that lumberjacks cut down the trees, which, in the form of logs, are transported to lumber mills where they are cut into timbers, planks and boards. But what do we know about the trees themselves? Did the great forests with which we are familiar always exist?

Men who make science their profession tell us that they did not. According to them, the first living things that appeared in the world were plants. Certain types of mosses and ferns existed before anything else.

Museums of natural history contain pieces of rock and anthracite taken from coal mines and pits, thousands of feet below the surface of the earth, which bear imprints of ancient club mosses and other fern-like plants. These specimens seem to offer sufficient proof that mosses and ferns lived before trees.

We are all familiar with types of trees called "conifers." Pines and spruces belong to the conifer family. Dwarfed cone-bearing trees, the ancestors of our conifers, were believed to be the first types of tree life to appear upon the earth. When people talk about the world as it was millions of years ago, they often call that period the "Age of Conifers."

Wood was used to make articles of utility long before man knew how to use any other materials. We have all heard of the "Stone Age," the "Brass Age," and the "Steel Age"; but the "Age of Wood" came first. Many kinds of wood are easy to work, and naturally the primitive people used the most easily worked materials. So, if you like to work with wood, you are just following a natural desire which was followed by your primitive ancestors millions of years ago.

Things to Know About Trees

You can obtain much useful information by studying trees. The tree is much like the human body. It is composed of many different parts and each part has its own important job. Like the human body, the tree can become ill; it can be wounded; it can die a natural death; or it can be killed outright.

Beneath the bark of the tree you find an interesting network of cells, annual rings, medullary rays, burls, and grains. All of these form parts of the life of the tree and each one contributes to its health, growth, and value.

Fingerprint experts tell us that of the two billion people living in the world, no two people have identical finger prints. The same is found to be true of sectional markings of trees. If you cut off a section through the trunk you will find that the inner markings of every tree are different. This condition accounts for the beautiful wood grain, always varied, which appears on the boards we use in making articles.

The cross-section of a tree trunk reveals at the center a small circular shaped section, known as the *pith*. As the tree grows, layers of *heartwood* develop around the pith, which, in turn, are surrounded by layers of *sapwood*.

Now, if you wish to become a student of trees, you will be interested in knowing that as far as the growth and life of the tree is concerned, both the pith and heartwood do not have any importance. But the *sapwood* which surrounds the heartwood does serve to carry food and moisture which sustains the growth of the tree. Year after year as the tree develops, adding a single ring each year to its circumference, the heartwood continues to increase in diameter. Young trees have no heartwood because the *growing sapwood* directly surrounds the pith center.

Between the bark and sapwood is found the *cambium layer*. This is the real life line of the tree. It is through the cambium layer that the growth actually takes place. The cells of this layer provide new sapwood on the *inside*, and on the *outside* increase the thickness of the bark.

The first American settlers knew how important the cambium layer was in the life of the tree. In clearing the forests for their farms, they simply *girdled* the standing timber, cutting a circle around the circumference of the trunk as deep as this life-giving layer. As a

A girdled tree.

Bottom left: A beautiful section of walnut grain. Each different wood has a special kind of grain. Certain sections of the tree are especially fine in the quality of their grain and surface features.

Section of a twenty-five year old tree.

result the foliage withered and the tree died. Consequently, the labor of clearing the land was greatly reduced.

Many precautions are taken by people who know trees to safeguard the cambium layer. Often where land has been filled adjoining old trees, the precaution is taken of building a retaining wall around the base of the tree so that the bark and the cambium layer will not become damaged by the fill. In the old days of horses and carriages, steel guards were placed around trees so that the hungry horse could not chew under the bark and thus damage the tree.

In studying the cross-section of a tree trunk, you will notice that there are a number of alternating light and dark rings. These markings are known as the "annual rings," and they are so called because one full ring is added to the circumference of the tree each year.

During the springtime when much moisture is present the cells are porous, soft in texture, light in color. As the season advances, and during the summer months, a narrow ring of dark and dense wood makes its appearance.

It is interesting to note that if the growth of the tree is checked in the middle of the sum-

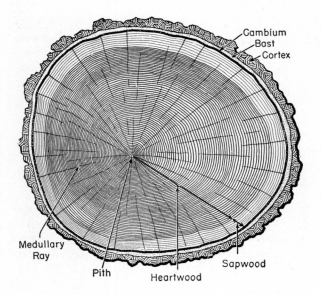

mer by unseasonably cold weather, severe drought, or caterpillar attacks, two small annual rings may be formed in a single season. These small, imperfect bands may be detected and you should add them as one in estimating the exact age of a tree.

Each annual ring, once it is completely formed, remains practically the same size and shape during the entire life of the tree. If a bullet were fired into the trunk of a tree it will remain lodged in a *specific annual ring,* at approximately the same distance from the center, and at the same height from the ground during the entire life of the tree.

Lumbermen tell about finding fragments of shells from ancient wars lodged in trees. These fragments remain entirely concealed within the

Below left: The burl: An abnormal growth on certain trees. It contains the beautiful grain so much sought after in the making of fine veneers.

Below right: Felling a large pine tree in the Lassen National Forest, California.

tree. Were it not for the discoloration of adjoining portions of wood, these odd bits of metal would provide an extremely dangerous hazard in later sawing operations, where large saws are used to slice the tree trunks into planks.

While discussing the structure of trees the *medullary rays* are of interest. These rays are small radial lines, or dense cells, which radiate in starfish fashion from the pith center to the cambium layer. They appear at right angles to the annual rings. Medullary rays show up most conspicuously on quarter-sawed, or quartered oak. On some other woods they are almost invisible.

Sometimes a cluster of buds remaining dormant, form beneath the bark of a tree, and develop into a protruding lump. This growth is known as a *burl*. Because of its exquisite grain burl wood is quite valuable.

Beautiful grain is likewise found in sections of the tree where limbs, branches, and trunks come together. It is at such places that the beautiful crotch wood is found. Here the wood fibers are very dense; which is nature's ingenious way of preventing the wood from splitting at the connection.

How Lumber is Made

The business of lumbering starts with the simple process of chopping down a tree. However, according to modern lumbering practice, this process is not quite as simple and straightforward as it may sound. In fact, the modern lumberjack must have a knowledge of quite a few subjects before he even goes out to start his work.

Everyone has heard of *forest conservation*. The lumberjack can tell you all about it; and before he walks out with his axe, there are many details regarding this subject that he intends to keep in mind. Unlike the Pilgrim Fathers who were privileged to go into the virgin forests, chopping at random and at will, and knowing that their most ambitious effort would hardly be noticeable because of the naturally abundant woodland, the modern lumberman must harvest and save his trees in much the same manner that a modern farmer harvests and saves his crops. Careless lumbering has destroyed countless acres of rich forest growth. But the lumberman has learned his lesson and now he goes about his job with far greater caution than he did in bygone years.

One of the first rules of lumbering is to cut down only the mature and fully grown trees. Care is taken to prevent damage to the smaller trees which must remain to replenish the forest.

Let us take the time to watch a lumberjack as he goes about his duties. After selecting a particular tree for felling, a deep "V" cut, or *undercut* as he calls it, is chopped on the side facing the direction in which the tree is to fall. Calling upon one of his companions to lend a hand with a large cross-cut saw, operations start on the side opposite the "V" cut. As the sawing progresses, wedges are driven into the saw cut, thereby preventing the blade from becoming bound or squeezed inside of the cut. Our lumberjack friend will tell us that these wedges

Logging in New Mexico. Down goes the tree!

also tend to tip the tree, thus causing it to fall in the right direction.

As the sawing nears completion and the trunk of the tree starts to shiver, the lumberjack voices loud shouts of "Timber!", and the tree crashes to the ground. It is then trimmed of all branches and sawed into regular log lengths. In due time these logs are transported to the lumber mill.

But this is only a very general description of how trees are felled. In preparing "spars" for lumbering operations, certain tall trees, notably the redwoods of California, must first be "topped" before they are cut down. In order to perform this extremely dangerous job, our courageous lumberjack must climb the tree to within a short distance of the top. In this hazardous position, held only by his climbing spurs and belt, the lumberjack proceeds to chop and saw off the top of the tree, working almost in mid-air. After the tree top has been "lopped," the trunk lurches back and forth, the lumberjack swinging with it, on his precarious perch. Is it any wonder that lumberjacks are often called "human flies"?

In northern sections of the United States and Canada the cutting of lumber generally takes place during the winter months. Lumber camps are located in the forest regions. It is here that our lumberjacks toil for long hours during the months of winter, felling trees in temperatures which often go far below the zero mark. Their work is paid for with plenty of good hot food, hot coffee, and relatively small wages.

How Logs Are Transported from Forest to Sawmill

Sometimes lumber is cut in forest regions which are near a river. In mid-winter the logs are carried or dragged by tractor, sledge, or specially built railway, to the river bank where they are held, waiting the spring thaw. They are then spilled into the river and floated with the current to the sawmill.

The process of floating the logs on the swiftly moving river current is indeed picturesque. Here we see the skill and daring of the lumberjack, with his companion the log driver, displayed in thrilling fashion. There is a great deal of danger lurking in the job of floating thousands of tree trunks on the flood current of a river.

The lumber rush begins during the early spring when the ice and snow of the timberland melts and adds its volume to the angry swirl of the swollen river. At the vital moment the logs are dumped into the water and areas of the river, filled from bank to bank with logs, become alive with this bobbing cargo, starting on its pell-mell journey to the sawmill. Then the lumberjacks, with a great deal of dexterity in their movements, rush back and forth over the logs swinging their peaveys (lumber picks) to prevent the possibility of log jams. A single error in judging the buoyancy of the logs or in picking an insecure footing may result in instant death.

Log jams are a constant menace. Frequently a single log becomes lodged on a shallow portion of the river bottom and snags the progress of all the timber following behind. Quick action is required because a log jam can become a serious thing. It may dam the entire river and cause floods over large areas. When a log jam occurs the lumberjacks must find the "king log." This is the single log which holds up the mass. If the king log cannot be moved with a peavey—a very dangerous undertaking—the jam must be dynamited.

Of course there are many different ways of floating logs on the river. In some sections they are chained together so as to form huge rafts. Such rafts are far more readily maneuvered than loosely floating logs. In some sections, notably in the South, the logs are chained and hauled by steamboat. Where water conditions permit, logs are floated all summer.

Top: Logs being loaded for transportation by horse-drawn vehicle. Note that the wagon has eight wheels.

Center: Logs being hauled by tractor. The usefulness of the tractor for this type of hauling is very great.

Bottom: Logs being loaded upon flat cars by use of derrick.

*Logs being loaded on flat cars by
use of derrick.*

*Railway ties (hewn in the forest)
ready to be floated down stream.*

*Floating logs being conveyed from pond
to sawmill.*

*Logs in pond adjacent to the mill. Note endless-belt action
of the conveyer.*

What Happens at the Sawmill

After the logs arrive at the sawmill they remain soaking for a while in a nearby mill pond. This is part of the seasoning process. It helps to prevent splitting or checking of the finished lumber. Afterwards they are picked up on a mechanical conveyer, a "jack ladder," as it is called, and carried inside of the mill where the sawing is performed.

The actual sawing of the logs into planks is a sight worth seeing. Huge single or double-edged band saws perform the job, the log being fed through the saw on a power-driven carriage. With the double-edged band saw it is possible to saw the log in both directions—both on the *forward* and *return* trip of the carriage.

Although these saws are gigantic in size, they may be adjusted to cut the logs into lumber of any specified thickness. There was a time when large circular saws were used but they have been replaced almost entirely by band saws, because the latter type is speedier and more economical.

There are, of course, many different ways of sawing a log. The two principal methods are known as *plain sawing* and *quarter sawing*. Plain sawed lumber is sliced from end to end along the length of the log.

Quarter sawing is the method whereby the log is first cut into four diamet-rical quarters. Each quarter is then sawed into planks at right angles to the annual rings of the wood and parallel to the medullary rays. Naturally a certain amount of wood is wasted through this method and there is also some sacrifices in the width of the boards. But quarter-sawed lumber, especially quarter-sawed oak, the grain of which is identified by the cross marking of medullary rays, is especially beautiful.

How Lumber is Cured, or Seasoned

After the planks have been sawed, they are stacked layer upon layer with spacers between the layers to permit ventilation and proper drainage for air seasoning. This first step in seasoning the lumber is quite important and the lumberman is extremely careful to see that every duty is properly performed. It would not do to have the rain collect in stagnant pools on the planks and so they are stacked on a

Above: Huge bandsaw—the type used for cutting planks—being sharpened. Sometimes these saws have teeth on both edges and are used to cut logs on both forward and return trip of the carriage.

Left: Walnut planks being cut by bandsaw. Note the heavy duty carriage which is used for accurate cutting.

An interesting scene, showing forest, stream, sawmill, and acres of stacked lumber. The photograph shows the Neils Brothers Mill, Libby, Montana.

Left: Lumber properly stacked for outdoor seasoning. Strips or spacers are placed between each layer to permit proper ventilation.

Above and left: Lumber stacked on conveyors, ready to be put into dry-kilns.

slope. A roof is often built over the stack for added protection against the elements. The process of air seasoning may be carried over a period of months, or years, depending on the thickness and kind of lumber.

Following the period of air seasoning, the lumber is again stacked with spacers between layers on carriages or cars for transfer to the dry-kilns.

We have all heard the term "kiln-dried lumber," but how many of us know exactly what it means? Let us consider this very important process in the treatment of lumber.

The dry-kiln is a large chamber similar to a tall and elongated garage. A batch of lumber is rolled into it on specially constructed carriages and the large sliding doors of the kiln are closed. Live steam is charged into the kiln, saturating the lumber uniformly with moisture. After a period of time the steam is turned off and the temperature inside the kiln is gradually increased. This process tends to bring about a slow and uniform drying action. With the temperature ranging from 140 to 160 degrees, the lumber remains in the kiln for several days, a week, or a month, until the moisture content drops to specified requirements. The lumber is then removed from the kiln.

The lumber is now ready to be placed in storage where a constant temperature and even ventilation is maintained. If it were not for both the seasoning and kiln-drying processes, lumber would warp, twist, shrink, and crack.

Lumbering is a Great World-Wide Industry

In the United States lumbering ranks third among the national industries. But we are by no means the only nation in the world wherein it figures prominently. Certain countries are noted for the lumber which they export. These exports form a large part of international trade.

Teakwood is exported from Siam to all parts of the world. While in the foregoing general methods of lumbering have been discussed, it is interesting to note that in Siam the elephant is still employed as a beast of burden in transporting the teakwood logs.

Japan and China provide a large part of the world's supply of bamboo. Heavy shipments of pine and fir come from Norway and Sweden. The West Indies, Central America, the Philippine Islands, and sections of Africa have long been famous for their mahogany exports.

Many of our extremely rare woods come from places which are themselves insignificant. Small and secluded islands and certain primitive inland regions are sometimes better known for the woods which they export than for anything else. It has been related that on the island of Cristobal, noted for its *lignum vitae*, a native coffee grinder was fueled with this expensive wood—firewood valued at approximately five dollars a stick in most countries! We import many of the rarer woods in bulk, that is, in log form. They are sawed into planks and veneers in our own lumber mills.

How We Save Our Forests

We hear a great deal about the scientific way of doing things. The scientific way is usually the best way, which is particularly true in regard to forestry. People cannot go out and chop down the timber in random fashion. If they did, it is quite possible that our great national forests would soon be destroyed. If, however, lumbering is performed in accordance with modern scientific practices there is little to be feared.

It is true that our old mature trees should be cut down. But the trained forester demands that the young and growing crop be allowed to remain in order to replenish the forest and to safeguard its life. In this way a fresh crop of timber is always available. Moreover, the proper cutting age of each tree may be scientifically determined, thus making it possible to harvest the trees when they have attained their most useful growth. The benefits of such practice become apparent when the tree is later cut into lumber. A better and more uniform quality of lumber is produced as a direct result.

Obviously, this practice also affects the set-up of lumber production. Mills and machinery may be arranged to handle logs which are cut to required specifications, thus eliminating much waste motion when the time comes to produce the actual lumber.

Forestry was not always conducted in this way. At one time our wooded sections were entirely cleared and as a result soil erosion set in, and the land became barren. It was discovered that the land needed its trees in order to remain fertile. Also, at the sources of large rivers and streams, forest areas help to absorb heavy seasonal rains, thus reducing the danger of flood.

In 1891, during the administration of President Harrison, Yellowstone Park Timberland Reserve was taken over by our National Government. This was the first of a series of steps to place forest areas under governmental management. Since that time there has been an increasing growth in the number of national forests. We now have nearly two million acres of protected timberland.

These protected areas are under the direct charge of the United States Forest Service of the Department of Agriculture. It is estimated that about one-fourth of our standing timber is thus protected. Indeed, we are very fortunate that our National Government has taken a hand in forest conservation. The value of the protected timberland will increase, and new areas being added will aid in reducing the danger of a lumber shortage. New growths are being developed scientifically with a view to bettering the quality of lumber and obtain a greater yield of desirable grades and sizes.

Top: The error of "clear cutting" timber. Note that the land has been cleared and no new growth is left to take the place of the original timber.

Center: The sensible way of cutting timber. The younger trees remain and will soon form a new growth of timber.

Bottom: Planting a forest. Photograph shows C. C. C. planting crew. Klamath National Forest, California.

Although several millions of dollars worth of good lumber is taken from these national forests each year, little harm is done because of the careful way in which lumbering is practised. Some of our finest and most stately trees are thus guaranteed lasting protection. Our oldest, largest, and most famous tree, affectionately known as "General Sherman" in the Sequoia National Park, California, is thus protected in its old age. This venerable giant, rising two hundred and eighty feet tall—*taller than the dome of our national capitol*—thirty-six and one-half feet in diameter, and approximately four thousand years old, is considered to be as live and healthy today as it ever was in the annals of our national history. Still another great tree, also under governmental protection, "Black Causeway," a gigantic redwood with a roadway leading through the center of its trunk, stands in stately and protected majesty within the precincts of one of our national parks.

We all realize the value of our forests as playgrounds and recreational areas. We know how important they are for the preservation of our wild life. We are also aware of their service in the prevention of soil erosion. All of these qualities provide additional reasons for us to be grateful that they are being protected from destruction.

What is a Town Forest?

A number of communities have their own "town forests." Millions of acres of woodland are now owned and controlled in this manner.

While the idea of town forests is somewhat new in this country, it has existed for centuries in certain parts of Europe. These forests serve as a good financial investment for the residents of the town which owns them. They provide a general community interest which in many instances rivals that of the other more commonly known town institutions.

Moreover, residents of the town are frequently permitted to help themselves to whatever cordwood or timber they need for home construction and household heating. The profits from this town enterprise are in some instances large enough to reduce or to eliminate entirely the burden of local taxation.

Some communities purchase barren land in the vicinity of their town limits and practice reforestation. Even when the purchase of a town forest is made solely for recreational purposes, the investment is worth while. Riding paths, ski trails, picnic areas, well-stocked trout streams, and the preservation of wild life, are among the possible advantages of such an enterprise.

Enemies of the Forest

The four chief destructive agents of forests and wood are: decay; the ravages of insects (termites and other wood pests); dry rot, attacks by rot producing fungi; and fire.

Of this list of destructive agents, decay is the most common. Trees are living things and as such they are sure to die. It is certain that they will eventually become decayed.

However, it is known that wood which is kept either *permanently wet* or *permanently dry,* will withstand decay over a long period of time. This rule holds true both in the living forests and in lumber which is used for building. The wooden *pile dwellings* of Switzerland, Ireland, Scotland, and elsewhere, were built on piles which remained submerged beneath the water level over a period of thousands of years and yet have retained a good state of preservation.

Termites are other vicious enemies of the forest. They bear the appearance of white ants. They were originally known for their destructive work in the timberland, but during recent years they have caused alarming damage to private dwellings and other wooden structures. The extent of their damage has been estimated in the vicinity of forty million dollars a year.

These insidious little pests go about their pillage in an extremely inconspicuous, not to say modest, fashion. They shun the light and imbed themselves inside the timber in swarms, performing their damage in such a way that their activity cannot be detected from the outside. Many instances have been cited where termites completely undermined a building before the owner was even remotely aware of their presence. Treatment of the wood with chromated zinc chloride or creosote oil, provides good protection against their damage.

Almost every one is acquainted with *dry rot*. This disease is actually a fungus growth, the spores of the fungi nestling in the crevice of the wood and, under certain conditions, germinating at an alarming rate. Dry rot provides as hidden an attack as termites, and, as in the case of termites, it is usually impossible to detect the damage (especially where the wood has been painted) until the outside surface crumbles. As the destructive fungi grow, a branch work of dead fibers spreads among the wood tissues, causing the wood itself to become like cork both in weight and strength. One of the most effective agents in preventing dry rot is *chromated zinc chloride*.

Fire is a great and commonly known enemy of wood. It is estimated that approximately 90% of all forest fires are the result of human carelessness. They are usually started when camp fires are not properly extinguished, when burning cigarettes are flipped carelessly from moving cars, by matches which were *supposed* to be extinguished, or by small grass fires which spread into forest regions during high winds.

All of these causes, every one based upon human carelessness, result in the starting of well over 100,000 fires a year. Each year, carelessness of this type causes the burning of enough timber to fill a string of freight cars extending across our country from the Atlantic to the Pacific. In actual value, the destroyed timber amounts annually to many millions of dollars.

This accounts for only the outward destruction by forest fires. The indirect damage cannot be estimated. As the flames roar through the dry woodland, everything containing life which stands in its path is destroyed. This includes human life, animals, and game, and practically all living plant growth. The beautiful wooded regions, verdant with life, is transformed into an ash heap of charred waste. Gone with the fire are millions of acres of our precious heritage!

It takes fully a half a century to restore land once ravaged by forest fire. With the natural ground cover removed, erosion sets in at an alarming rate, streams quickly vanish during dry seasons, and floods become the aftermath of heavy rain. All of these misfortunes are the inevitable results of forest fire. A large percentage of them have been caused by a small flame that was not properly guarded by human hands.

Easy as it may seem for us as individuals to guard against forest fires, and despite our confidence that we shall never let a fire, even a small one, get away from us, it becomes apparent that we are not very careful in this respect. Probably in most instances we can blame our overconfidence for what has happened. Perhaps the attitude of the average person may be summed up in the statement "I am always careful with fire. If everyone were as careful as I am there never would be any of these fires started." Many persons who have felt this way and who have expressed themselves practically in these words have unconsciously and unintentionally caused the most devastating fires.

A raging forest fire in the Willamette National Forest, Oregon. Each year thousands of acres of timber are destroyed by fire.

Fire control is taught to members of C. C. C. Camps. When proper steps are taken, fire damages can be greatly reduced.

Timberland that has been ravaged by fire. Note the dismal condition of this hillside that once was a beautiful dense forest.

Below: Erosion—this is what results when forest land is carelessly stripped of its standing timber. Note how the soil "slides" and "creeps" over the treeless area.

Below: Fire-fighting truck and appliances.

Rare Woods and Where They Come From

It is a well-known fact that certain rare woods are so valuable as to be almost worth their weight in gold. Because of their beauty and value these woods are used sparingly.

The metal craftsman saves his precious gold and platinum for *plating*. Cheaper metals are plated with precious metals in order that the beauty of the precious metal may appear upon the surface. In like manner the wood crafts-man making a beautiful article of wood often covers the surfaces of his common woods with a thin layer, or *veneer*, of precious wood.

Veneering is by no means a modern practice. The finest examples of cabinet work, dating back to the time of the Revolutionary War, were veneered. The idea that veneering is a cheap process intended only to disguise inferior workmanship is by no means true. On the contrary, veneering is a widely accepted practice.

Were it not for the practice of veneering, it would be impossible to produce the exquisite surface effects found on furniture of better quality. Some woods are so very rare that they could not be obtained in sufficient quantities were they not thinly sliced and used as veneers.

Select, or prime, cuts of wood, used for veneering, form only a very small part of the total bulk of the tree. These prime cuts, unusually beautiful in their distinctive grain and surface characteristics, must through necessity be spread over as large an area as possible. They are therefore sliced into thin layers or *flitches* of veneer. The select portions of the tree include the *crotch* areas, the *burl,* and *stump wood.*

In cutting veneers, a razor-sharp knife is used which simply peels off thin flitches, or slices, of veneer from the circumference of a log by means of a mechanical slicing process. Each flitch is specially treated for preservation and stored in a manner which insures proper climatic control.

From the craftsman's point of view the practice of veneering is indispensable. Rare and beautiful woods simply could not be obtained in sufficient quantities if they were not conserved and used as veneers.

The job of finding the precious woods from which the veneers are to be cut involves a search of the entire

Top: A rapid acting veneer slicer for cutting especially long logs. This huge machine can handle logs up to sixteen feet in length.

Center: A veneer slicer. By slicing stump wood, crotch wood, and burls into thin layers and using these as a surface veneer, hundreds of square feet of beautiful grained veneer may be cut from one small piece of timber.

Bottom: A plywood veneer cutter. When a continuous strip of veneer is peeled from the circumference of a log, it is referred to as rotary-cut veneer.

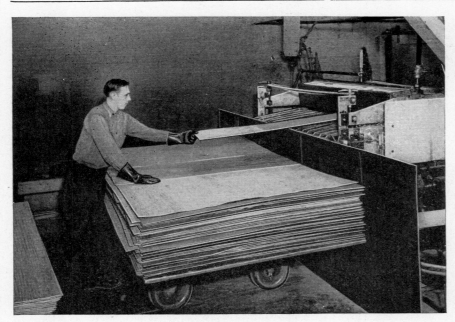

The making of plywood. Thin sheets of wood are glued together so that the grain in each layer runs at right angles to the grain in the next layer.

world. Such precious woods come in great variety. The places of their origin cover the four corners of the earth. Most of us are acquainted with such valuable woods as mahogany, walnut, teak, lignum vitae, ebony, and others. But these classifications hardly scratch the surface when the entire list is taken into consideration.

Among the most exquisite woods will be found the beautiful light colored *Harewood*, with superb delicate grain, which is imported from England; *Carpathia Elm*, the burl of which is unmatched in its subtle tracery; *Tamo* from Japan; *Figured Satinwood*, which is brought to us from Ceylon, India, and the East Indies. Then there is the lovely chocolate colored *Orientalwood* which grows largely in Australia; *Padouk* from Burma; and *Thuya* from Algiers. South America and East Africa export the exotic *Zebrawood*.

From Hawaii comes the Koa log; while in the damp tropical jungles of Brazil thrives the Rosewood tree. From this wood is manufactured the beautifully tinted rosewood veneers found only in the costliest of furniture. These woods and countless others have interesting stories about their growth and development. Many rare woods are used in tables and other furniture displayed in the art shops of our large cities. In part, these exquisite woods comprise the treasure trove of the wood craftsman.

Manufacture of Plywood

But the practice of veneering is not necessarily restricted to the rarer woods. In the manufacture of plywood, where alternating layers of veneer are laminated one on top of the other, with the grain of each layer running across the grain of the adjoining layer, is seen another example of the use of veneers.

Plywood has come to be a very popular product. One way in which plywood veneers are obtained is in itself extremely interesting. For this purpose the original log is mounted in a huge lathe and after being reduced to uniform diameter, a continuous sheet of veneer is stripped from its surface. It will be observed that the plywood veneer is cut from the log in much the same manner that wrapping paper is drawn from a large roll. As the log revolves in the lathe, sharp cutters peel a continuous thin sheet of veneer, which is then cut into the required lengths.

During recent years plywood has been adopted to an infinite variety of new uses. Because it is made of thin sheets glued together with the grain crossed, it is not handicapped by a *single* direction of grain, and thus the structural weakness of ordinary lumber is eliminated. Moreover, plywood itself may be veneered with a more valuable type of wood to create a rich surface effect.

Manufacture of Paper

Not only is the tree chopped down, sawed into planks and used *directly* for making things, but the properties of wood are utilized as well in the manufacture of a great many products. Often in their finished appearances these products bear little or no resemblance to the original wood from which they are made.*

Large stacks of pine pulpwood ready to be ground into pulp. Enormous quantities of wood are used each year to supply the needs for paper, composition boards, and other wood products.

The most important of these by-products of the forest is paper. Paper-making, together with the manufacture of associated synthetic wood products, is rated as America's fourth greatest industry.†

Thousands of acres of our forests are cut down each year in order to provide wood for the paper industry. This industry in itself is the second largest user of wood in this country.

To obtain a clear idea of the large amount of wood that is actually used in paper-making, it will be interesting to note that many of our larger metropolitan newspapers keep entire forests for their own exclusive use. Each year their printing presses consume the wood from large areas of timberland.

* The United States Department of Commerce lists around 5,000 different industrial uses for wood. It is used in the manufacture of approximately 200,000 different articles.

† Census of Manufacturers, 1935, published by United States Department of Commerce.

While paper is considered one of the chief products of wood, science in our modern time has created a number of other products which depend upon wood as their chief ingredient.

Wood in the Manufacture of Rayon

Imagine the surprise with which our ancestors would greet the information that cloth, and very beautiful silky cloth, can be made of wood! Yet the soft and lovely fabric known as *rayon*, commonly used in making clothing and other cloth materials, is manufactured from the cellulose of wood pulp.

Each year two hundred thousand tons of rayon cloth are produced. Thus we learn that great regions of woodland are utilized in the making of cloth and clothing. It is rather startling to realize that we wear "wooden clothing!"

The manufacture of rayon is a subject of special interest. Unlike silk and cotton, rayon is a fiber which cannot be found in natural form. It is produced by a chemical and mechanical process. Its chief ingredients are the cellulose of cotton linters (the short fibers which cling to the cotton seed) and wood.

In manufacture, the pulverized raw material first undergoes a series of chemical treatments until it is converted into a thick, "honey-like" liquid known as *viscose*. This solution is forced through a "spinneret"—a nozzle, perforated with tiny openings. It issues from the nozzle in extremly fine strands, or filaments. These filaments are twisted together to form a thread of rayon yarn. The yarn, in turn is worked, purified, and wound into convenient forms and is then ready for use in the making of different types of rayon fabrics. Rayon yarn is extremely uniform in quality. Its whiteness resists aging or dulling.

The usefulness of rayon is demonstrated by the number of different textured materials which it can be made to resemble. This variety includes satins, crepes, velvets, sheers, moires, and even knitted fabrics. Moreover rayon is used for making towels, sheets, napkins, ribbons, bathing suits, dresses, hosiery, handkerchiefs, trimmings, lace, draperies, upholstery, and innumerable other types of fabrics which would otherwise require very special and distinctive materials.

A rayon spinning machine in action. Note the many thin lines of rayon thread leaving the chemical bath. These tiny silken threads are made from wood.

Wood in the Manufacture of Cloth and Clothing

Through a process similar to that used in producing rayon it is possible to change wood pulp into a thread which may be treated and woven in such a way that the finished cloth approaches the warmth of wool. Thus, blankets, suits, overcoats, and other apparel used to preserve bodily warmth can be produced from wood.

Wood veneer, laminated with a transparent cellulose acetate plastic, is used in the manufacture of hats and other accessories. The transparent plastic coating provides a strong yet pliable surface, making possible individual shaping of brims and crowns. Veneers of birch, tigerwood, and African mahogany are frequently used with the plastic material in making hats, handbags, cigarette cases, and compacts. The natural grain of the wood tends to give these articles an exceptionally interesting effect.

Cellophane is Produced from Wood

Cellophane, that transparent material for which we have found so many uses, is likewise produced from wood. Wood plastics are used in a number of commercial products. Another process is used in the manufacture of nitroglycerin and dynamite.

There are several interesting processes brought out in the production of cellophane. Pure spruce wood pulp is first steeped in a caustic soda solution. This treatment causes the pulp to be converted into alkali cellulose. The sheets of wood pulp thus treated are then shredded into a white and fluffy material which resembles bread crumbs. Another chemical called "carbon disulphide" is added to the fluffy pulverized cellulose, causing it to change to an orange color. It is then placed in huge tanks where it is dissolved in caustic soda. The solution within the tanks is carefully controlled until it ripens into *viscose*. Following this step, the viscose is chemically coagulated and after a series of rolling operations thin sheets of cellophane are developed.

The slogan "wrapped in cellophane" is one which has become almost as common as the ordinary salutations of the day. This material is used not only to protect the freshness of countless thousands of products but it has also found its way into numerous other fields.

Cellophane is extensively used for decorative purposes. Textile manufacturers have even gone so far as to have the cellulose film woven into cloth. It is used in the manufacture of wall coverings, rugs, curtains, even in making shoes and handbags. Every day a number of new uses are being found for this very remarkable product.

The making of cellophane (cellulose film). The cellulose film above is being drawn from an acid bath. This is part of the treatment necessary to make smooth, strong, transparent cellophane—so unlike the wood from which it is made.

Other Products of Wood

Then too, there are various types of composition board and insulation board used in house construction, which have been developed from wood pulp. During recent years scientists have even found a use for wood in the manufacture of synthetic sponges.

Composition board which is made of shredded wood fiber provides an extremely practical base for plaster. It is also extensively used for sheathing houses. In addition to its many other advantages, it provides a high degree of insulation and when used as sheathing it may be applied in a much shorter time than the conventional type of sheathing board.

Of course, this treatment only highlights a few of the commonly known products which are derived from wood. We all know that such commodities as rubber, turpentine, methyl alcohol, tung oil (a subject in itself), dyes, and various staple foods, are all direct products of the tree. Scientists are constantly on the alert to discover new ways of making things and so we may expect further and even more startling discoveries in the future.

Molded Plywood and Compregnated Wood

Through the introduction of resin glue an entirely new type of plywood, known as *compregnated wood,* has been produced. The wood plies are glued together in standard fashion with the grain of each layer running crosswise to the next. With resin-glue between the layers the plies are subjected to tremendous pressure, forcing the glue completely through each layer. Under pressure the compregnated plies are compressed to half their normal thickness. By regulating the pressure during the gluing process, the finished product can be made to equal the strength and hardness of many types of metals. Also, areas of the wood can be given additional pressure, or additional plies may be added, to increase the strength or thickness at certain vital constructional points.

Compregnated plywood may be molded to almost any desired shape during the gluing process. It can be shaped to form the hull of a small boat or the fuselage of an airplane. Moreover, the molded unit can be made in one piece and in many instances does not require any structural reinforcement.

Science Discovers a Way to Bend Wood

Recently a research scientist who was trying to find a better way to season wood, happened upon a process whereby standard boards could be bent and twisted almost as easily as rubber. When making this discovery the scientist placed a board in a solution of *urea,* allowing it to become thoroughly soaked. When the board dried it was heated for proper seasoning. After the board was removed from the oven the sheet appeared—to the amazement of the scientist— to be quite flexible.

This process should be of especial interest to the layman and woodworking student. It is simple to follow: Select a board that is not too thick and soak it thoroughly in a solution of urea. Then let it dry thoroughly. Following this process, place the board in an oven and as it heats, the chemical change takes place in the fibers of the wood. The wood can be easily shaped while it is still hot. After cooling, the wood retains its new shape. The use of this process serves as a decided boon in the making of furniture and other articles where bent or curved shapes are required.

Wood and the Future

Those of us who love wood as a material for work and construction, will rejoice in the increased importance which the forest product has taken in our modern civilization. We are amazed by the many new uses to which wood is being put. Hardly a month goes by that the scientist does not develop a new product from the tree.

But it is probable that in the future limitless variety of new products will appear employing wood as their basic ingredient. It is likewise probable that conventional wood construction, as we know it today, will be replaced in time by entirely new types of joinery. Already we have observed the way in which *compregnated plywood* is molded and shaped to any desired structural form. Possibly the wooden home of the future will be stamped out in sections and fabricated in mass production for quick and economical assembly.

All of this may indicate that in time, lumber will be handled and formed as a flexible material, to be manufactured into products through processes similar to those now employed for shaping sheet metal and plastics. Certainly there would be many advantages to this type of manufacture, especially in the case of furniture where one-piece construction would eliminate existing weakness of joinery, lumber preservation and finish. Economy of manufacture and economy of materials would also serve to recommend this idea.

In summing up, it does not seem too far fetched to conjecture that our great great grandchildren, living in another century, may not be able to use lumber or boards as *direct* building materials, but, instead may recognize the tree only as the living source of a variety of products used in building as well as in numerous other enterprises. Thus, in time lumber, as we know it, may become an obsolete material. But the tree shall continue to be used for the manufacture of myriads of new products and it is probable that the woodworker of the future shall proceed with his job in a manner quite different than the general practice of today.

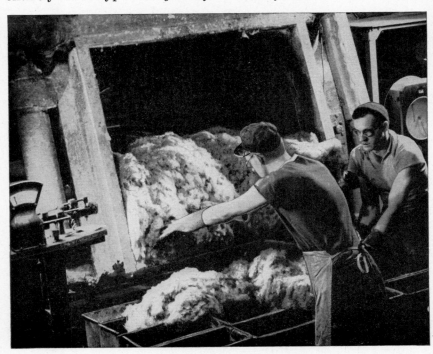

Manufacturing man-made sponges from wood. The picture shows the mixture being placed in molds.

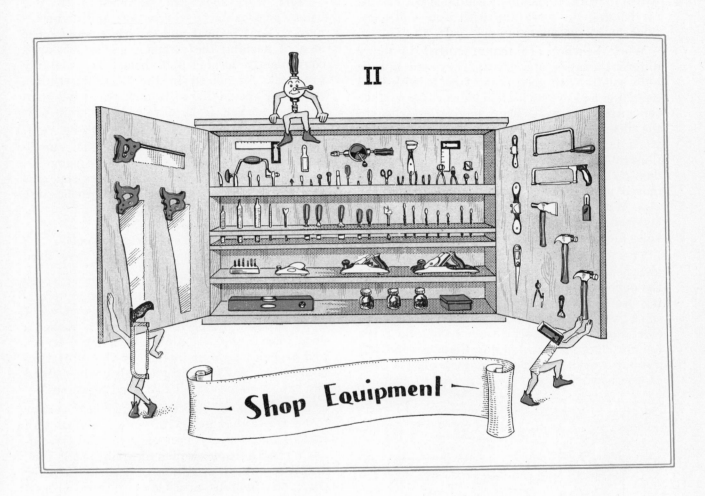

Shop Equipment

The Woodworker's Work Bench

It goes without saying that among the woodworker's first needs is a good solid bench on which to work. It should be equipped with a vise for holding the work and with slots and holes for keeping the common hand tools.

Work benches are manufactured in many different shapes and sizes. They are always built solidly with good heavy tops to withstand pounding and to provide a good working surface for cutting, as well. They may be attached to the floor so as to remain stationary while work is in progress. The vise on the bench illustrated is equipped with an "adjustable dog"; that is, a piece of iron which can be moved up and down in the outside jaw of the vise. With this dog boards may be firmly held between it and a bench stop which fits into the holes along the edge of the bench.

The woodworker often prefers to make his own bench, rather than buy one. Thus, he has the opportunity to use his originality in designing useful features to his bench. For instance, some woodworking benches have drawers to store supplies and tools. Others have lockers below for clothing and supplies. Plans for making a simple workbench appear in the project section of this book.

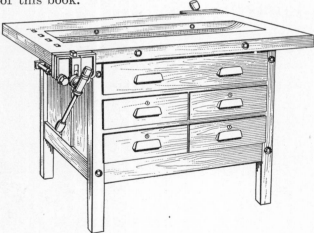

A Handy Place to Keep Tools

Neatness and tidiness are very important in the woodworking shop. In fact, the success of the work depends a great deal upon these qualities. The person who has spent half an hour hunting for a tool which "I had in my hand just a minute ago," realizes the importance of having a definite place for keeping each implement and the further importance of *always keeping it in that place*.

Most workshops are equipped with tool boards and cabinets where tools and materials may be kept in neat and orderly manner. The idea of keeping the common hand tools on a conveniently located tool board is especially practical. As shown in the title illustration, each tool should have its own exclusive spot, and the worker, if he always keeps it in that spot, always knows just where to look for it.

The combination of tool board and supply cabinets, which the title illustration suggests, should serve the needs of the industrial arts or home workshop ideally. Work benches are usually made from 30 to 36 inches high.

An Introduction to Woodworking Tools—
Their Names and How They Are Used

You don't *have* to know the name of every woodworking tool in order to use its successfully. Nor do you *have* to know the name of every process you perform. Still, it is rather a good idea to get acquainted with these terms, and probably as your interest in the subject increases, you will become naturally curious about the proper names of all tools and processes.

Indeed, you will find that it is an easy matter to become acquainted with your equipment. In fact, it may only be necessary to read the following paragraphs which describe each tool, and study the illustration of each one. After that you won't be satisfied to just go around calling a **saw**, a saw; a **chisel**, a chisel; or a **file**, a file. You will discover that there are many different types of saws, as there are chisels and files and other tools, and that each type has its own exclusive name and use.

So just look them over and get acquainted with them. Then some time later, when you find yourself at a loss for a name, simply go back to these pages and refresh your memory. Of course, it is not possible to show and describe *all* tools in these pages, but since the woodworking tools that *are* used in connection with a work bench all come under the general classification of *hand tools,* it is a comparatively simple matter to consult a manufacturer's catalog and find the correct name of any woodworking tool.

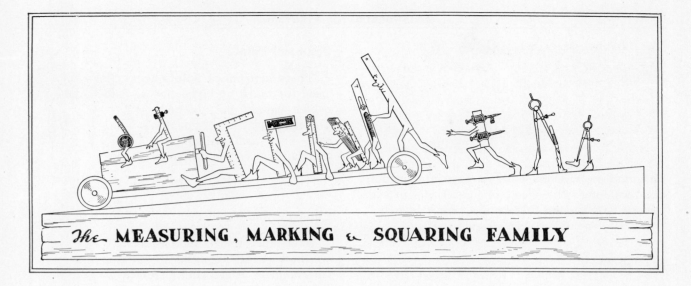

The MEASURING, MARKING & SQUARING FAMILY

Try Square

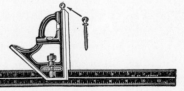

This little tool is as important to the woodworker as the compass is to the mariner. Using it as a check and a guide, you can always tell if you are right or wrong. It is used for marking lines square across the work—a very important function in woodworking. It is equally as important in checking the squareness of boards and construction.

As shown, the try square consists of a metal blade, fitted so as to form a perfect right angle to the straight edge of a heavier piece of wood or metal. The blade is usually stamped in one-inch graduations and their fractions, which makes the try square a measuring tool as well as a squaring tool.

Combination Square With Level

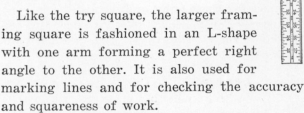

This very useful tool serves three purposes: (1) That of a straightedge ruler; (2) a marking and gauging square; (3) a level. It is especially useful in carpentry work where joining parts must be tested for *level* as well as for *square,* and for a 45° bevel. A small pointed scribe used for marking accompanies the model shown.

Framing Square (Steel Square)

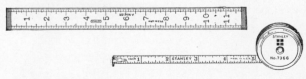

Like the try square, the larger framing square is fashioned in an L-shape with one arm forming a perfect right angle to the other. It is also used for marking lines and for checking the accuracy and squareness of work.

The carpenter greatly depends upon this type of square when he is building a house. He uses it for laying out angles, foundations, and framework. The two arms of the framing square are stamped in various fractions of an inch. They are also marked with computing tables, which are used by the carpenter in many different phases of his work.

Rules and Rulers

An important item in any shop is a good quality straightedge bench rule. These rules are manufactured of either wood or metal. They are used to check work for *straightness* and to measure and mark straight lines.

Included in the other types of rules used in shop work are the *folding two-foot rule;* the

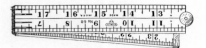

pull-push rule, made of steel tape and usually six feet long; the wood or metal *zigzag rule* which likewise unfolds to a six-foot length.

Straightedge

This very necessary tool is made either of wood or metal and ordinarily varies in length from one foot to three feet. Usually it is not stamped for measuring and, therefore, is used exclusively for marking straight lines and for checking the straightness and accuracy of work.

Marking Gauge

The marking gauge is used for making lines at a uniform distance, in from the edge of a board or piece of work. Practice is necessary in order to learn how to use it properly. The adjustable marker can be set for the required depth of marking.

Bevel Gauge

The bevel gauge is used to mark and check angles. The blade can be adjusted and set to any desired slant. When being used it is held against the work like a try square.

Trammel Points

These sharpened points are used for marking large circles which cannot be spanned by the ordinary compass or dividers. They are adjusted on a wooden bar to the desired radius.

Compass and Dividers

Ever since kindergarten days, we have been acquainted with the compass. It is a simple device for marking circles or parts of circles. Dividers serve the same purpose, only they are made entirely of metal and their pointed ends scratch the marking rather than penciling it. Dividers are also used for dividing lines into equal parts, and for setting out or measuring distances.

Scribers and Bench Knives

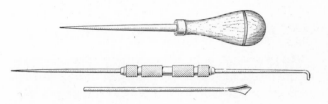

A scriber consists of a piece of tool steel ground to a long, tapering point and hardened. The scriber shown at the top is fixed in a handle for convenience in using. It is used to draw lines on surfaces. It can draw a very fine line. Another form of scriber shown in the lower illustration has a hollow knurled sleeve in which two scriber points are clamped by means of nuts. At the bottom is shown a knife point which may be substituted for one of the points.

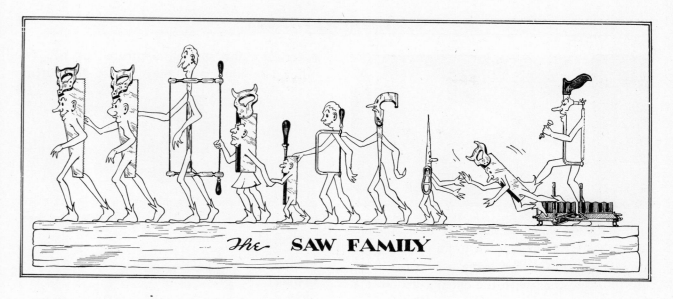

The SAW FAMILY

Special Uses for Saws

As mentioned before, saws are made in many different types, shapes, and sizes. Moreover, each type of saw has its own specific use, and certain jobs in woodworking require the use of that kind of saw *exclusively*. For this reason it cannot be properly said that a saw is a *saw*; but rather that it is one of a large and important family.

Section of Bronze Saw from Ancient Nineveh

These primitive ancient saws were cast in crude stone molds.

Stone Mold for Casting Bronze Saws

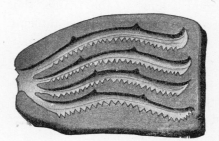

This ancient mold originated in Sweden.

Crosscut Saw

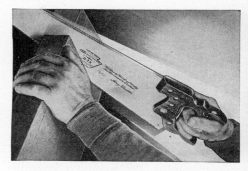

The crosscut saw is one of the "old reliables" of the woodworking shop. As the name indicates, it is used for cutting across the grain of the wood.

The saw teeth are set alternately to the right and left. The illustration shows how they are shaped so as to form sharp cutting points along the outside edge. Saws of this type are made in various sizes. The fineness or coarseness of the cutting edge is determined by the number of teeth per inch.

A number of other saws, bearing different names, have teeth which are shaped for crosscutting.

Ripsaw

In the language of the woodworker, when a piece of wood is sawed with the grain it is *ripped*. The ripsaw has teeth which are especially shaped to perform this particular type of cutting. The illustration shows the way in which

 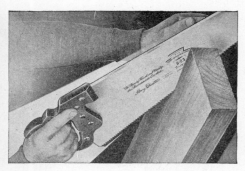

each tooth is shaped so that it is perpendicular at the front, and sharpened to an even edge at the cutting point. When being used, these teeth bite into the wood with the cutting action of a series of small chisels.

Ripsaws are made in different sizes; their teeth varying in coarseness for either fine or rough cutting.

Backsaw

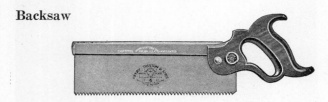

As the name indicates, the backsaw is made with a rigid steel reinforcement attached to its top edge to form a "back." The teeth of the backsaw are shaped like those of the crosscut saw. Having a thin blade and fine teeth, it is well suited for accurate and precise cutting.

Cabinet Saw

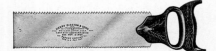

This saw bears some resemblance to the backsaw but lacks its rigidity. It can be used to cut entirely through a piece of wood. Saw teeth on opposite edges are sharpened for different cuts. The handle is adjustable for position, when either edge is being used.

Miter Saw

The miter saw is simply an oversized backsaw. Ordinarily, however, it is only used in a

miter box for special, accurate cutting. The miter box illustrated may be set for cutting

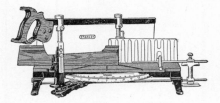

at various angles. It holds and guides the miter saw so as to insure accuracy, even for the inexperienced woodworker.

Coping Saw

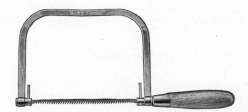

Coping saws are used for cutting curves, roundings, and special shapes. There are two distinct types, namely: the *wire frame* coping saw and the *rigid frame* saw. Each of these types may be fitted with either fine or coarse blades. The ends of the blades are made with pin fittings, loops, or lock loops, which hold them in place in the frame.

Because of its flexibility, it is considered better to attach the blade in the wire frame saw, so that the teeth point toward the handle. The cutting is then performed on the *draw stroke*. However, the blade of the rigid frame saw is attached in the opposite direction because the rigidity of the frame permits accurate cutting on the *drive stroke*. The latter type of saw offers the advantage of a pivoting blade which may be turned at different angles to the frame, thus making the cutting of long curves less difficult.

Turning Saw

Like the coping saw, the turning saw is designed for cutting curves, scrolls, and roundings. It is used chiefly on heavier work where long fast strokes and less accuracy of cutting is permissible. The thin blade is removable. It can

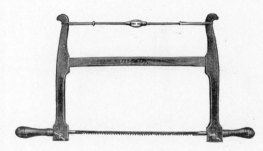

be pivoted between the handles. Usually the saw is used so that it cuts on the pulling stroke.

Dovetail Saw

This little saw is closely related to the backsaw. It is lighter, however, and possesses a thinner blade and finer teeth. The handle is round, to provide a delicate grip for fine cutting. This saw is used where absolutely precise and delicate cutting is required.

Compass Saw

With a blade resembling the beak of a swordfish (the shape incidentally which was probably used when saws first originated) this type of saw is commonly used for making "cutouts" on the inside surface of a piece of work. A hole is first bored inside the portion which is to be cut out. The pointed compass saw is pushed into the hole to start the sawing operations.

Keyhole Saw

Although it is smaller in size, the keyhole saw is used in the same manner as the compass saw. For this reason it is generally employed for finer work where the compass saw would be too big and clumsy for the job.

Hack Saw

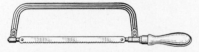

While essentially designed for cutting metal, this tool comes in for a variety of uses in the woodworking shop. The hack-saw frame is de-

signed in a number of different ways, some with pistol grips, others with handles similar to those used on a conventional saw, others with turned handles. Blades are detachable and can be obtained with teeth of varying coarseness.

Sawing Operations

In sawing, the saw handle should be grasped lightly and easily, with the forefinger extended along the side. The general tendency when first using a saw is to hold it too tightly and to depend too much on the muscles of the arm to give it movement and direction. As the saw cuts while it is being pushed away from the workman, the tendency at first is to press the teeth forcibly into the wood during this part of the movement. This pressure is unnecessary, as it does not increase the cutting speed and makes it difficult to guide the saw properly. By grasping the saw lightly, in fact, in what seems at first to be a loose manner, and putting no more pressure on the teeth than comes naturally with the back-and-forth movement of the body, the best results in the way of speed in cutting and guidance are obtained.

Before the cut is started, a line is marked on the wood with a lead pencil to serve as a guide, and the cut is started by drawing the saw toward the operator, as this gives a groove of sufficient depth to keep the saw in place. The cut is made along the waste side of the marked line, and just away from it.

At times, the saw may tend to run off the line, in which case the blade should be twisted gently, so as to change the course to the proper one. It should be noted that the more nearly the line of the saw teeth is perpendicular to the face of the work, the fewer are the teeth that are actually cutting and the smaller is the effort required to do the work. This is true of both the rip and the cross-cut saw. By lowering the handle and putting more teeth in action, the workman will find that his labor is increased, as the effect is then the same as if he were cutting through thicker stock. In general, the more nearly upright is the position of the saw, the less will be the effort required to do the work. An angle of 45 degrees with the surface of the work may be taken as a good angle for rip saws.

The PLANE FAMILY

There are various sizes of planes: little planes, big planes, and medium-size planes. There are also many different types of planes and each type is used for its own special work.

All planes are assembled of a number of different parts. Each part serves to make the plane cut smoothly and efficiently. Most types of planes may be adjusted for a desired depth of cut. The cap which is adjusted over the cutting edge of the blade provides a smooth and even cut, and prevents the blade from sticking and roughing the work.

Jack Plane

The jack plane is so named because the woodworker uses it in a variety of ways, especially for rough or preliminary work. While there are actually forty-six different parts to this plane, the worker need only become acquainted with the working or regulating parts. These are: (1) The *cutting blade* or plane iron; (2) the *adjusting nut*, which is turned to raise or lower the blade; and (3) the *adjusting lever*, which regulates the blade so as to make possible an even or slanted cut.

The cutting blade or *plane iron*, as it is usually called, is guarded with a metal cap which is adjusted on top of the blade to within about $\frac{3}{32}$ of an inch of the cutting edge. As already noted, this cap eases the cutting action by curling and breaking off the wood shavings evenly, thus preventing splitting or splintering of the wood.

Smooth Plane

This useful little plane is somewhat smaller than the jack plane, measuring between 6 and 10 inches in length. It is a fine utility tool, especially useful for planing end grain, chamfers, and other edge shaping.

Jointer Plane

When a fairly long board must be planed absolutely straight and square along the edge, it is easier to obtain a straight and level surface with the jointer than with any other type of plane. All planes when set for a small cut and pushed evenly along the edge of a board, cut so as to make that edge straight and even. However, the longer the plane, the easier it is to produce an exactly level edge. While sizes vary, the most popular type of jointer plane is 24 inches in length.

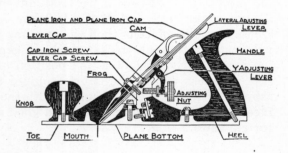

PLANE IRON AND PLANE IRON CAP
LEVER CAP
CAP IRON SCREW
LEVER CAP SCREW
FROG
KNOB
TOE   MOUTH   PLANE BOTTOM   HEEL
CAM
LATERAL ADJUSTING LEVER
HANDLE
Y ADJUSTING LEVER
ADJUSTING NUT

Fore Plane

This plane may be aptly referred to as a "junior" jointer plane. Measuring 18 inches in length, it is slightly shorter than the conventional jointer plane. It is used principally for planing edges of medium length.

Block Plane

The little block plane is particularly useful in planing end grain, inasmuch as its blade is tipped at a lesser angle for this type of cutting. It is also well adapted to small work where precision is essential. The popular type of block plane is 6 inches in length. It is held in the palm of the hand.

Router Plane

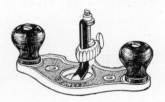

Having two knob handles, the router plane hardly resembles a plane. However, it is listed under this heading and it is used for routing out grooves in the surface of a board. It is especially useful in making dado joints and small panels.

Circular Plane

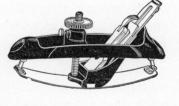

This tool was especially devised for shaping round edges. Its shape adapts it for planing either convex or concave surfaces. This plane may be adjusted so that the flexible bed will conform to circles of various sizes.

Rabbeting Plane

If the edge of a piece of board is to be rabbeted, this type of plane may be used. The side guide and the cutting blade may be adjusted so as to cut rabbets of varying widths and depths. The plane is useful, as well, for various types of edge shaping.

Plane Gauge

The plane gauge, which may be fastened to any standard size of plane, is very helpful, especially for the beginner. It is used to hold the plane for cutting at any desired slant and thus greatly helps the accurate cutting of bevels and chamfers. When set at right angles to the bottom of the plane, it can be used as a guide for straight cutting.

Combination Plane

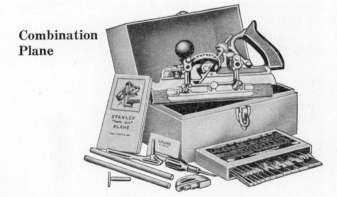

This interesting type of plane, with its many adjustments and its variety of cutters, may be used to produce a great number of edge shapings. In fact there are well over 100 different shaped cutters which may be used with a plane of this type.

The BORING FAMILY

Like the saws and planes, the borers form a large and thriving family. Of course, they are all used to make holes in wood.

There are two distinct types of *holders* used in boring. These are known respectively as the *brace* and the *drill*.

Brace

The brace is a crank-shaped tool which is used to hold various types of boring and utility bits. Some braces are made with a *ratchet* attachment which permits use of the brace in a confined space or position, where a complete revolution of the brace is impossible. A knurled ring on the crank permits the use of the brace in either direction.

Drill

(Hand Drills and Automatic Push Drills)

Drills are separated into two types, hand drills and push drills. Not to be confused with the household egg beater, the hand drill works on about the same principle. The action of cranking a geared side-wheel causes the drill to revolve and to drill holes.

The push drill turns automatically when being pushed into the work. When it is released and

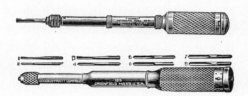

drawn away from the work, the drill revolves backward. This type of drill is especially useful when a number of small holes must be made.

Auger Bit

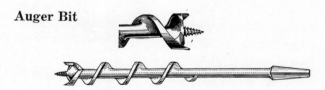

This is the type of bit commonly used for boring various sized holes in wood. It is spiral shaped, having a screw point (commonly known as a *spur*).

The cutting action is provided by a pair of sharp *nibs*, or cutters which, with two sharpened *side lips*, bore cleanly into the wood.

Auger bits are commonly made in sizes ranging from $\frac{3}{16}$ inch to $1\frac{1}{4}$ inches. The size of the bit is stamped on the square end (shank), which fits into the brace. All size graduations are based on the $\frac{1}{16}$ inch fraction, the size being stamped in the numerator of the fraction.

Forstner Bit

This style of bit has a variety of special uses. For certain types of work it has some advantages over the ordinary auger bit. Its unusual shape and cutting action make it very useful for boring holes near the end of a board—where the auger bit might split the wood. It is also especially useful for boring into end grain, and also when a hole already bored is to be made larger. This bit can also be used to bore a hole along the edge of a piece of stock where a portion of the bit is not working in the stock, or to bore two holes that partly lap or cut into each other.

The fact that this bit lacks a pointed spur is indeed a help when holes are to be bored *almost* through the stock. Like the auger bit, the Forstner bit is graduated in size by sixteenths of an inch.

Expansive Bits

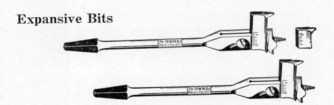

Bits of this type can be adjusted to bore any desired size of hole. Expansive bits are obtainable in two separate sizes. The smaller and lighter size is fitted with a cutter which may be adjusted to cut holes from 1 inch to 2 inches in diameter. The larger size bit is fitted with cutters which bore holes up to 3 inches in diameter.

Countersink Bit

When a "pilot hole" has been bored to receive the unthreaded stem (shank) of a flat-head screw, something must be done so that the head of the screw will "seat" evenly into the hole. For this purpose the countersink bit was invented. It spreads the surface of a small hole to receive the screw head.

Gimlet Bit

Where a series of small holes are to be bored in hardwood, the gimlet bit is extremely useful.

Bradawl

This handy tool is used for piercing small holes. It can be used for making pilot holes for smaller sized screws. During recent years it has been replaced, largely, by the automatic push drill.

Bit Extension

As the name indicates this implement is simply an extension rod which fits into the brace to extend the regular length of the boring bit for especially deep boring.

Bit Gauge

To permit the woodworker to bore holes to a desired depth, *and no deeper*, the bit gauge has been invented. It can be adjusted to any desired depth. The gauge should not be forced too tightly against the stock, as this action not only damages the surface of the board, but also causes the gauge to slip to a greater depth. When using, remember that it is a *bit gauge* and not a *bit stop*!

Screwdriver Bits

When steady pressure is to be applied, especially on larger sized screws, the screwdriver bit is the answer. Used with a plain or rachet brace, this bit provides for a degree of driving pressure that would otherwise be impossible to obtain. Like standard screwdrivers, screwdriver bits may be obtained in various sizes.

Doweling Jig

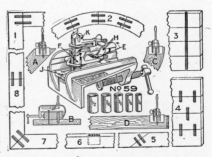

The doweling jig is an extremely important device to have on hand when absolutely straight and accurate boring must be accomplished. As the name implies, it is especially useful for boring holes for dowel joints.

The FILE FAMILY

History of Files

The file is one of the oldest tools known to history.

To abrade, or file, ancient man used sand, grit, coral, bone, gritty woods, and stones of varying hardness in connection with sand and water.

Crude as were these abrading instruments, and slow and laborious as must have been their use, they nevertheless served primeval man well throughout the Stone and Bronze Ages. Up to the time of the discovery of iron, natural abrasives were used extensively. Copper, and later bronze, did not permit of sufficient hardening to be used as a material for the making of artificial files, although attempts were made to use both for that purpose.

Among the earliest known examples of artificially made metal abrading tools, for which a date can be fixed, is a bronze file which was dug up in Crete by an expedition from the University of Pennsylvania and is now in the Museum at Candia. This prehistoric file believed to have been made about 1500 B. C. possesses an astonishing likeness to the half-round file of today. The Egyptians are also known to have made small rasps of bronze, about 1200-1000 B. C.

First Iron Rasps Made by Assyrians

The Assyrians, credited by historians as the first race to work with iron, made a straight rasp of iron an excellent example of which has been found, and which was in form very similar to the modern rasp. These files date back to the 7th century B. C.

Machine-Cut Files

About the year 1490 A. D. we find the first attempt to cut files by machine, an invention of Leonardo da Vinci, famed for his sculpture and paintings and also renowned as a musician, scientist, engineer, and mechanic.

The first machine which actually cut files was probably made by Chopitel, a Frenchman, in 1750. Later machines, numbering a dozen, were invented between the years 1756 and 1862, mainly by Frenchmen.

It is interesting to note that the first American machine for cutting files was made in 1836.

How Files Are Named

Three details must be specified to describe a file correctly. These are length, shape, and cut.

Length

Files are designated as so many inches long, but this length does not include the *tang*, or that portion of the file which is inserted into the handle.

Shape or Kind

Files are classified according to their general shape. For instance, they are divided from the form of their cross-section into three general classes: quadrangular or square, circular, and triangular. In addition, many additional odd and irregular forms of cross-sections are being used. Files may have parallel edges or may taper slightly through the latter half of their length, opposite the tang. Sometimes files taper in thickness as they taper in width.

Cross-Sections of Files

Cut

The cut of a file refers to the parallel series of teeth on the file. For example, single-cut files have parallel lines of teeth running diagonally across the file face. When there is a double series of teeth crossing each other at an oblique angle, the file is said to be double-cut. The cut of files is divided with reference to the *character* of the teeth, into *single, double, rasp* and *curved*; and with reference to the coarseness of the teeth into *rough, coarse, bastard,*

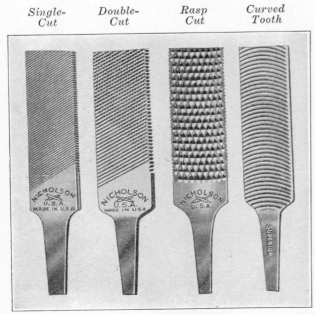

Single-Cut | Double-Cut | Rasp Cut | Curved Tooth

Typical File Cuts

second cut, smooth, and *dead smooth.* Single-cut files are used with a light pressure to produce a smooth surface finish; or they may be used to produce keen edges on knives, shears, saw teeth, or other cutting implements.

Double-cut files are usually used under heavier pressure, for fast metal removal where rougher finish is permissible.

The rasp cut consists of a series of individual teeth produced by a sharp, narrow, punch-like cutting chisel. It is an extremely rough cut and is used principally on wood, hoofs, aluminum, lead, and other soft substances for fast removal of material. Rough, coarse, and bastard cuts are used on heavier classes of work, and the second-cut, smooth, and dead-smooth files for finishing on more exacting work.

Inserting Files in Handles

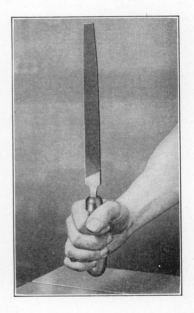

Good judgment and caution should be used in inserting files in their handles, for they are b r i t t l e and break easily when s t r u c k with another metal object. The accompanying illustration shows the correct method of attaching a file handle.

Files are just as useful in woodworking as they are in metal work. They are used in the smoothing steps which follow after a piece of wood has been roughly cut. There are a number of different sizes and shapes of files. Their surfaces vary in texture for different kinds of use.

Files should be well taken care of; should be kept in a dry place to avoid rust; and should be brushed and cleaned frequently with a file card. Different types of files are illustrated and their use explained.

Rasp

Strictly speaking, the rasp does not belong to the file family. However, it is shaped and used like a file. The triangular shaped projections or teeth which appear on its surfaces cut into the wood. It is used only for rough shaping.

Flat and Half-Round Files

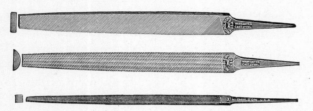

Each of these files have their specific uses. The half-round file is used for work that curves inward, and the flat file for work that curves outward, as well as for straight work.

Round or Rat-Tail File

The round or rat-tail file is used for shaping curved parts, or in holes and indentations where the flat file could not be used.

Triangular Tapered File

This type of file is really more of a metal working tool. However, it comes in handy around the woodworking shop, especially for cutting nails and sharpening certain tools.

Auger Bit File

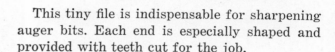

This tiny file is indispensable for sharpening auger bits. Each end is especially shaped and provided with teeth cut for the job.

File Card

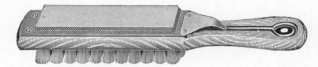

When files become clogged with wood dust, there is nothing more useful than a stiff wire brush for cleaning them. The *file card* is especially designed for the job. It should be kept handy when files are being used.

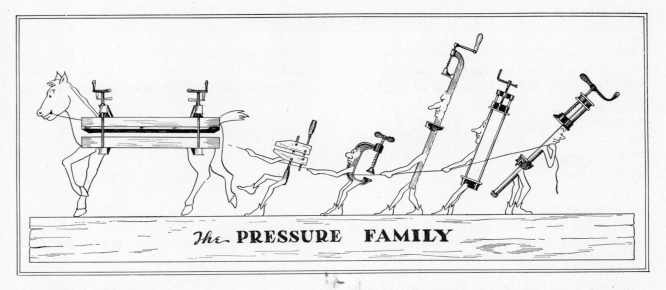

The PRESSURE FAMILY

When making articles out of wood, it is often necessary to press and hold together the different parts for a certain length of time. The gluing together of a piece of furniture calls for the use of clamps to hold the parts together while the glue is drying. Likewise, it is often desirable to hold a board in a special manner while the work is being done. For all of these purposes, clamps are very necessary in the workshop.

Clamps

(Hand Screw—Wooden)

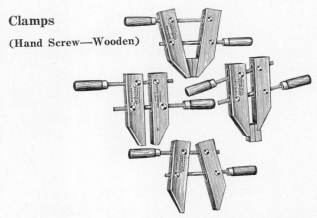

Here is a type of clamp that fulfills a countless number of purposes in the woodworking shop. As shown in the illustration, it is adjusted with parallel screws. The screw clamp serves to apply pressure on even or uneven surfaces. In use, the object is to obtain pressure with leverage from the back screw. These clamps vary in size from 6 to 18 inches.

The clamp illustrated is also known as a ball-and-socket hand clamp. It differs from the parallel clamp in that one half of each screw has a left-hand thread, whereas the other half has a right-hand thread, and in that the nuts through which these screws pass consist of balls fitting in sockets. Owing to this method of construction, work of almost any shape can be held. The upper and lower views illustrate settings of these clamps to hold work having non-parallel sides; the left-hand view shows a clamp set for parallel sides; and the clamp in the right-hand view is set to operate with one jaw in advance of the other.

Wooden Clamp for Light Duty

(Parallel Clamp)

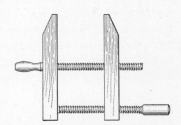

The form of wooden parallel clamp shown is very useful for general purposes. For light work in a woodworking shop a number of them should be on hand. They are readily adjusted to clamp the work.

"C" Clamps

(Carriage Clamps)

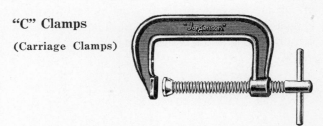

This type of clamp serves in a number of ways around the shop. While the "C" part is amply strong, the woodworker should avoid

putting too much pressure on the screw or there
may be a tendency to warp or "spring" this
part. They vary in size from 3 to 12 inches.

Adjustable Bar Clamp

(Cabinet Clamp)

The long, crank-handled, adjustable bar clamp
is another of the woodworker's standbys. It is
used to join boards together, or to obtain even
pressure over broad surfaces. Clamps of this
type are obtainable in sizes ranging from 2 feet
to 8 feet. Of course, each size of the clamp may
be adjusted to any spread less than its total
length.

Double Bar Clamp

Like the cab-
inet clamp, this
clamp is used
principally for joining boards together. The
double bars straddle the connecting boards and
thus an even pressure may be applied along each
surface of the board. This pressure helps to
prevent the boards from buckling when pressure is applied, an advantage that the single
cabinet clamp lacks. These clamps vary in
length from 2 feet to 5 feet.

Steel Pipe Clamp

This clamp dif-
fers from the
standard cabinet

type only in that a steel pipe forms its back-
bone as shown. The adjusting parts consist of
an adjustable end stop, and a crank screw which
is fastened to the opposite end. These parts are
attached to standard plumbing pipe of any de-

sired length. This type of clamp is particularly
handy for the workman who needs clamps of
varying lengths and who does not want to purchase a number of different size cabinet clamps.

Miter Clamps

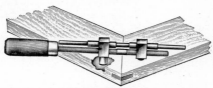

Miter clamps find their principal use in applying pressure to miter joints. They are especially

helpful in the construction of various types of
frames where even corner pressure is essential.

Veneer Press

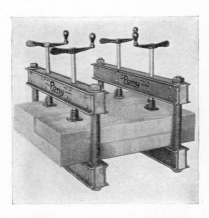

The process of veneering is quite easily performed with the veneer press. The construction
of this equipment guarantees uniform pressure.

Of course, in the absence of a regular press,
clamps of various types may be used to apply
pressure.

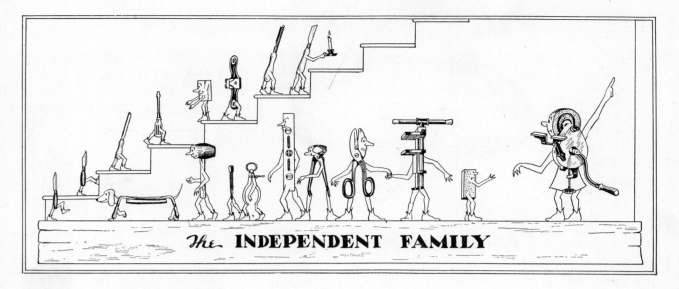

The INDEPENDENT FAMILY

While the tools which follow are listed as being "independent," they all form part and parcel of the essential group of hand woodworking tools.

They are placed separately, however, because in most instances each particular tool is in a class by itself and, therefore, is not a member of any of the foregoing families.

Chisels

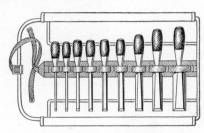

Chisels are among the most necessary tools in woodworking. They are commonly made with either wooden or composition handles. The widths of the blades range from 1/8" to 1" by eighths, and from 1" to 2" by fourths. There are two types of construction employed in the making of chisels, namely, the *tang* and the *socket* types. The tang chisel is made with a tanged, or pointed end which pierces into the handle. The socket type reverses the process by having the handle fit into the socket collar on the blade.

It will also be noted that the chisel blades vary in shape, some types being beveled along the sides as well as the cutting edge. Mortise chisels, used in making mortise joints, have perfectly flat blades usually a trifle thicker than the other ordinary types. Of course, the blades of all chisels are sharpened on a bevel from one side only.

It is a very good idea to use two hands when operating a chisel. The work should be held securely in a vise or with clamps so that both hands of the worker are free to handle the chisel.

Gouge

Gouges are sharpened in two different ways, either from the outside edge or from the inside. They range in size from 1/8" to 1" by eighths, and from 1" to 2" by fourths. While the standard types of gouges are manufactured with straight shanks, there is a separate type made with a bent shank. The latter is more practical for deep cutting.

Spokeshave

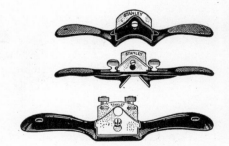

This tool is used primarily for shaping and smoothing edges. As the name implies, it was originally designed to make oval-shaped spokes for wagon wheels.

As indicated in the illustrations, spokeshaves are made in a number of shapes, sizes, and designs. They are obtainable in straight, hollow, and convex forms. Some types provide for adjustment of the blade in a manner similar to that of the plane blade.

Cabinet Scrapers

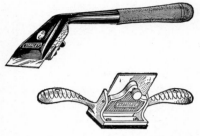

There are several distinct types of cabinet scrapers. However, they are all used for the same purpose, which is to scrape the surface of a board. The experienced craftsman often prefers to use the scraper blade alone, without a handle. Two different types are illustrated.

Screwdrivers

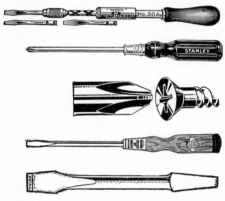

The screwdriver has long been known for its utility value around the home as well as the shop.

The hand automatic screwdriver which drives screws with a *pressing* action, is especially helpful. In using this tool, however, you must be careful not to pinch your finger. As previously noted, screwdriver bits are manufactured to fit into the conventional type of brace.

Knife

Two kinds of knives are commonly used in woodworking, one for scribing lines and one for whittling. The sloyd knife originated in Sweden, where it was used by the founders of the Sloyd school. The stencil knife, which has a triangular point, is used wherever a sharp pointed cutting knife is required.

Draw Knife

The draw knife is shaped somewhat like a pair of bicycle handlebars. The cutting knife spans the handles and the cutting action is produced by *drawing* the knife. This type of knife is generally used for cutting wood roughly to

size, and since it is not a precision tool, its use must necessarily be restricted to rough cutting only. Caution should always be observed to avoid drawing the blade in such a way that it may slip and cut into parts of the body.

Carving Tools

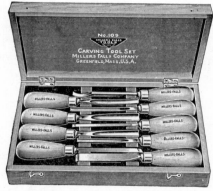

As illustrated, carving tools are made in varying shapes. Like the instruments of the dentist, or the clubs of the golfer, each separate carving tool has been designed for a specific type of cutting.

Hatchet

Both inside and outside of the woodworking shop the well-known hatchet is one of the most useful implements. As a woodworking tool, strictly speaking, it serves for the roughest sort of shaping.

Hammer

The hammer hardly requires any introduction—most of us have been familiar with it since infancy. However, it is interesting to know that hammers may be purchased in varying sizes ranging in weight from 7 to 20 ounces. There are two working parts to the hammer, the head for driving nails, and the claw for pulling them.

Mallet

This handy tool is used most frequently for striking chisels or gouges. It is also used to tap parts of a project together during the assembly process. Mallets are made in various shapes and sizes. Those of more recent manufacture have heads made of hard composition rubber, thus to protect the work or tools.

Nail Set

In order to drive the heads of nails below the surface, it is necessary to use either a *nail set* or a slightly larger size nail. Finishing nails of recent manufacture have small indentations on the head which provide for the use of a pointed nail set.

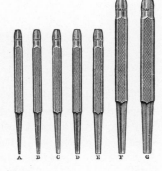

Calipers

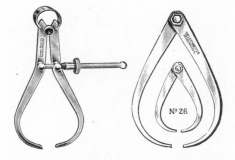

The round or turned parts of wooden articles are most easily measured with calipers. In wood turning, it is necessary to use calipers frequently when turning or shaping wood to a desired diameter. In use, the arms of the cali-

pers, at the curved tips, are pressed lightly against the wood at the point being measured. The separation between the tips is then measured. *Inside calipers* are used to gauge the size of inside surfaces.

Spirit Level

If you were to take a bottle or test tube of water and fill it so full that the water came to within a small space of the cork; and were then to place this bottle on its side, you would find a small *unfilled* space gliding along the top. Regardless of the position of the bottle the unfilled space would always remain *level*. It is on this principle that the carpenter's level functions. Instead of employing a bottle, a small glass tube partly filled with alcohol and sealed is inserted in a metal or wooden mounting and the unfilled part of the tube, or "air bubble," indicates the level qualities of the object being checked.

Pliers
Combination Pliers

Combination pliers have many general uses in the shop. The slip joint permits two positions.

Round Nose Pliers

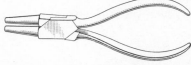

Pliers with round jaws are used for forming loops of wire. They are also used in radio repair, reed, and upholstery work.

Side Cutting Pliers

Side cutting pliers are used for cutting wire and removing cotter pins. This tool is also used in electrical construction work and for miscellaneous purposes.

Carpenter Pincers

Carpenter pincers are found to be very valuable in removing brads and small nails. Usually one of the handles is formed in the shape of a tack puller and the other handle is shaped in the form of a screwdriver, making the carpenter pincers a very valuable utility tool.

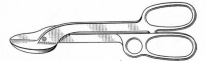

Scroll Pivoter

The scroll pivoter operating on the pivoting principle enables one to cut intricate shapes out of sheet metal, such as circles, scrolls, or squares, as easily as cutting along a straight line.

Vise

The vise is a very necessary article in woodworking. Work must be held and the vise is the instrument that holds it. There are several varieties of vises, each possessing its own particular merit. One of the common types is illustrated.

Oilstone

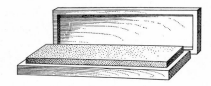

Sharp tools are essential in woodworking. In order to keep them keen it is necessary to have a sharpening stone on hand. The oilstone serves this purpose to perfection. It is made either of natural stone or artificial stone. Ordinarily the oilstone is made in rectangular shape, having one coarse and one smooth side.

Another form of oilstone called the *gouge slip* is used for sharpening gouge chisels and other curved cutting edges.

Tool Grinder

The tool grinder has a place in the woodworking shop because it is used for grinding the edges of chisels, plane blades, knives, and other cutting tools, in the first steps of sharpening. Such grinding is necessary to *hollow grind* the cutting edge and remove nicks which would otherwise remain after the ordinary process of sharpening.

Let's Go to Work!

One of the most important things in woodworking, as in any other endeavor, is a proper knowledge of *how to get started*. The beginning woodworker, finding himself in a fully equipped shop, is apt to become confused by all the tools and materials and finished work which confront him. Indeed, he may even become a little bit discouraged. After examining the work of the experienced craftsman, he may be inclined to wipe his forehead and say, "Whew! I could never do work like that!"

However, the beginner really need not become discouraged, because after he gets acquainted with the work he is bound to find that all those things which seem so difficult and confusing at first are actually quite simple. In order to get started all he needs is the ambition to make something out of wood.

It is always advisable to start on a simple type of project, something that does not involve the more complicated woodworking processes. Plans and working drawings of many simple "easy-to-make" project ideas can be found in project books and homecraft magazines. In order to get started on one of these projects, it is first necessary to know how to read a working drawing.

Reading a Working Drawing

Before doing anything or making anything, it is necessary to have a plan. If you were to start out on a long automobile trip, you would probably figure out the way you were going to go before you started. You would consult a road map and this would give you a *plan* of your route. In like manner, the company that builds a skyscraper, a steamboat, an airplane, or anything else, must have a plan to work by before any of the actual construction takes place. So too, the woodworker must first have a plan of the article that he is going to make. In woodworking, the plan is usually referred to as a working drawing.

The woodworker's working drawing shows all the dimensions as well as the construction of the article being made and, by studying it, the worker can determine, ahead of time, what the thickness, width, and length of each part of the article should be. Also, he can decide upon a method of attack for making the article; what parts to make first, what parts to put together first, and other important information of this nature.

A plan known as an *orthographic projection* is used in the preparation of working drawings. By this method three separate views of the article are drawn, namely, the *front view, top view,* and *end view*. Ordinarily these three views are drawn at right angles to each other; the top view occupying the top left corner of the paper, the front view immediately below it, and the end view in the right-hand lower corner. In instances where the article being made is identical in appearance when looked at from both front and end, the end view is not drawn.

The illustrations on the next page show the method whereby working drawings are prepared. In the working drawing, the *top view* of the five board stool is shown as though the actual top were X-rayed, revealing the dimensions and construction of the parts below the top. Similarly, the front view reveals the sizes and hidden construction of the front. Likewise, in the end view all of the end construction is shown. In this way both the size and the shape of every piece of wood used in making the article are accurately revealed.

It will be noted that all hidden construction, joints, and pieces that lie beneath each view of the article are shown with dotted line. Moreover, the dimensions of each piece are clearly indicated with arrows and figures. Even the position and size of every nail and screw are given.

Not only does a good working drawing show full dimensions and construction of every piece in the article, but it also shows the shape of curved and scrolled parts. This is generally done by "graphing out" the scroll; which simply means that lines are marked in the manner illustrated for the curved edge. From this a full-sized pattern is laid out in squares of the size indicated. The points where the line of curve crosses the lines of the squares are spotted off on the pattern and thus the curved line may be accurately drawn.

HOW TO READ A MECHANICAL DRAWING

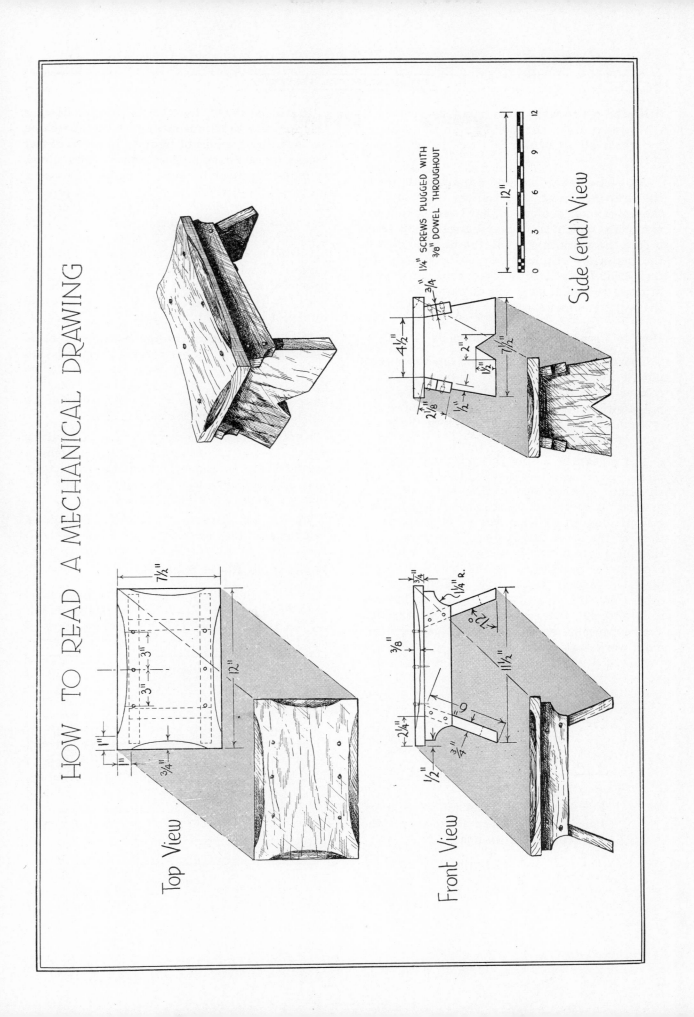

Top View

Front View

Side (end) View

Working drawings, like maps, are drawn to scale and a scale rule is shown on the drawing by which all measurements can be accurately checked.

As well as showing how the article is made, the drawing assists the worker in estimating the exact amount of wood, hardware, and other materials which the job requires. Thus even before the work is started, the finished cost of the materials required can be accurately determined. In fact, it is often considered good practice to make out a bill of materials before the work commences.

How to Prepare a Bill of Materials

There are several different methods employed for making out bills of materials. The cost of lumber used in a project may be computed either by figuring in terms of board feet or square feet. Three satisfactory methods are suggested herewith.

The system of listing the price of lumber in terms of square feet makes possible a very simplified method of figuring the cost. This method is becoming increasingly popular because it does away with many of the complications of the other two systems. Simply by multiplying the number of pieces by the width of each piece, *in inches,* by the length of each piece, *in inches,* by the cost per square foot, over a denominator of 144 (square inches per square foot), the cost is arrived at through simple cancellation. In practice this easy formula works out as follows:

Legend

N = number of pieces
W = width in inches
L = length in inches
C = cost per square foot in cents

$$\frac{N \times W \times L \times C}{144} = \text{cost in cents}$$

For 6 boards, 4″ wide and 22″ long, at 12 cents per square foot, we get the following substitutions:

$$\frac{6 \times 4 \times 22 \times 12}{144} = 44 \text{ cents}$$

It will be noted, however, that in following this formula, fractions of an inch might well be avoided. But the idea of figuring in terms of full inches (considering all fractions as full inches) is quite practical because it makes allowance for any waste which may occur in the process of cutting the lumber. Moreover, if fractions less than $\frac{1}{2}$″ are dropped and those over $\frac{1}{2}$″ are considered as full inches—$5\frac{5}{8}$″ listed as 6″, while $5\frac{3}{8}$″ listed as 5″— the sum will be approximately correct. It will be further noted that in order to arrive at the number of square feet in the total, it is then only necessary to divide the total cost by the cost per square foot.

It is often practical to figure out the cost of one large piece of lumber before it is cut up into smaller parts. Obviously it is much simpler to figure the cost of the original board than to figure individually the cost of a number of small pieces of varying widths and lengths.

Another method commonly used in figuring out the cost of lumber is to multiply the length by the width in inches, divide the product by 144, and multiply the result by the cost per square foot for each inch of thickness.

($W \times L$ (in inches) $\div 144 \times$ cost per square foot for each inch of thickness.

Filling Out a Bill of Materials

In most Industrial Arts shops it is customary to make out a full bill of materials of each project that is made. This bill often contains a

Project No. 12

GREENWICH PUBLIC SCHOOLS
MANUAL ARTS DEPARTMENT
Bill of Material

Name John Jones   School Center   Grade 8
Article Utility Box   Bench No. 12
Material Cherry   Approved by A.B.C.

Name of pieces	No.	TxWxL	Sq. Ft.	@	Cost	Check
Bottom	1	$\frac{1}{2}$ x 8 x 12		.14	.09	
Sides	2	$\frac{1}{2}$ x 1¾ x 12		.14	.05	
Ends	2	$\frac{1}{2}$ x 1¾ x 7		.14	.03	
Handle	1	$\frac{1}{2}$ x 2¾ x 11½		.14	.04	

Received Payment A.B.C.
Date 4/26/44

Total Charge $ .21
I approve the above charge
John Jones Sr.
Signature of parent or guardian

listing of the screws, hardware, sandpaper, and miscellaneous items which the job required.

It is customary to list lumber dimensions in the sequence of thickness, width, and length. Moldings and trim are listed by the linear foot.

In addition to a complete listing of stock used, the bill of materials may call for the student's name and grade; type of wood; name of project; date of beginning work on project; and materials used. All of this information is required in order to prepare a complete record. The bill of materials illustrated here has proven to be very satisfactory.

It will be noted that this is simply an accurate record of the cost of those items required in construction. Its purpose and function is similar to that of an ordinary grocery bill or milk bill. Naturally, this listing may be prepared before starting the project, while the project is in progress, or after completion.

How to Order Lumber

To the average inexperienced person, the ordering of lumber sometimes seems to be quite an involved and complicated matter. Of course, the lumber dealer will cooperate in seeing that the correct material is supplied. However, it is well to be able to call off the complete order.

Lumber can be purchased in various grades, thicknesses, widths, and lengths. Obviously for cabinet work only the better grades are suitable. So the average home or school woodworker will be interested in purchasing only the finer grades of lumber.

Government specifications require that various grades of lumber be listed under definite specifications, such as No. 1 clear pine, No. 2, No. 3, and so on. It will be best for the individual doing cabinet work to tell his dealer the kind of work he is going to do and to specify his own requirements regarding clearness, freedom from warps, cracks and checks, and degree of seasoning and kiln-drying.

Having determined the basic matters regarding the *quality* of lumber required, make a bill of materials of your various parts, and determine how many of these parts can be made from a single piece of lumber of specified thickness, width, and length. For instance, if you are making a table you may require as many as three different thicknesses of the same type of lumber. The legs may require stock 1¾″ square. In ordering material for these legs, specify the dimensions of a single piece of 1¾″ stock that is sufficiently long and wide to allow for cutting out the four legs a trifle over their finished size requirements. *Always allow ample room for sawing and planing to actual finished size.*

In many communities, for a nominal milling charge, the lumber dealer will cut your parts to size. This is often an important help, especially where many parts must be cut and where power machinery is not available.

How to Saw Lumber to Size

When the project to be made has been decided upon, the first job will be to cut the lumber to proper size. At this point it is necessary to cast a glance toward the lumber pile and determine the types of lumber which it contains. If the lumber is of a superior quality, kiln-dried, and smoothly surfaced on both sides, it will be an easy matter to get started. Even if the lumber is rough surfaced, there is no cause for alarm. Rough or smooth, the preliminary cutting steps may be proceeded with in easy fashion.

It is wise at the start, however, for the beginning woodworker to use a soft, even textured species of wood. A good grade of white pine serves admirably. This, and similar softwoods, cut and shape easily. They do not offer the beginner too much resistance.

Having selected a piece of lumber, the next step consists of using the woodworking tool called the *square,* for squaring up the ends of the piece of lumber. As described before, the square is used for marking lines and checking edges at perfect right angles. It is a very important tool.

Before using the square, the end of the piece of lumber is carefully examined for *checks and splits.* The end of a board will often be found to be slightly damaged in this way. Therefore, assuming that the long edge of the board is perfectly straight, the very first job in cutting lumber to size is to mark a line square across the end of the board so as to margin off the damaged portion.

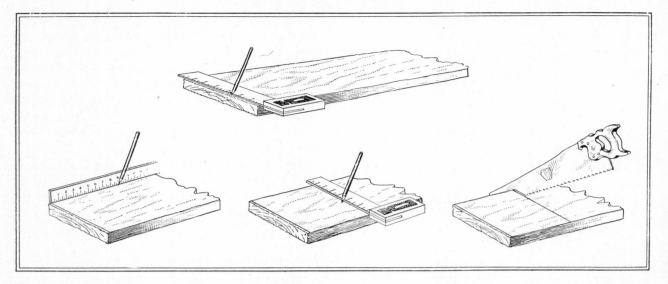

The original squared line which has been marked across the end of the board serves as a starting point. A rule is used to measure off from this line the length of the required board. It is good practice to mark the exact length. A line is then marked square across the board at the required length.

Now, all is ready to saw off the piece that is needed. The sawing is performed slightly outside the squared line with a crosscut saw. It is easier to guide the saw if the board is held flat. In sawing, it is good practice to hold the thumb lightly against the side of the saw. This will prevent the saw from jumping back, which might injure the hand or mar the work. Saw with a slow, even drive. When the end of the cut is reached the board must be supported so that it will not break off and splinter.

After the piece of lumber has been sawed slightly outside the squared line on both ends, it is possible to proceed with the following steps so as to square the piece to the required size.

Directions for Squaring a Board to Exact Size

The Four Squaring Steps.

Suppose the working drawing indicates that a board measuring exactly ¾ inch thick, 7½ inches wide, and 12 inches long is required; that the board be perfectly square and cut to these exact dimensions.

Assuming that the face of the board is smooth and level, the first job will be to plane one of the edges perfectly straight and square. Using a jack plane, the blade is set for a shallow cut, and the plane is driven evenly along the edge.

Now, experience has taught us that to use a plane properly, with the grain, it is necessary to have it set to the proper cut; and as a general thing, it is wise to set it for a shallow cut, so that it does not peel off too heavy a shaving. The plane should be held evenly on the edge, and driven along with a uniform pressure from end to end. As the planing is continued, the edge is checked with a square and straightedge. The job is not completed successfully until the entire edge has been planed perfectly square to the face of the board, and perfectly straight lengthwise along the board.

After this, one end of the board must be planed square to the first edge and square to the face. Right here the special job of planing end grain will be met. However, this is not too difficult to perform if the plane is set for a shallow grazing cut. Extreme care must be practiced to avoid splitting the end grain. The plane must not go all the way across the end in one cut, but from both edges toward the middle.

However, if the board is extra wide, so that some of the width will later be taken off to make the board the proper width, a corner notch can be made on the further corner of the end. This notch makes it possible to plane the end all the way across in one direction without splitting.

With one edge and one end planed true and square, the other end may be planed square to the first edge, and to the face, and to the exact length required.

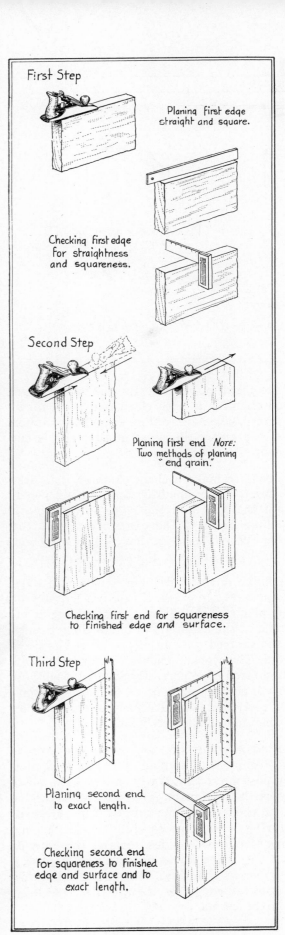

First Step

Planing first edge straight and square.

Checking first edge for straightness and squareness.

Second Step

Planing first end Note: Two methods of planing "end grain."

Checking first end for squareness to finished edge and surface.

Third Step

Planing second end to exact length.

Checking second end for squareness to finished edge and surface and to exact length.

Fourth Step

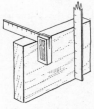

Planing second edge straight and square, and to exact width.

Checking second edge for straightness and squareness, and to exact width.

Fifth Step

Planing first surface smooth and level.

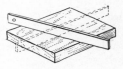

Checking first surface with straight-edge for smoothness

Sixth Step

Planing second surface smooth and to exact thickness.

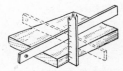

Checking second surface for smoothness, level and exact thickness.

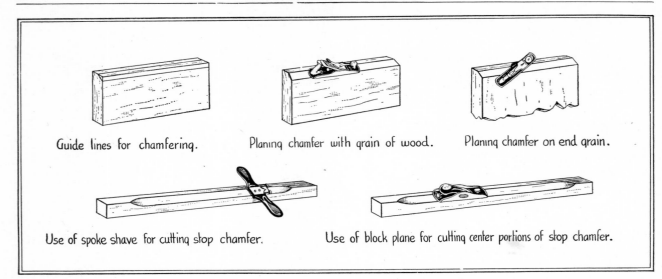

Guide lines for chamfering.   Planing chamfer with grain of wood.   Planing chamfer on end grain.

Use of spoke shave for cutting stop chamfer.   Use of block plane for cutting center portions of stop chamfer.

The final step in squaring the edges is to plane the opposite edge to the exact required *width,* straight and square.

It should be noted, however, that if the board is rough-surfaced, or if it must be brought down to a required *thickness,* one surface is planed before the "four squaring steps" can be undertaken. This operation is performed by securing the board in a flat position and planing one surface until it is perfectly level and smooth. The "four squaring steps" are then followed to bring the board to exact width and length. Planing the other surface to thickness is all that now remains to be done. The required thickness is marked around the edge, *away from* the finished surface. This is usually done with a marking gauge. The opposite surface is then planed *level and smooth* to this thickness.

Summary (Squaring to Length and Width)

First Step—Finish one edge.

Second Step—Square one end.

Third Step—Square other end *to exact length.*

Fourth Step—Finish other edge *to exact width.*

Chamfering and Beveling

If the sharp corner is removed from a piece of wood, the result is more pleasing to the eye. One of the most common ways of performing this is to chamfer, or cut away, part of the edge. A good chamfer is both clean and accurate in appearance. The bevel differs from the chamfer in that the *entire* thickness of the edge is cut to a slant.

In order to make a clean chamfer it is first necessary to mark chamfer lines with a pencil on both the *face* and the *edge* of the board. These lines indicate the exact margin of the chamfer. When the edge has been evenly cut away to these lines, the chamfer is finished.

When the chamfer is planed along an edge that runs *with the grain,* it is only necessary to set the plane to a small cut, and holding it on the angle of the chamfer, to plane along evenly until the desired portion of the edge has been removed. The worker should endeavor to keep the chamfered edge perfectly flat and clean and not to wiggle the plane so as to cause unevenness or rounding. It is extremely important that the plane blade be perfectly sharp.

The chamfering of *end grain* requires a special technique. The plane must be held in a paring position so that it will shear off the wood partly with the grain, and not splinter the grain at the end of the stroke. This type of chamfering is most successfully performed by working from both sides toward the middle so that the plane blade never actually passes entirely across the edge. The small block plane is favored for end-grain chamfering, especially when there is a narrow edge to be planed.

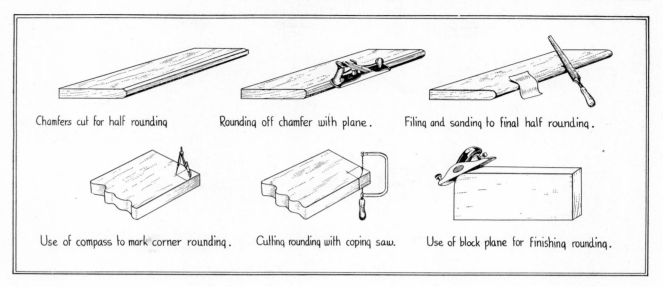

Chamfers cut for half rounding.   Rounding off chamfer with plane.   Filing and sanding to final half rounding.

Use of compass to mark corner rounding.   Cutting rounding with coping saw.   Use of block plane for finishing rounding.

Stop Chamfers

When a board is to be chamfered only partly along its edge so that end portions remain sharp, a stop chamfer is used. Ordinarily, after the work has been marked, a spokeshave, or a chisel, is employed for the cutting. However, if the stop chamfer occupies a reasonably long spread, it will be possible to use a block plane to cut the middle area. As in the case of the regular chamfer, work of this particular type should be well marked and performed in a careful manner. Where the plane and spokeshave are used, each tool should be set for a shallow cut.

Rounded Edges and Corners

When a half-round is required along the edge of a board, it is first necessary to mark the amount of rounding required. This marking is done by making pencil lines along the center edge of the board and along each opposite face, equal distances in from the edge. With these lines as the main guides, the work is proceeded with in two steps.

The first step involves the cutting of a regular straight chamfer at *half* of the span of the final rounding. With the plane set for a very small cut, the final rounding is accomplished in a series of graduating *rounding* cuts to the line of marking. The edge, which is now roughly rounded, is further smoothed with a wood file and is then sanded to a smooth, perfect rounded edge.

Rounded corners are first marked with a compass or are traced from circular templates. A coping saw, bandsaw, or scroll saw may then be used to remove the excess portions. Care must be exercised to cut just outside the rounded marking. The work is then planed, filed, and sandpapered to the final shape of rounding.

How to Bore Holes

Almost everyone is acquainted with the brace and auger bit. At some time or other we have all found a use for this important combination. There are, however, a number of other tools used for boring holes. It is well to know about them and to understand their use.

Using a Drill

In making holes of small diameters, either the *hand automatic drill* or the *push drill* is used. The hand automatic drill is operated in much the same manner as an egg beater, and accommodates drills in a variety of small sizes. Good results may be obtained by holding the drill steady and turning the operating crank evenly, at the same time maintaining a slight, even pressure upon the handle.

The push drill is especially helpful where a number of small holes must be drilled for screw fastenings, or for similar volume work. It will take drills in assorted small sizes. Through the simple action of pushing the handle, the drill automatically twists and drills a hole.

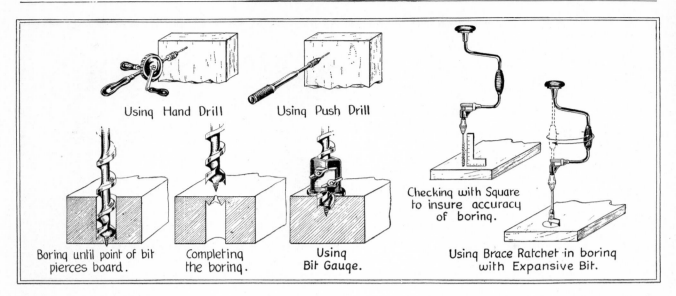

Using Hand Drill   Using Push Drill

Boring until point of bit pierces board.   Completing the boring.   Using Bit Gauge.

Checking with Square to insure accuracy of boring.

Using Brace Ratchet in boring with Expansive Bit.

Brace and Auger Bit

While the action of the brace and auger bit is more or less self-explanatory, still there are many people who experience difficulty in using these tools properly. In the first place, the bit should be placed in the brace in such a way that it is held firmly and securely. This means that the end of the bit should be inserted into the chuck or holding part of the brace, *as far as it will go.* When the bit is in action, and if a hole is to be bored entirely through the wood, the worker should stop turning when the point, or spur, of the bit appears through the opposite side of the board and then re-bore from the opposite side to finish the hole. Otherwise, the board may splinter on the opposite side.

For straight boring, the brace must be held so that the bit is perfectly perpendicular, and at right angles to the wood. The knack of holding it in an accurate position is soon acquired. However, it is well at the start to test the position of the bit with a try square, as the work progresses.

When boring holes of a diameter greater than 1″ the expansive bit is generally used. After it has been adjusted to the required size, the boring continues in the manner already described. However, when using an expansive bit to bore a large hole, it is sometimes advisable to use the ratchet adjustment on the brace, making part turns with the ratchet. Otherwise the resistance to the wide spread cutter would make steady and accurate work difficult.

Likewise, when the screwdriver bit is used, the ratchet attachment assists greatly. Small turns on the brace make the driving of large stubborn wood screws possible, after all other methods have failed.

Using the Bit Gauge

When holes of an exact required depth must be bored, the bit gauge comes in very handy. This little device which is attached directly to the bit, permits the bit to enter the wood to the adjusted depth. Care must be taken, however, to watch the gauge so that it does not scratch or mar the wood after the required depth has been reached.

Marking and Cutting Curves and Scrolls

Ordinarily a *template,* or "pattern," is used to mark scrolls on a piece of wood. In making a template, first lay out squares on a piece of bristolboard or similar material, as shown in the illustration. These squares should correspond to the size indicated in the working drawing. The exact line of the desired curve is transposed from the working drawing and "spotted off" on the squares of the template. After this operation, the several points are connected by a free flowing line representing the desired curve. The bristolboard template is then cut out with a pair of scissors, a sharp knife, or razor blade.

After the template has been made, it is used to mark the scroll on the work. In the absence

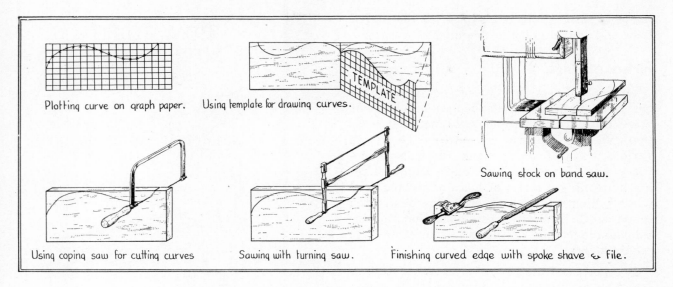

Plotting curve on graph paper.   Using template for drawing curves.

Sawing stock on band saw.

Using coping saw for cutting curves   Sawing with turning saw.   Finishing curved edge with spoke shave & file.

of a machine bandsaw or jig saw, the actual cutting is performed by hand with a coping saw, turning saw, compass saw, or keyhole saw. Each of these is well adapted for its own particular job.

Turning saws are admirably suited for the type of scrollwork wherein long deep curves are to be cut. Because of its wider and coarser blade, however, it is impossible to obtain as fine a cut with the turning saw as with the coping saw. Therefore, provision must be made in cutting for final working and smoothing to the desired scroll.

The coping saw is probably the most popular of the saws used for cutting curves. While using this tool, the work should be clamped in posi-

tion so that the blade may at all times cut absolutely perpendicular to the surface. By maintaining an evenness and uniformity of cutting thrust, keeping the saw blade absolutely straight and level at all times, the resulting cut will be perfectly square and very little dressing up will be required. All sawing should be carefully performed just at the outer edge of the desired line, thereby preventing any change of the pattern curves. This method also eliminates a great deal of the work involved in finishing off curved work with other tools.

As shown in the illustration, a spokeshave of the straight or convex type, a file, and sandpaper are indispensable in finishing curved areas. Sharp edges should be avoided. A round-

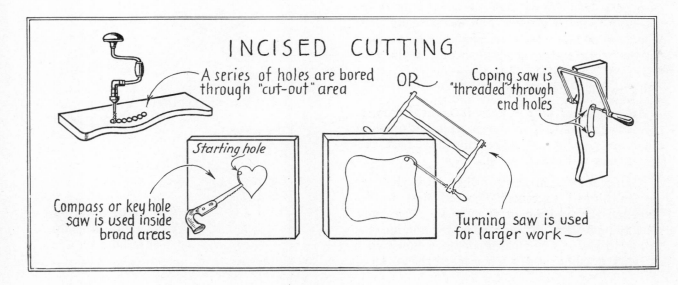

INCISED CUTTING

A series of holes are bored through "cut-out" area   OR   Coping saw is "threaded" through end holes

Starting hole

Compass or key hole saw is used inside broad areas

Turning saw is used for larger work —

ing of at least $\frac{1}{16}$ inch tends to soften the curved lines and adds dignity to the finished work.

Incised Cutting

It is often necessary to cut out spaces and curved shapes *inside* the edge area of a piece of wood. Cut-out handles and other incised decoration call for this type of cutting. There are various ways of going about this job. Sometimes it is desirable to bore out a handle shaping by making a series of holes of the required width which eclipse each other to remove the center stock. Following this operation, the inside handle may be chiseled and shaped to exact requirements.

In other cases the power scroll saw or coping saw may be "threaded" through a hole which has been bored within the cut-out area. The stock is then sawed out in regular fashion from this starting hole. Turning saws may likewise be taken apart so that the blade can be threaded through an inside hole. This saw is especially helpful for such cutting in heavier stock, or where the margin between the edge of the stock and the cut-out is greater than can be normally spanned by a coping saw.

Keyhole and compass saws are especially designed for inside cutting and can be used to very good advantage where holes and shapes are to be cut out in central areas of broad surfaces. Of course, these saws are apt to make a rough cut, but they are invaluable where the span or the spread of work is so great as to prevent the use of a loop frame type of saw. This is especially true on work which has already been constructed and where the tool must be brought to the work rather than the work to the tool.

How to Fit Butt Hinges

In attaching butt hinges it is necessary to inset each leaf to a thickness equaling one-half the thickness of the hinge knuckle. These cut-out insets are called *gains*.

Gains are cut in both of the pieces that are to be hinged together. Proceed first to determine the position of the hinge. Then mark out the position of each gain by holding the hinge in place and marking along each end with a sharp pencil or knife. Then mark the depth of

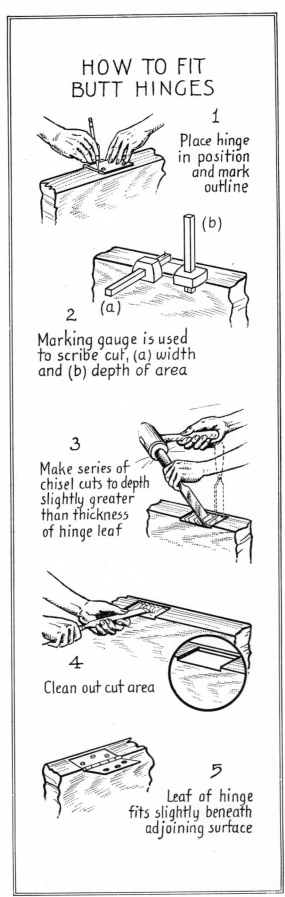

HOW TO FIT BUTT HINGES

1 Place hinge in position and mark outline

2 Marking gauge is used to scribe cut, (a) width and (b) depth of area

3 Make series of chisel cuts to depth slightly greater than thickness of hinge leaf

4 Clean out cut area

5 Leaf of hinge fits slightly beneath adjoining surface

Squaring top line of taper.

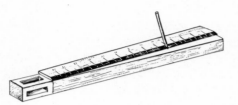

Marking taper on one side.

Marking tapered side for second taper.

Finishing second taper.

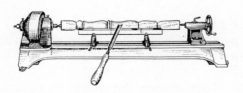

Leg being turned on lathe.

the area to be cut out, which is equal to slightly more than the thickness of the hinge leaf. This is marked on each of the pieces that are to be hinged together.

In cutting out the gain, the chisel is placed in an upright position on the line which locates one end of the hinge. The mallet is then used to drive the chisel as deep as the line which marks the depth of the gain. Next, a series of chisel cuts is made within this area, as shown in the illustration. After these cuts have loosened up the area to be removed within the gain, a sharp chisel is used to clean out the area. The gain is cleaned so that the hinge leaf fits within it snugly and evenly. The hinge should not be forced into the cut-out area.

Holes for the hinge screws are drilled as described for driving screws. As a rule, it is advisable to drive only one screw in each hinge leaf, so that the fitting of the hinge may be tested. If the fitting functions properly, the rest of the screws are driven. If not, the depth or position of the hinge leaf is adjusted before driving the remainder of the screws.

How the Legs of Tables and Chairs are Shaped

Legs of chairs and tables are shaped in three general ways, namely, round (turned), curved (cabriole), square (straight or tapered). Obviously the square type is the easiest to make, although frequently the least desirable. However, there is no difficulty attached to the making of any of these types, provided, of course, that they are devoid of elaborate decoration and carving.

The perfectly square leg is simply cut to length, planed to the required thickness, thoroughly sanded, and thus considered complete.

The *tapered leg,* however, requires additional treatment. In most cases the taper, or slant, is cut on two sides of the leg only. Thus the leg is first pencil-marked on one side to the desired amount of the taper. A ripsaw, or better still, a band saw, may be employed to remove the extra wood outside of the taper line. A plane is then used to smooth the tapered side down to the line.

When one side has been finished, the adjoining side of the leg is marked. This side in turn is carefully sawed and planed. It will be noted that in assembly, the two tapered sides generally remain on the inside, to improve the appearance of the article and to give it a splayed effect.

Turned legs are made on a lathe. Naturally, the work involved may be simple or difficult depending on the type of design and the skill of the worker at lathe work. Turning is explained in the section on lathe work (page 102).

Cabriole legs, because of their appearance, seem hard to make, yet when it comes right down to the actual work of making them they are not at all difficult. A template, or pattern, is first made of the curved cabriole shaping. This pattern is carefully marked on the two opposite faces of the square piece of wood from which the leg is to be made. The leg is then cut outside the marking and smoothed down with a spokeshave, file, and sandpaper to the cabriole marking. After this primary

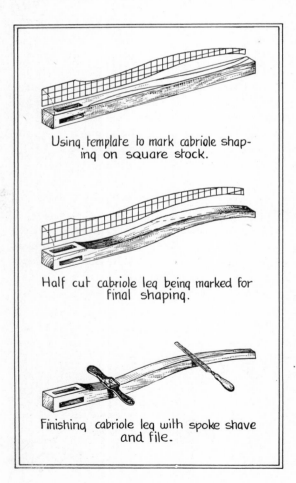

Using template to mark cabriole shaping on square stock.

Half cut cabriole leg being marked for final shaping.

Finishing cabriole leg with spoke shave and file.

shaping, the pattern is again marked on the two opposite sides of the leg that have already been shaped. The cutting and smoothing is performed as in the primary step and thus the cabriole shaping is accomplished.

Often, however, the cabriole shaping must be further shaped and rounded. This operation is performed with a sharp spokeshave, file, and sandpaper.

Simple Edge Shaping

The tops of tables, chests, and stools are generally embellished along the edge with some special type of treatment. This treatment may vary from simple rounding or sandpapering of the edges, to involved and elaborate carving and scalloping.

One of the most common of these treatments is referred to as the "thumb edge." As indicated in the illustration, the usual thumb edge requires a straight top cut, or shoulder, and a gently sloped and rounded edge. If the worker decides to make this edge by hand he should proceed in the following manner.

First mark a marginal line at the required distance (usually as deep as the thickness of the wood) in from the edges that are to be shaped. Proceed then to saw along this line, on the surface, to a depth of $\frac{1}{8}$ inch or slightly less. This process is most easily accomplished by first placing a board on the line and securing it in place with a clamp. This board then acts as a guide for sawing the shallow shoulder.

After the shoulder cut has been accurately made, several additional saw cuts should be made to the necessary depth, on the portion of the edge which is to be rounded off later. With a sharp plane, preferably a rabbeting plane, the stock outside of the shoulder is then leveled off. Following this operation, the edge is pencil-marked to the required amount of sloped rounding and either a rabbet plane or block plane is used to make the rounding. In doing this, the edge is first chamfered and then rounded off. The opposite, or bottom, edge is then given a $\frac{1}{8}$-inch rounding. A wood file and sandpaper are used to give the thumb edge its final shape and smoothness. A rabbet plane may also be used to make the shoulder cut, as shown.

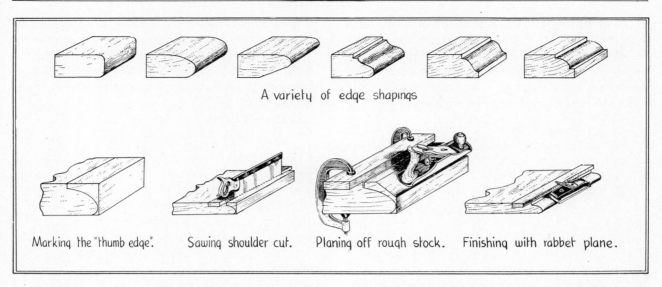

A variety of edge shapings

Marking the "thumb edge". Sawing shoulder cut. Planing off rough stock. Finishing with rabbet plane.

Of course, if the thumb edge is made on a circular saw, the work is greatly simplified because the primary shoulder cuts may be machine-made and all the excess stock can be removed by making a number of trips across the circular saw. Only the finishing work need be done by hand.

A typical assortment of edge moldings are shown in the accompanying illustrations. They may all be successfully shaped by hand.

Seat Weaving

The weaving of seats for stools and chairs presents itself as a fascinating activity which most children, as well as adults, enjoy. The work itself is extremly simple. In fact, it is necessary to learn only a few basic techniques in order that the weaving of seats of stools and chairs may be performed in a really skillful manner.

Because of the fact that round and flat fiber of the manufactured type is now available for immediate use, the task has been greatly simplified. It is no longer necessary for the worker to be hampered by the short, stiff, natural strands. Sturdy strands are now produced in lengths measured in hundreds of feet and, in addition, they are soft and pliable. They are also made in an interesting assortment of colors.

Caning is generally used on seats of three different types, namely, square, rectangular, and Windsor (irregular shaped).

In making the article to be caned, the rails may be set in from the edge of the legs a distance which is at least equal to the thickness of the weaving cord. This arrangement causes the outer surface of the weaving and the edge of the leg to line up in the finished article. It is well to remember that the edges of rails which are to support the weaving cord should always be rounded. This rounding greatly lengthens the life of the woven seat, inasmuch as it reduces the tendency to cut or break the fiber composition along the sharp edges.

The fibers most commonly used for weaving purposes, now commonly referred to as art fiber, are of two basic types, the *round* cord (referred to as rush) and the *flat* cord. Of these two types, the flat cord is slightly easier to handle and requires a little less skill in application. On the other hand, the seat woven correctly with rush has greater strength and, more important still, it carries the impression of being extremely quaint and authentic.

Rush weaving was frequently done in the Colonies long before the Revolutionary War. In contrast to the weaving cord used today, the rush fiber of Colonial days was made by the laborious task of twisting together long strands of soft pliable grass. It is interesting to note that in the appearance of the finished seats, there is little difference between the seats of old and the seats of today, especially when one uses a prepared cord which has been correctly colored.

Let us now begin the actual job of weaving a seat with flat cord. This weaving fiber is produced in standard ¼-inch width. A great many people prefer to use two colors, each color being woven across the other. Two colors make possible the weaving of interesting designs.

Due to the fact that four widths of flat cord are required for each inch in width, it is easy to compute the approximate length of cord needed, always allowing a few extra feet.

The first step is to tack one end of the flat cord beneath the end rail, snugly against the leg of the article. Then wrap the fiber right around the end rails, from one to the other, just as you would wrap cord around a block of wood. This first step is really not weaving, but merely wrapping. Be careful to avoid twisting the fiber and see that it is snugly wrapped so as to cover the entire seating area. After as many wrappings have been placed as the end rails will conveniently accommodate, the remaining end is tacked securely beneath the end rail. This operation completes the first of the two necessary steps.

We are now ready to begin the second, or weaving step. Cut off about 8 or 10 yards of flat cord of the desired color. Tack one end beneath the side rail, snugly against the leg. Then pull the flat fiber through the fingers so as to remove all twists. Now the real weaving begins—over five strands—under five strands —over five strands—under five strands—over the remaining number of strands. Weave the bottom in the same manner as the top. You have now woven the first strand.

The second strand is woven just like the first, excepting that the fiber "enters" and "leaves" so that it is always one strand nearer the person who is weaving. That is, we progress one strand each time so as to get a diagonal effect. The same is done for weaving the next strand, and the next, and the next, and so on until the short piece of flat cord has been used.

We are now ready to splice another piece of fiber to the first woven length. The weaving fiber is then cut off under the seat so that the splice will be concealed inside the bottom strands. About one inch at the ends of each of the joining cords should be unwrapped to form a flat "fan" shape. By placing a drop of glue between the ends, twisting them roughly together, and then wrapping the entire area tightly with fine thread, a secure splice is formed. The weaving process may then be continued until the top has been completely woven and the remaining end of the flat cord has been tacked securely beneath the rail.

This simple type of caning provides an interesting diagonal pattern. Various types of geometric designs are made possible by slightly adjusting the length and width of the area for weaving, so as to fit the specified number of strands needed for each individual design. The fact that the flat cord is provided in ¼-inch width, makes it easy to figure the sizes necessary for accommodating a specific number of strands.

Interesting variations in design, such as those illustrated, may be worked out. Plot the design you wish to use on graph paper and count the number of strands both lengthwise and crosswise. Diamond-shaped patterns, patterns with radial lines, in fact, simple block initials may be woven into the design.

For *rush weaving,* take an entire roll of fiber of the desired color and diameter and tack one end tightly against the under side of the left end of any rail. Sometimes the entire area can be woven without a single splice. When a splice is necessary, however, it is made in exactly the same manner as suggested for splicing flat cord.

The cord is (1) tacked beneath the rail, (2) it passes over the top of the rail which is directly opposite, (3) down under it, and (4) up over the end of the other rail which is attached to the same leg. This process is repeated for the remaining three sides. Thus is concluded the first trip around the outer edge of the seat.

This same process is repeated again and again until the diagonal corner lines meet snugly in the center.

In a rectangular stool the width will naturally be completed before the length. This remaining area is then filled in by simply passing the round fiber back and forth, over the side rails. Be sure that the cord is kept taut

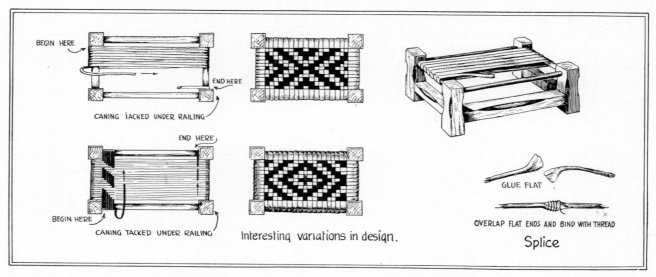

BEGIN HERE
END HERE
CANING TACKED UNDER RAILING

END HERE
BEGIN HERE
CANING TACKED UNDER RAILING

Interesting variations in design.

GLUE FLAT
OVERLAP FLAT ENDS AND BIND WITH THREAD
Splice

at all times and that the work is carefully done, so that the diagonal corner lines will be straight and neat. After the weaving process is completed, adjust the woven surface carefully with a pointed stick or screwdriver so as to make the cords line up in an orderly fashion. Sitting on the newly woven top helps to pull the strands into their required positions. In order that there may be less sagging, soft paper is sometimes carefully packed beneath the layers during the weaving operation.

The weaving of an irregularly shaped seat requires the weaving in of the wide area so as to form a regular square or rectangle. This weaving in is easily done by tacking the round fiber to the inner edge of the side rail, near the widest part, weaving across the wide area to the other side and then securing the remaining end to the inner edge of the other side rail. Then weave another strand across the wide part—and another—and another—until the remaining area has four right angles. The regular opening is then woven just as any other square or rectangular area would be woven.

For several reasons, the woven seat should be protected with a suitable preparation. Because these materials are relatively porous, thin clear glue is frequently used as the sizing, or priming coat. This may be applied with a brush just as a coat of varnish is applied. The sizing provides an excellent base for a coat or two of white shellac or clear varnish. Many people

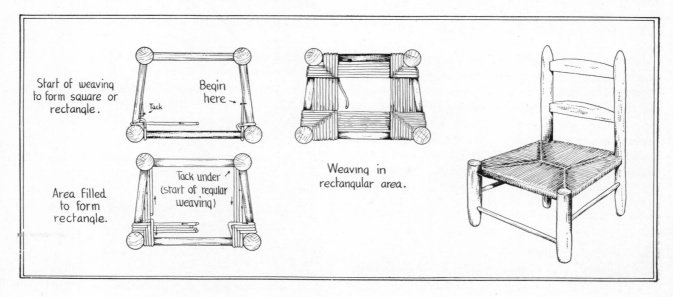

Start of weaving to form square or rectangle.

Tack

Begin here ➔

Area filled to form rectangle.

Tack under (start of regular weaving)

Weaving in rectangular area.

prefer to omit the glue and use only shellac or varnish as a protective finish of pleasing effect.

Simple Upholstery

Upholstery is an art in itself. In fact, the professional upholsterer carries on a type of work which is quite different from woodworking. Yet at times it is necessary to know something about upholstery in order to construct certain kinds of woodworking projects. For this reason only the simplest types of upholstery will be discussed.

Seat pads for chairs may be easily upholstered in the following manner. First, it is necessary to stretch alternating layers of upholsterer's webbing across the open part of the seat frame. The webbing is tacked securely to the surface of the frame. A double layer of muslin is then laid over the webbing and tacked at the edges over the surface of the frame. Hair, down, kapok, or sea moss is used as a filling for the upholstery and is carefully packed above the muslin. This filling, in turn, is covered by another double layer of muslin which is tacked along the edges of the frame to provide the cushion. The final covering fabric is then stretched over the pad and tacked at the edges.

Sometimes a thin layer of cotton is laid on top of the pad between the last muslin covering and the fabric covering.

An excellent example of simple yet attractive upholstery, is displayed by the small footstool illustrated. This footstool is upholstered with a roll edge pad. Webbing is first attached crosswise from the aprons, as shown. A roll of stuffing is then made to cover the sharp upper edges of the rails. The roll is pocketed beneath a strip of burlap 3 or 4 inches wide, which has previously been tacked in, along the upper rail at the desired point of overlaps. A fold about ¼-inch wide should be made on the edge of the burlap so that the tacks will hold better. The roll should be as hard and even in size and shape as possible. It is put in place in the burlap casing, which, in turn, is tacked on the upper edge of the rail. The footstool will require a roll 1 inch in diameter.

Horsehair, moss, kapok, or down is used in the fill. This material is pressed down tightly and covered with muslin, which is secured with

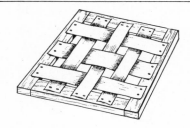

Burlap webbing stretched and tacked over seat frame.

Double layer of muslin spread over webbing and tacked to edges of frame.

Filling packed over muslin and ready to be covered by top layers of muslin.

Layer of cotton placed over muslin.

Seat frame after upholstered covering has been applied and tacked beneath.

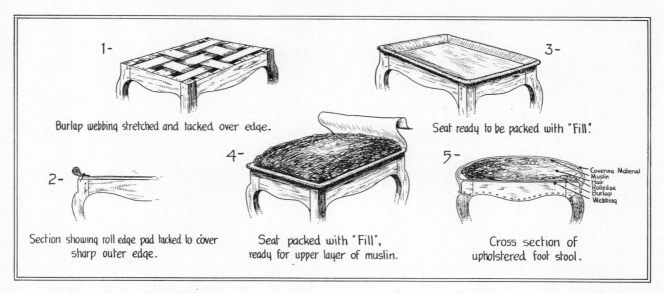

1- Burlap webbing stretched and tacked over edge.

2- Section showing roll edge pad tacked to cover sharp outer edge.

3- Seat ready to be packed with "Fill".

4- Seat packed with "Fill", ready for upper layer of muslin.

5- Cross section of upholstered foot stool.

Covering Material
Muslin
Hair
Rolledge
Burlap
Webbing

tacks along the outer surface of the apron. The fabric cover is then cut, hemmed, and carefully tacked on. Usually, all edges are covered with upholstery braid, and sometimes special upholstery tacks, with large heads, are used to secure this braid. These tacks give a decorative appearance to the finished piece.

Simple Decorative Processes

Inlaying

Many types of work require the use of inlays as part of their decorative treatment. Ordinarily, inlaying is not too difficult a process, but, because it is one of the finer practices of woodworking, it demands strict adherence to the rules of precision and accuracy. Sharp tools are, of course, a primary requisite in the performance of this work.

The straight inlay is first marked out with a sharp pencil and straightedge, as shown in the first illustration. Care must be taken to inscribe the exact location and width of the inlaid portions. Absolute accuracy may be obtained by adjusting carefully the straightedges so that they fit snugly against a strip of inlay. Straightedges are then fastened along the inscribed lines. Several perpendicular cuts are made along each edge with a sharp knife. By grooving out the section between the straightedges with a sharp chisel, to a depth which corresponds to the thickness of the inlay, the chan-

nel is finished and the edge guides may be removed.

After the channels have been made and the strips of inlay cut to the desired length, thin glue is spread on these strips and they are lightly tapped into the groove with a small hammer or mallet. Care must be exercised at this point to avoid breaking the inlay. The entire surface, or the inlaid strips, as desired, are then covered with paper to prevent the glue from adhering to the clamping boards, which are used to distribute even pressure while the glue is drying. It is unnecessary to use clamps if grooves are cut with absolute precision. When the glue has set, the entire surface should be thoroughly sanded.

Veneering

Veneering is an art which dates back many centuries.

The veneering process demands careful workmanship, but it is by no means too difficult for the amateur to undertake.

It is necessary first to lay out the pattern in which veneers are to be combined on the surface which is to be veneered, as shown in the first step of the illustration. The cutting is performed with a straightedge and a sharp veneering knife. Although veneers are only about $\frac{1}{32}''$ thick, care must be taken to cut this minute edge perfectly square.

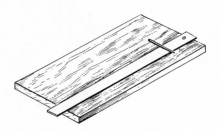

Marking out area to be inlaid.

Clamping straight edges to exact width of inlay.

NOTE: STRIP OF INLAY SHOULD FIT SNUGLY BETWEEN THESE CUTTING GUIDES.

Cutting shallow channel for inlay.

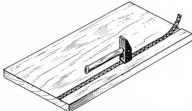

After covering with thin coat of glue, inlay is lightly tapped in place.

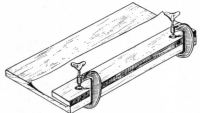

Method of clamping inlay.

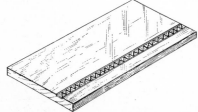

Inlaid surface as it appears when completed.

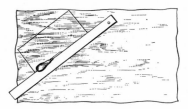

Cutting veneer with straight edge and sharp veneering knife.

Matched veneering with edges cut true and square.

Veneer seams held with veneering tape.

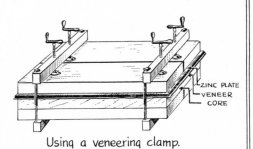

ZINC PLATE
VENEER
CORE

Using a veneering clamp.

TOP BOARD
ZINC PLATE
VENEER
CORE BOARD

Using "C" clamps for gluing veneered stock.

Diamond Matched.

Veneer cut from "Crotch."

Veneer cut from "Burl."

Spotting off spaces for reeding.

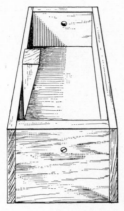

Reeding box. Note wedge for holding work stationary.

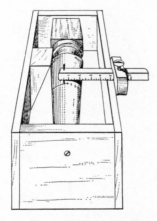

Use of reeding box and marking gauge for accurately marking reeds.

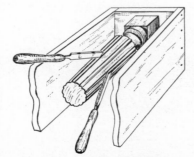

Cutting the reeds with veining tool and skew chisel.

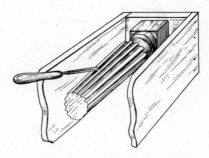

Cutting flutes with gouge.

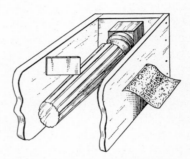

Finishing work with scraper and sandpaper.

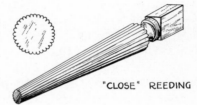

"CLOSE" REEDING

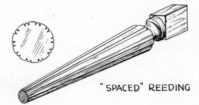

"SPACED" REEDING

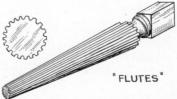

"FLUTES"

Finished examples of reeding and fluting.

Where matched veneers are being used, each separate piece is joined to the others by gluing veneer tape or narrow strips of wrapping paper over the joint.

Glue is never applied to the veneer itself, but to the surface on which it is to adhere. A hot zinc plate may be placed directly over the veneer and above this a board, either flat or curved, conforming to the surface. This board is either clamped or placed in a veneer press and allowed to stand for at least twenty-four hours. Naturally, the veneer should be applied as soon as possible, before the glue has started to congeal.

Reeding

Reeding is a decorative process which is especially attractive when used on the legs of certain types of chairs and tables. The process itself is not very difficult, but it does require patience and skill.

When reeding is to be applied to a piece of turned work a special reeding box should be made to hold the work. Such a box consists only of two sides and two ends without top or bottom. The turned piece is placed in the box and held by a single screw at each end. Care should be exercised to attach the turned piece in the exact center of the reeding box.

The circumference of the turning is then marked off for the desired number of reeds. This marking is most easily done by taking a small strip of paper, equaling in length the circumference of the turning. The strip is then divided and marked to the desired number of reeds. It is then wrapped around the turning and the marks are transferred to the circumference of the work.

The marking gauge is used to make the *vertical* marking along the turned piece. The gauge is held so that it presses evenly along the edge of the reeding box and is adjusted to scratch a straight vertical line along the center of the turned piece. Thus the position of each reed is clearly marked on the turning.

The turning is then wedged firmly in the reeding box and each vertical scratch mark is V-cut, to start the shape of the reed. Each V-cut is then carefully shaped and mounded with a

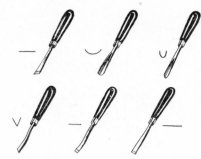

Set of carving tools.

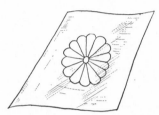

Design drawn on paper.

Use of carbon paper for transferring design.

Incising outline of design with "v" or veining tool.

Scooping design with gouge for finished effect.

sharp chisel to form the individual reeds. The cutting steps are followed by careful sanding.

Flutes

Flutes require the reverse treatment of reeds; that is, they are scooped out rather than mounded. The fluting process may be performed with a sharp gouge. Extreme care must be exercised, however to keep each flute of uniform depth and shape. A router plane, equipped with a round-nosed cutter, may also be used to perform the fluting process.

Both reeding and fluting may be most easily made with a routing machine. Such a machine carefully operated eliminates much of the chance element and assures absolute uniformity of work.

Simple Carving

Carving is a most entertaining occupation. It is not difficult to learn and yet it provides an excellent opportunity for self-expression. Like all other phases of woodworking, successful carving is largely dependent upon sharp tools. The variety of carving tools has already been noted. They form part of the craftsman's kit.

A typical example of simple carving is shown in the illustration. This type of carving is performed by first making a pattern of the desired design. The outline of this design is then marked on the wood. The design can easily be transferred through the use of carbon paper. Along the edge marking the design is lightly incised with a V-cut carving tool. The inner portions are scooped out carefully with a sharp round-nosed carving tool. Care must be exercised to cut from alternating ends of the scooped out portions. The beauty of this type of carving is dependent, naturally, on the worker's ability to handle his tools skillfully.

Simple carving of this type is suggested as a beginning step. Other elaborate forms may be attempted as the skill of the worker increases.

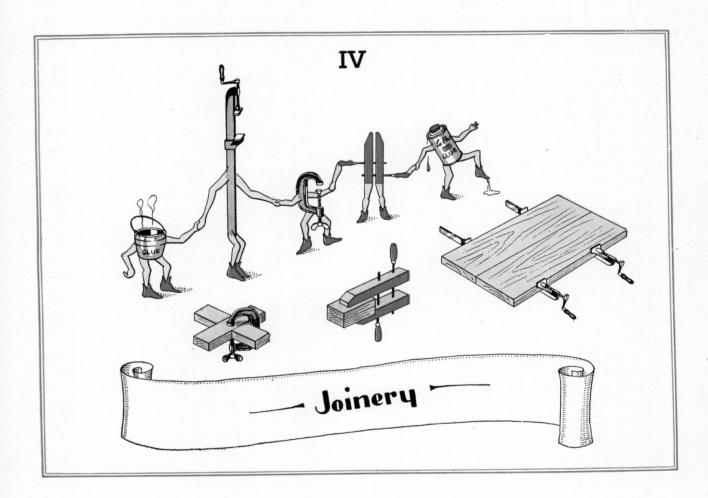

IV

Joinery

What is Meant by Joinery?

The common dictionary definition of the word "join" is set forth as follows: "To set or bring together; connect; combine." The term "joinery," as applied to woodworking, follows the same definition.

An article made of wood can be no stronger than the *joints* which hold it together. It is necessary, therefore, to secure all wood joints in the strongest possible manner. We cannot merely put wooden parts together and expect them to stay together, *if they are not fastened securely*. From the very beginning the worker should get the habit of making good, stout, secure joints. Actually, little extra effort is required to accomplish this end and the result may double or treble the life of the things you make.

Many sturdy pieces of Colonial furniture, dating back well over two hundred years, are still in use because of the excellent joinery employed by old-time craftsmen. We can profit by their work if we wish to produce articles of lasting sturdiness and strength.

There are many different types of joints, each adapted to certain specific needs. Frequently nails are used to make joints, sometimes screws. Other types of work call for glue, hinges, dowels, mortises, and tenons; or frequently a combination of several fasteners. Let us consider some of the general methods of joinery.

Nails

Nails are probably the most common and best known type of wood fastener. The relative strength of nails and the ease with which they may be used, accounts for their wide usage. They are most commonly used, of course, in carpentry and building where speed and strength of construction go hand in hand.

Nails range in size and style from the smallest of brads and tacks to the heaviest of railroad and construction spikes.

The subject of nails would not be complete unless a few words were said in regard to their sizes. Long years ago there originated the term "penny" to tell the sizes of nails. In its abbreviated form, it is marked by the letter "d." It is interesting to note that these terms still exist

and that we speak of 6d or 10d nails. For regular usage, nails range in size from the tiny 2d nail to the huge 100d spike.

Many different types of nails are made from several kinds of metal; iron, copper, and steel. There are nails with galvanized coating to retard the destructive action of rust. There are nails bent in the shape of a "U" with both ends sharpened, which are known as staples and which come in a variety of sizes. There are shingle nails, roofing nails, casing nails, and cut nails. Even carpet tacks, upholstery tacks, lath nails and shoe nails belong to the nail family and each is made for a specific use. All of these types are shown.

Brads might roughly be referred to as small finishing nails. They differ principally in size rather than in style or use. The small head found on finishing nails and brads tends to hold and yet minimizes the danger of splitting the wood when it is driven beneath the surface.

The nail most commonly used when it is not necessary to conceal the head, is the common wire nail. Usually the diameter of the head is approximately three times as great as of the nail itself. The enlarged head serves to prevent the head of the nail from being drawn through the board. Sometimes the large flat head is *set* and is then concealed just like a finishing nail. This type of nail eliminates the danger of a small head being drawn through a soft board. Securing soft cedar siding to the side of a house is probably one of the best examples of the use of common wire nails in which the heads are set and concealed.

For certain types of work, the heads of the nails are allowed to remain exposed; while in other instances they must be set beneath the surface. This practice permits them to be covered and concealed by putty and paint.

The finishing nail is easily set beneath the surface with a *nail set* or, sometimes, by using another larger nail. This latter practice is permissible when using finishing nails of the variety which have heads with depressed centers.

Nails driven in at a slight angle provide greater holding strength than those driven straight into a board. This is especially true when driving nails into end grain. The practice of sloping the nails is known as *toeing*.

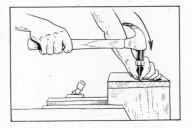

Correct method of holding nail
and hammer.

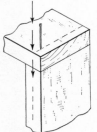

Sighting nail
to exact
center of edge.

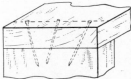

Nails "toed" at angle for
greater holding strength.

Setting nails with a nail set.

Pressing fill substance with thumb and
"planing off" with putty knife.

An inexperienced person usually finds that some nails have a nasty way of creeping out through the side of the board when nailing into thin stock. This fault is caused by incorrect aiming when driving the nail. Sighting along a nail is similar to aiming a rifle. Always be sure to stand in a position which permits sighting carefully over the edge of the thin stock. Start the nail so that it will be in direct line with the center of the thin board. Except in rare cases of hard, sloping grain, the nail will then continue indefinitely through the center of the stock.

One mistake which is commonly made is to start the nail so that it is headed in the wrong direction. Even after the exposed part of the nail has been straightened, the remainder of the nail may follow the incorrect direction set by the point. The nail point then splits out through the surface of the board.

For certain types of fastening, especially in rough work, it is necessary to drive a nail clear through the joining pieces of stock and to bend over the point on the opposite surface. This is known as clinching. Thus with the head on one end and a bent-over point on the other, the nail resembles a small bolt or rivet in its holding strength.

Use of the Hammer in Drawing a Nail

It is well to remember when attempting to draw or pull a nail with a claw hammer that a block of wood placed beneath the head of the hammer not only protects the surface of the board, but also provides greater pulling leverage, and thus makes the operation much easier.

Making a Nail Joint

When making a joint with nails the following considerations should be kept in mind. The application of glue before assembly tends to strengthen the joint. Nails placed directly in line with the grain and close together tend to split the board. Whenever possible, stagger the nails. When large nails are used near the end of a board or when the wood is extremely hard, drill holes (slightly smaller than the nail) to prevent splitting. Use judgment in deciding upon the sizes of nails to be used.

Wood Screws

In many instances screws are used for the same purposes as nails. However, they are threaded metal fastenings which offer distinct advantages over nails. By using screws the strain caused by heavy hammer blows is eliminated. Screws have much greater holding power than nails, they may be removed with greater ease, and frequently they are needed to harmonize with cabinet hardware and special fittings. Their chief disadvantage lies in the fact that they are more expensive than nails and require more time and effort to apply.

Screws are made in a variety of styles and sizes, and are made of several types of metal. The one style most widely used is the *flathead bright screw.* In addition to this well known type, we have the *roundhead, oval head, and square head* (commonly known as the *lag screw.*) Unlike the other types which require the use of a screwdriver, the lag screw has a square head which requires the use of a wrench. This head permits greater ease in driving extremely large screws.

To meet the many needs, screws are also manufactured in a variety of finishes: galvanized, nickel-plated, brass and bronze finishes, blued, japanned, the common bright finish, and even the tinned finish for ease of soldering. Obviously, solid brass and bronze screws are indispensable for wet fittings in that they defy rust. Other types of finishes tend to resist rust.

Wood screws are also made in various lengths and diameters. Inasmuch as screws are made from wire of graduating gauges, the gauge of the wire used determines the diameter of the screw.

The *Phillips screw,* a comparatively recent development, differs from the conventional screw in that the center of the head is slotted crosswise. Its advantage lies in the fact that it may be readily driven without fear of "burring" or breaking the head. Likewise, the appearance of the cross-slotted head makes it suitable for exterior or exposed use.

Rivets and Bolts

For sturdy construction, rivets and bolts far surpass the strength of nails and screws. In using them, it is necessary to drill a hole cor-

Correct method of drawing nails.

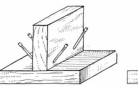

"Toenailing" an end fastening.

Drilling hole in hard wood to prevent splitting.

How to "clinch" a nail.

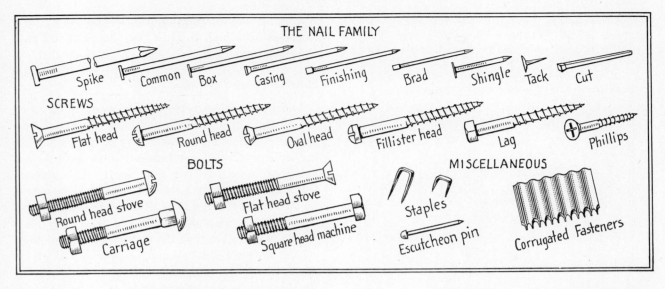

THE NAIL FAMILY

Spike   Common   Box   Casing   Finishing   Brad   Shingle   Tack   Cut

SCREWS

Flat head   Round head   Oval head   Fillister head   Lag   Phillips

BOLTS   MISCELLANEOUS

Round head stove   Flat head stove   Staples

Carriage   Square head machine   Escutcheon pin   Corrugated Fasteners

responding in size to the diameter of the rivet or bolt all the way through the connecting pieces of wood.

The rivet and bolt differ principally in that the rivet is held in place with a washer and a clinched end, whereas the bolt requires a conventional nut and washer. Consequently, a bolt can easily be removed by merely unscrewing the nut; but to remove a rivet it is necessary to file or grind off the rivet burr.

Rivets are manufactured in a variety of styles and sizes and are usually made of relatively soft metal, so as to permit the making of a flattened, or clinched end. Copper rivets (which, of course, do not rust) are used in the construction of boats. The rivets used for wood construction form an interesting contrast to the large metal rivets which are used in building skyscrapers and huge bridges.

To meet the many needs which arise, bolts of several types are available in a variety of lengths and diameters. The types most commonly used are *machine bolts*, *stove bolts*, *machine screws* (with round and flat heads), and *carriage bolts*. They range in length from tiny bolts and machine screws which are but a fraction of an inch long to those which are measured by the yard. Likewise, they are made in diameters which fit the most exacting engineering requirements.

Corrugated Fasteners

Corrugated fasteners are often used for rough work and for concealed construction. Among their many uses, we find that of making plain butt joints and miter joints, especially when one has to perform an adequate job in a short time.

These metal fasteners come in a variety of sizes. The one edge is sharpened (either with a plain edge or with a saw edge) to facilitate their being hammered into the wood. Also, they are produced with tapering or parallel corrugations. Those of the former type tend to pull the boards firmly together, thereby making a tight joint.

The worker should be careful to see that the adjoining boards are in correct position before driving this type of fastener. Once driven into place, the fastener is hard to remove without breaking off the adjoining sections of wood which it secures. For fine cabinet work, the corrugated fastener is rarely used. Many other methods of joining are preferable.

Recently a new type of wood fastener made its appearance. Known as the "Teco Fastener," it has virtually revolutionized heavy wood construction. The simple device of an attached ring causes this fastener to sustain heavy stresses that would be impossible with ordinary bolt construction.

Hinges

There are numerous types and kinds of hinges. Most of them are designed for special use. Some of the decorative types in use today date their origin back several centuries. Most common of all hinges is the *butt* type. These hinges are used principally for attaching doors

The "Teco" Fastener

and table leaves. They are manufactured in two types, namely, the *fast-pin butt hinge* and the *loose-pin butt hinge*. The loose-pin type is

commonly used for attaching doors. After this hinge is attached, the pin may be removed and the door detached.

How to Drive Screws

Driving small screws in soft wood is an easy job. A light tap of the hammer starts the screw and the screwdriver then drives it home. For larger screws and for harder wood the process becomes more involved. Frequently three operations are necessary to avoid splitting the wood or twisting off the screw. First, a hole should be drilled to accommodate snugly the shank, or unthreaded portion of the screw. Next, the edge of the hole should be *countersunk* as shown in the illustration, to accommodate the head of the flat-head screw. Lastly, a small pilot hole should be drilled to receive the threaded portion of the screw.

Using a lubricant on screws greatly expedites the work of driving them into place. Various types of waxes, oils, and special mixtures are frequently used. The lubricant can best be applied by simply dipping the threaded section of the screw into the preparation.

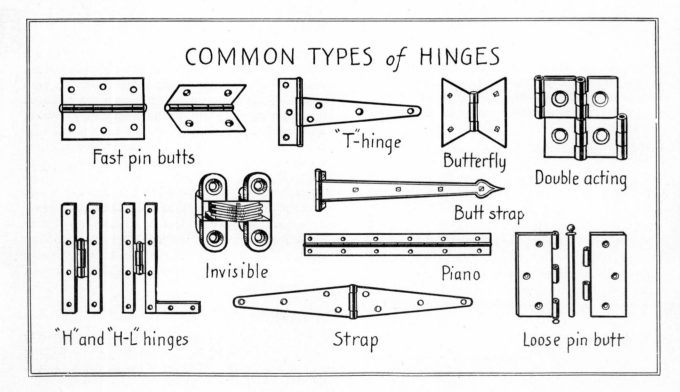

COMMON TYPES *of* HINGES

Fast pin butts

"T"-hinge

Butterfly

Double acting

Butt strap

Invisible

Piano

"H" and "H-L" hinges

Strap

Loose pin butt

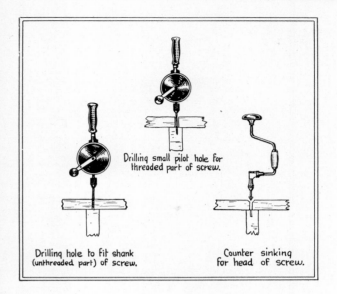

Drilling small pilot hole for
threaded part of screw.

Drilling hole to fit shank
(unthreaded part) of screw.

Counter sinking
for head of screw.

Counter Boring and Plugging

In most cases it is desirable to conceal the heads of screws. This is readily done by counter boring, that is, drilling a hole approximately halfway through the board with a bit, large enough to accommodate the head of the screw. After securing the screw, it may then be concealed, or covered over with a wooden plug. After the counter boring is finished, the respective holes are drilled for both the shank and the threaded part of the screw.

Now let us consider the plugs which are used to conceal the screw heads. For ordinary shop use we might list them in the following manner: First, there is the *boat plug*, or *surface*

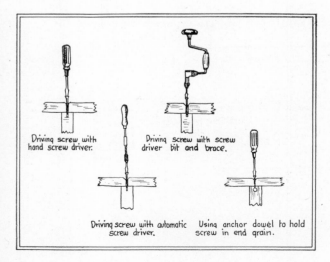

Driving screw with
hand screw driver.

Driving screw with screw
driver bit and brace.

Driving screw with automatic
screw driver.

Using anchor dowel to hold
screw in end grain.

grain plug. When it is cut from the same type of wood with a special cutter, the wood grain can be matched so as to make the plug almost invisible, after the sanding operation.

Next, there is the *end grain plug*, cut from an ordinary dowel, which when sanded level gives an interesting effect. The end grain of the plug usually absorbs a little more stain than the surrounding area, causing the small decorative plug to be slightly darker. This gives the piece of furniture the interesting effect of being "pegged."

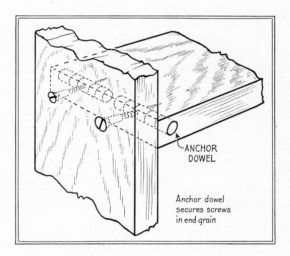

ANCHOR
DOWEL

Anchor dowel
secures screws
in end grain

Third, we have the protruding end grain plug, again cut from an ordinary dowel. The plug is cut long enough to extend approximately one-eighth of an inch above the surrounding surface. It is inserted after the surface of the article has been thoroughly sanded. This protruding end is then nicely decorated by cutting the edges irregularly with a sharp chisel. Quaint pegged effects are likewise obtained by using the square or irregular plug. These plugs should be cut to fit snugly within the bored area.

Wood plugs should always be glued securely in place.

Glue and Cement

Various kinds of glues and cements are needed in school and home shops. For the sake of convenience, they may be listed as liquid glue, animal glue, vegetable glue, casein glue, and the new Weldwood resin glue. Each offers certain advantages and certain disadvantages. Cements may be purchased under a variety of trade names, and like glue, certain preparations have specific uses.

Liquid glue is commonly used. This glue is the kind which comes in small cans ready for immediate use. Its greatest asset is its convenience. This kind of glue absorbs moisture readily and thus during damp summer days, especially along the sea coast, it tends to return to its liquid state. Consequently its holding qualities are greatly impaired when exposed to moisture. The slowness with which it dries permits ample clamping time.

Animal glue, as the name implies, is made from the gelatin of various animals. It is sold in flake or granulated form and must be soaked in water and heated in a double-boiler glue pot or other suitable receptacle. Boiling impairs its strength and should be avoided. This is the type of glue one usually finds in the familiar glue pot of the school shop or of the woodworking plant. It congeals rapidly and therefore no time must be lost in placing the glued stock in clamps. Avoid using it upon cold surfaces. Like liquid glue, this adhesive is also affected by the presence of excessive moisture.

A type of glue which is rapidly becoming more and more popular is the waterproof glue. For marine work and construction jobs which are subjected to extremely damp climates and conditions, it is unexcelled. One type of waterproof glue is really the finest of *casein* glues. Like the other members of the casein family, it is made primarily from cow's milk and caustic lime. The glue sets up slowly, allowing ample time for the clamping operation. Probably its chief disadvantage lies in the fact that it must be prepared daily. Also, it has a tendency to stain the stock somewhat more than other glues.

Recently a type of glue appeared on the market that just about revolutionizes all previous ideas of the holding power of glue. Known as *Weldwood plastic resin waterproof glue*, this product is a genuine urea-formaldehyde plastic. It belongs to the famous modern family of synthetic resins, familiar to all under a wide variety of trade names. This glue comes in powder form and is mixed with water. It dries by chem-

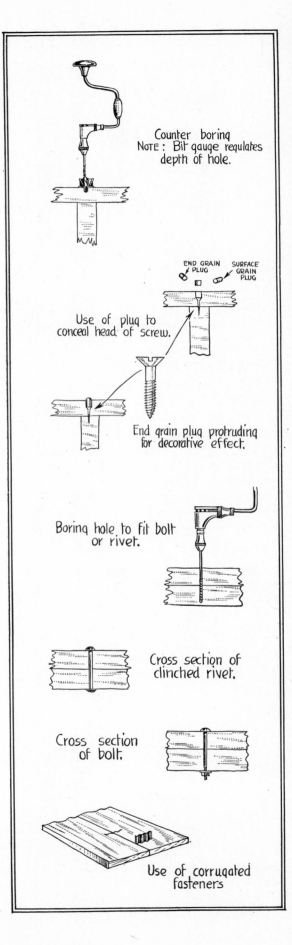

Counter boring
NOTE: Bit gauge regulates depth of hole.

END GRAIN PLUG   SURFACE GRAIN PLUG

Use of plug to conceal head of screw.

End grain plug protruding for decorative effect.

Boring hole to fit bolt or rivet.

Cross section of clinched rivet.

Cross section of bolt.

Use of corrugated fasteners

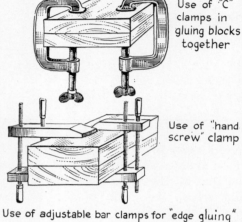

Applying glue to edges of board for butt joint. NOTE: Glue is applied to both edges

Use of "C" clamps in gluing blocks together

Use of "hand screw" clamp

Use of adjustable bar clamps for "edge gluing"

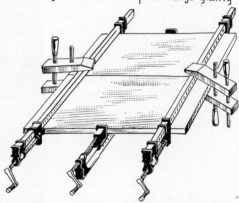

NOTE: Hand screws are used to prevent "buckling"

Assembly of rails and posts, properly clamped

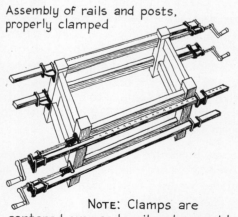

NOTE: Clamps are centered over each rail and assembly checked for squareness

ical action, not by the evaporation of the water with which it is mixed. Its holding power is practically unlimited. As the name indicates it literally *welds wood* together and depends on no special conditions for its effectiveness.

Applying Glue and Cement

Regardless of the kind of glue or adhesive used, there are a few simple directions which must be followed in order that a secure joint may be made. First, make sure that the surfaces to be glued together fit perfectly and that they are free of grease, wax, dirt, or any other foreign matter which might weaken the holding strength of the glue or cement. After applying a thin layer to both surfaces to be glued, the pieces should be pulled securely together with suitable clamps. This process tends to force all excessive glue or cement from the joint and holds the joint until the glue has dried and gained full strength. It is always well to allow ample drying time while the work is in the clamps.

Glue must always be of correct consistency. If it is too thick it will not readily penetrate the pores of the wood, and if too thin it will be absorbed and thus leave a dry joint with little strength. The wood should not be too cold or certain kinds of glue will be chilled, thereby causing them to congeal. This chilling greatly impairs their penetrating powers. Also, place the work in clamps as quickly as possible after applying the glue, before the glue has started to congeal. Good glue properly used makes a tremendously strong joint.

Regardless of the kind of glue or cement you have selected for the job, *don't spread it over the outside surfaces of the finished article.* Smeared glue or cement is very difficult to remove. It mars the wood and spoils what might otherwise be a perfect surface.

Peg-Leg Construction

The use of "peg-leg construction" provides an extremely strong and effective means of securing legs of stools, tables, and kindred articles. The results are pleasing and usually very secure.

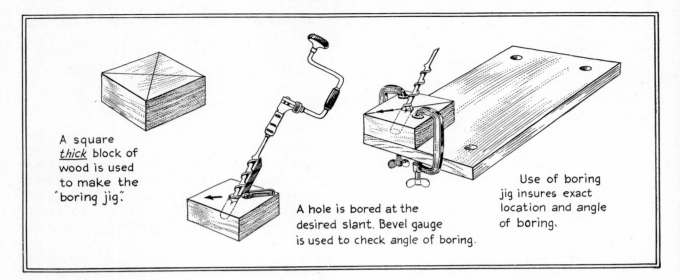

A square _thick_ block of wood is used to make the "boring jig."

A hole is bored at the desired slant. Bevel gauge is used to check angle of boring.

Use of boring jig insures exact location and angle of boring.

In the event that the plan calls for a thin board for anchoring the legs, place a batten reinforcement so that it will be concealed underneath, thereby increasing the thickness of the board at the places where the legs are secured. Repeated tests have proved that peg-leg construction, executed in the proper manner, with good solid wood, will withstand successfully all ordinary hard use.

The job of boring the holes for the legs is extremely simple. In order that it may be done accurately, prepare a jig by boring a hole of the desired size through a small block of wood. Bore at the proper location and hold the brace and bit so as to bore at the desired slant. A bevel gauge may be set to the desired angle and used as a guide. This block of wood then becomes the "jig" and can be clamped upon the board for boring each of the required holes. In this manner the jig guides the bit so as to insure identical locations and splays for each of the legs.

The legs are then shaped. Next, the top of each leg (the section which is to become the tenon) is made to fit the prepared holes. The tenons may be made to fit the borings either through the use of a lathe or simply by whittling carefully with a knife. A file may be convenient for the final fitting. Be sure that each tenon fits snugly within the hole.

If a tenon wedge is to be used, run the saw down the center of the tenon, lengthwise, to about two-thirds the length of the tenon fitting.

This permits spreading the tenon to receive the wedge. It is always well to make the saw kerf, or cut, so that all the wedges line up nicely in a position across the grain of the adjoining board.

After the wedges have been prepared, place glue upon the sections to be fastened together. Tap the legs into position and then drive the wedges securely into place. The protruding ends of the legs and wedges may then be cut off and sanded flush with the surface of the board. Otherwise they may be allowed to protrude slightly, and then decorated by making irregular cuts with a sharp chisel. This is known as a through, or open, tenon.

Sometimes it is desirable to make a hidden, or blind, tenon instead of the usual through type. In this case, the holes must be carefully bored so as not to extend through the top. After the fittings and hardwood wedges have been made, apply glue and assemble. The wedge, which is placed at the mouth of the saw kerf, is pushed into place as the leg itself is forced into the mortise. Obviously, the wedge causes the tenon to spread and assume a slight fan shape. For a secure fitting, it is customary to enlarge slightly the inner part of the mortise to permit wider spreading of the tenon.

Sometimes holes are bored through the edge and hardwood pins are glued and driven through the completed wedged tenon joint so as to provide even greater strength.

Sawing slot   for wedge.

Wedging the tenons.

A - Sharpened wedge is driven into slot.
B - Protruding wedged tenon is sawed
     flush to surface.
C - Smoothing tenon with plane and
     sanding block.
D - Tenon smoothed off flush to surface.

Method of sawing ends of legs even
to floor.

Sawing Jig

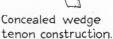

Concealed wedge   Tenon is held
tenon construction.   with "pin".

Dowel Joints

Dowels are small round sticks made of hardwood. They are used in a variety of ways. Usually they are produced in lengths of three feet and in various diameters to meet their many needs.

Dowels are commonly used to reinforce butt joints. Also, they are frequently used as a substitute for mortise-and-tenon joints. Dowels may also be used to strengthen miter joints, to secure legs and other fittings to turned columns, for strengthening square, circular, and irregular forms, and for numerous other purposes.

The correct use of dowels may be explained under a few simple headings. First and most important of all, *be sure that the location of dowel holes, of one member, match identically the location of the dowel holes of the corresponding member*. To insure accuracy in this respect, it is only necessary to place the pieces to be joined together, side by side, and then carefully measure and mark off identical points. When the corresponding points match perfectly, it is obvious that the drilled holes must also match perfectly.

Next in importance is the problem of drilling *straight holes* so that the dowel will not be forced into a bent position when the boards are drawn together with clamps. To assist in accurate drilling, a *doweling jig* (an adjustable metal holder for guiding the bit) offers a great deal of help. However, if a drilling jig is not available, stand directly in line with the edge of the board, sight the bit just as you would aim a rifle, and drill carefully. It might be well to stop drilling now and then and look at the job from different angles in order to be sure that the bit is held perfectly straight.

After the holes have been correctly drilled to the required depth, cut the necessary dowels approximately one-eighth inch shorter than the combined depths of the corresponding holes. This process permits a slight clearance and thereby prevents the danger of having the dowels jam. It is advisable to cut or file a small glue channel or spiral extending the full length of the dowels, especially when the dowels are an extremely tight fit. Dowels may be purchased which are prepared with a spiral glue channel. Otherwise, if the excessive glue and air cannot escape, the dowel may act like a tightly fitting piston and thus jam while being forced into the hole.

When gluing a dowel joint, be sure to place a thin layer of glue over both edges which are to be joined, over the entire surface of the dowels, and also inside the holes which are to receive the dowels.

Lap Joints

In construction work it is frequently necessary to have two boards cross each other on the same plane so as to form an even surface. To do this, it becomes necessary to cut away the upper half of the stock from the one member and the lower half of the stock from the other member, at the point of intersection. Then, when these two lapped pieces are put together, the upper and lower surfaces become perfectly flush.

Lap joints, as such, are very easy to make. Probably the most important detail to stress is that all measurements be carefully made and that cutting lines be sharp and accurate. This is really half of the battle. Before proceeding with the cutting operations, always hold the members together in order that the accuracy of the lines may be checked. It is then merely a

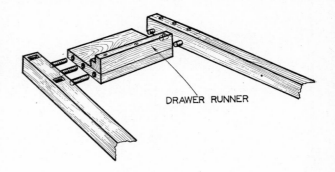

DRAWER RUNNER

matter of removing carefully the stock within the area of the lines so that the members may cross to form a snug joint.

The lap joint may be cut in several ways. A series of saw cuts extending in depth to the center line may be made within the limits of the side lines. The opening is then carefully dressed to the required lines with a sharp chisel. The sawing should be performed with either a hand saw or by making several cuts on a circular saw which has been set to the correct depth.

Several types of end laps may be cut directly by using the saw for cutting, both from the surface and from the end. In other cases the stock may be removed with bit and chisel, depending upon the nature and location of the joint. There is hardly one set rule for performing this operation, inasmuch as each craftsman follows his own particular rule for getting the greatest degree of accuracy with the least amount of unnecessary effort.

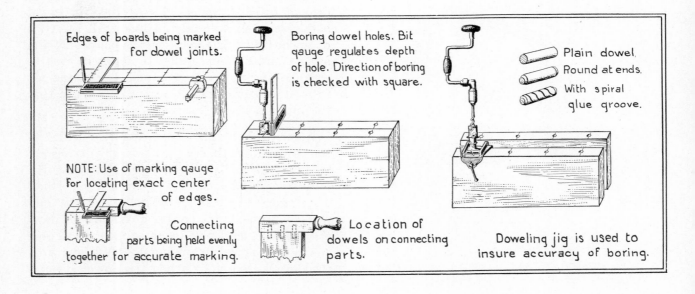

Edges of boards being marked for dowel joints.

Boring dowel holes. Bit gauge regulates depth of hole. Direction of boring is checked with square.

Plain dowel. Round at ends.

With spiral glue groove.

NOTE: Use of marking gauge for locating exact center of edges.

Connecting parts being held evenly together for accurate marking.

Location of dowels on connecting parts.

Doweling jig is used to insure accuracy of boring.

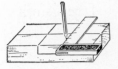

Pieces held side by side for marking center cross-lap joint.

Use of saw and chisel for removing "cut-out".

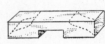

Cut-cut is made on top and bottom of connecting pieces.

Cross-lap members assembled.

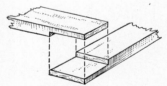

End-lap joint.

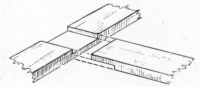

Middle-lap joint.

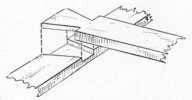

Dovetail Halfing joint

An error to guard against in this type of construction is that of making the opening too large, thereby causing a loose and sloppy joint. As long as the fitting is too tight it is a simple matter to enlarge gradually the opening with a chisel, until a perfect fit is made. But when the cut has been made too large, the best thing to do is discard the work and start again.

Lap joints are made in a variety of styles. There is the *center lap* where the members intersect each other at the centers; the *cross lap* when they cross somewhere between the center and the end; and the *end lap* where the ends are lapped over each other. These types are also combined in several different ways. In addition, there are *dovetail halving* joints of several varieties which are described with dovetail joints. Lap joints and dovetail halving joints are usually secured with glue, but concealed screws may also be used when additional strength is required.

Dovetail Halving Joints

This type of joint provides extra strength at a middle lap point of construction. It has an advantage over the conventional middle lap joint, in that it offers greater resistance to pulling strain. Moreover, it is quite easily made.

The work is started by marking out the cut-out part of the joint. This marking is done with a bevel gauge and square. After the cut-out has been marked, it is carefully sawed with a sharp backsaw. The cutting should be kept inside the marked lines. A number of saw cuts should be made within the marked area. The part that has been sawed is then carefully removed with a sharp chisel and the walls of the cut may be pared off until they are clean and even.

In making the end dovetail which fits into the cut-out, the joining piece is accurately marked at the end to the same dimensions as the cut-out. It is then sawed to the half thickness indicated by the marking. The final step is to make shoulder cuts at the base of the dovetail marking, and to saw the dovetail shaping. It is then finished with a sharp chisel and assembled to the first piece. The final fitting of the joint is made with thin cuts to avoid marring the corners. A tight fit is recommended, even though the joint is further held by glue or screws.

Grooved Joints

There are several different types of grooved joints, some running with the grain and others extending crosswise, either directly or on a slant. In some instances, certain of these joints are concealed, while others may remain exposed. As shown in the accompanying illustrations, good craftsmanship demands the frequent use of grooved joints in a variety of interesting and effective ways.

Let us first consider the simple *rabbet joint*. This joint is the square-edge cutting found usually on the backs of picture or mirror frames. It is put there so that the glass and other necessary fittings may be recessed into the frame. This is probably the most common of its many uses. Obviously, the rabbet should be carefully marked off and cut before assemblying the various parts.

The process of cutting a rabbet is very simple indeed. Actually, only two cuts across a circular saw, which has been set to correct depth, with the ripping fence set to the proper width, will perform the job in the shortest possible time. Also, routers and shapers are frequently fitted with blades and may easily be adjusted for the rapid cutting of rabbets of varying sizes.

Then again, clamping a straightedge board to the desired lines (one at a time) will serve as an excellent guide for the backsaw in making the necessary rabbet cuts. For small rabbets which are to be made in soft wood, one can easily make the cuts by tracing the two respective lines of the rabbet with a sharp, thin-blade knife, until the perpendicular cuts meet at the inner edge of the rabbet. Marking gauges which have been sharpened to a razor edge are also efficient for cutting rabbets in soft stock. A sharp chisel is used for making the rabbet smooth and accurate.

Next in order, let us consider the regulation groove joint. This joint is the type of recess needed to accommodate the tongue of the board in "tongue-and-groove" fittings; as a fitting into which panels are set; as the groove into which drawer bottoms are placed; and as a fitting for the use of splines and other interesting types of construction. The tongue-and-groove joints of

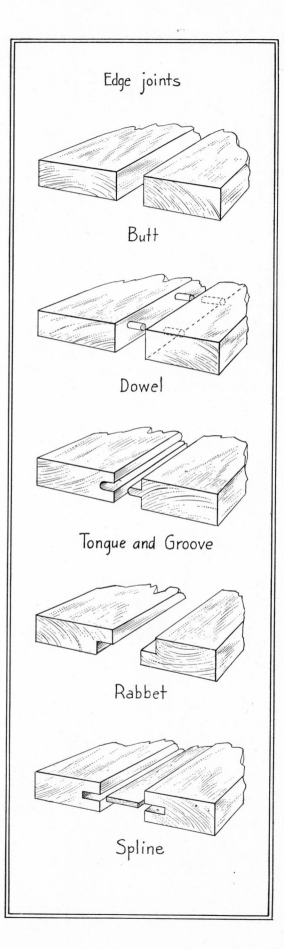

Edge joints

Butt

Dowel

Tongue and Groove

Rabbet

Spline

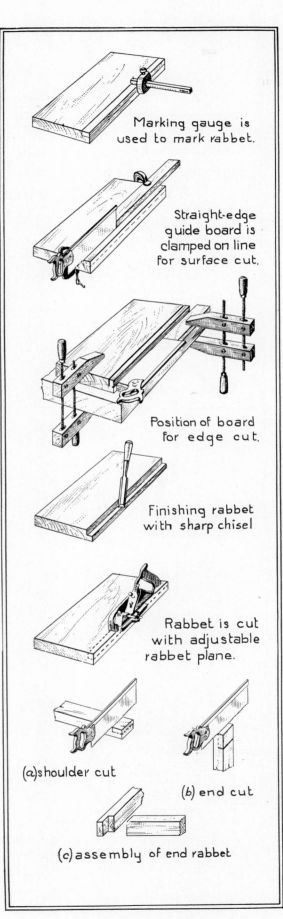

Marking gauge is used to mark rabbet.

Straight-edge guide board is clamped on line for surface cut.

Position of board for edge cut.

Finishing rabbet with sharp chisel

Rabbet is cut with adjustable rabbet plane.

(a) shoulder cut

(b) end cut

(c) assembly of end rabbet

flooring boards, sheathing boards, and other kinds of stock lumber have probably been noticed.

The groove itself, regardless of whether or not it is to be centered on the edge of the board, can be made with a dado head circular saw, a shaper, a router, or a simple tongue-and-groove plane.

Cutting a groove requires several trips across a circular saw, properly set, to remove the stock within the marked portion. Shapers, routers, and tongue-and-groove planes (combination planes) may be adjusted for grooves of the specified width and depth. A rabbet on each side of the piece will form the tongue.

When it is necessary to make short grooves without this special equipment, the job may be done with ordinary shop tools. A saw, a sharpened marking gauge, a knife, and a small chisel may be used for the job in much the same manner as that outlined for the hand-cutting of rabbets.

Cutting Dadoes

Dadoes are grooves cut *across the grain* of the board. They may be either visible or concealed in the finished article. The former are generally known as "open," or "through" dadoes; whereas the latter are placed under the heading of "blind," or "gain" dadoes. The grooves into which the shelves of bookcases and cabinets are ordinarily fitted, constitute the most common use of the dado joint.

The first step in the making of an open dado is to measure carefully and mark clearly the section of stock which is to be removed. Check the accuracy of all measurements. A few cuts across the circular saw, properly set, will automatically remove the stock to form the required dado. Otherwise, several careful cuts with a small hand saw, to the prescribed depth, makes it easier to trim the dado to the exact size with chisel and router. In this latter practice, a wooden straightedge, clamped to either side of the dado measurements, guides the saw and prevents it from slipping beyond the limits of the dado. For shallow dadoes in soft wood, a sharp knife can easily be substituted for the small hand saw in making the necessary cuts.

The process of making a blind dado is not quite as simple. Here, inasmuch as the groove does not extend entirely across the board, the use of a circular saw or a hand saw is somewhat limited. In wide stock, they may still be used for cutting part of the distance in much the

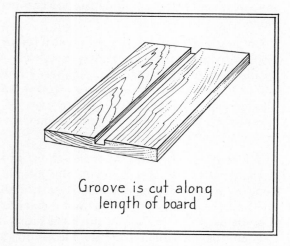

Groove is cut along
length of board

same manner as for a through dado. Boring a series of holes which correspond to the width and depth of the desired groove, is quite effective in removing the bulk of the surplus stock. The chisel is then the most effective tool for trimming it to exact size. Routers and router planes of various types greatly facilitate the task and make speedy and accurate cutting possible.

Miter Joints

Diagonal joints which are commonly used for fastening together the strips of wood used in making picture frames and mirror frames, are known as miter joints. This type of joint is also basically used in the application of different kinds of trim and moldings, for cove and quarter-round fittings, and in many other cases where no end grain is to remain exposed at the joint.

In order that the strength of miter joints may be increased for greater structural support, various methods of reinforcement are used. Of these, some may be easily reproduced by craftsmen, while others call for complicated cuts which can be performed only through the use of special machines and cutters. Blanket chests and cedar chests of the commercial type

Measuring and marking the dado.

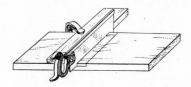

Use of saw and straight edge for cutting dado.

Finishing dado with chisel.

Blind dado roughly cut to size with brace and bit.

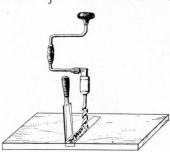

Use of router plane.

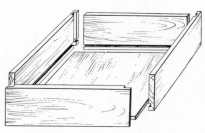

Common drawer construction showing assembly of dados, grooves, and rabbets.

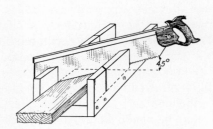

Sawing a miter with a home made miter box.

An adjustable iron miter box.

(Actual measurement of picture) "a" "a" "a"

Finding exact length and width for cutting mitered picture frame.

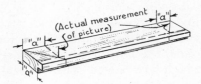

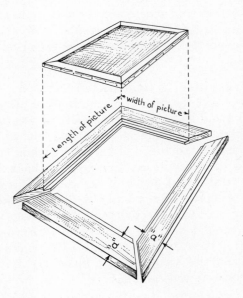

length of picture   width of picture

Picture frame cut to exact size and ready for assembly.

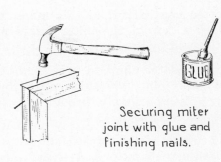

Securing miter joint with glue and finishing nails.

NOTE: Piece is held so that it slightly overlaps second piece to which it is being nailed.

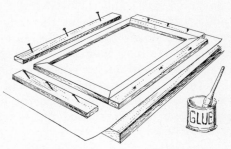

GLUE

Method of clamping picture frame after glue has been applied. Frame is placed on paper to prevent glue from sticking.

Making spline cut in miter joint.

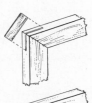

Inserting hardwood spline.

Miter joint held with dowels.

Miter corner joint secured with spline.

are often constructed in this manner. Let us consider a few of the miter joints most frequently used by craftsmen.

First, and the simplest type to make, is the plain miter joint, which is secured in not too sturdy a fashion simply through the use of glue and a nail or two.

The cutting of the joint should be performed on an adjustable miter box of the conventional type or, if none of these are available, on a handmade miter box. This simple device can be made by fastening two hardwood side boards to a bottom board; and then carefully measuring and cutting saw kerfs at the required 45-degree angle, down through the side boards. These saw kerfs may then be used to guide the saw for subsequent miter cuttings. The accuracy of the miter joints which are cut on this device depends a great deal upon the accuracy of the guiding saw kerfs and the construction of the miter box.

Not all miters, however, are cut at the same angle. A 45-degree saw cut is necessary for making a four-sided mitered frame, a 30-degree saw cut for an hexagonal frame or column, and a 22½-degree angle for preparing an octagonal fitting.

The ordinary miter joint can easily be strengthened by the use of a slip-feather; thereby producing a *slip-feather miter joint*. This contrivance is nothing more than a thin strip of hardwood which is inserted in a saw kerf, across the outer edge of the joint. When properly glued into place, the joint will withstand far more hard use because of this reinforced fitting.

Long miters, which are frequently used in constructing chests, columns, and similar articles, are reinforced with a spline. These joints are referred to as *spline miter joints*. This thin spline of hardwood, with a grain which extends across the joint, is inserted in prepared saw kerfs extending all the way down the center of the miter length.

Solid miter joints are fairly difficult to make and consequently require good workmanship. Various types of clamps and clamping devices are available to facilitate the task of assembly.

When these devices are not available, small strips of wood may be nailed at right angles on a board or on a bench top to accommodate the frame after the miters have been treated with glue. The frame may then be wedged into place and should be allowed to remain in this position until the glue has set. In this practice, a saw kerf can then be made after the assembly, in order that the miter joint can be strengthened with sturdy slip-feather construction.

Mortise-and-Tenon Joints

The mortise-and-tenon joint is one of the most commonly used joints in woodworking. It is the type of construction generally used for fastening rails and aprons to the legs of tables, stools, cabinets, and benches. Such joints when properly made with full snug fittings, wedged and pinned, represent construction of the strongest and best type.

Mortise-and-tenon joints, like many other types of joints, may be made in a variety of interesting styles. The *blind* and *through* mortise-and-tenon joints, the *pinned* and *wedged* types, the kinds which are keyed with an exposed wedge (either vertical or horizontal), in fact, even the *slip joint* is a close relative of this family.

Marking off the stock and making the necessary cuttings for mortise-and-tenon joints requires no great skill. If a circular saw and a machine mortiser are available, the task is especially easy.

The first step is to mark off carefully the exact size and location for each mortise. Check so as to avoid an error either in size or location. This being done, take a brace and bit which correspond to the width of the mortise and bore a series of holes so as to produce the exact length, width, and depth of the mortise. A bit gauge, properly clamped to the bit, will assist in boring to the correct depth. This boring operation should actually remove all the rough stock. It is then merely a matter of trimming out the mortise with a sharp chisel so that it will be exactly true and square.

The machine mortiser, or drill press, fitted with a hollow chisel mortising bit, simplifies the

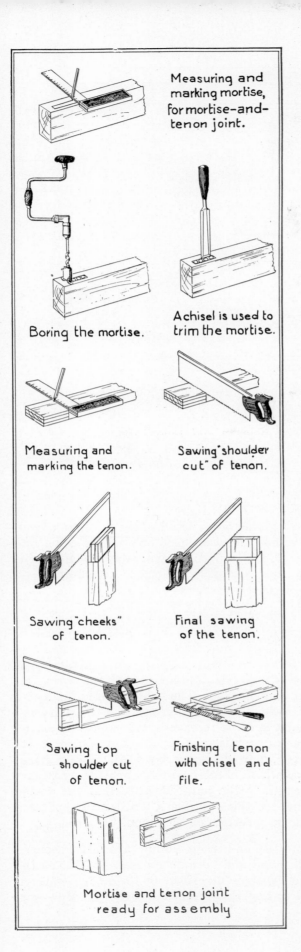

Measuring and marking mortise, for mortise-and-tenon joint.

Boring the mortise.

A chisel is used to trim the mortise.

Measuring and marking the tenon.

Sawing "shoulder cut" of tenon.

Sawing "cheeks" of tenon.

Final sawing of the tenon.

Sawing top shoulder cut of tenon.

Finishing tenon with chisel and file.

Mortise and tenon joint ready for assembly

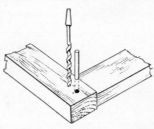

Use of tenon pins to reinforce mortise – and – tenon joint.

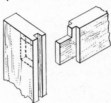

"Drawbore pins" used to secure joint.

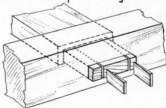

"Haunched" mortise and tenon, cut to fit panel groove.

Wedged mortise and tenon.

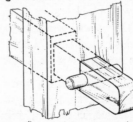

"Keyed" mortise and tenon. (Horizontal wedge)

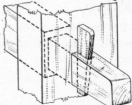

"Keyed" mortise and tenon. (Vertical wedge)

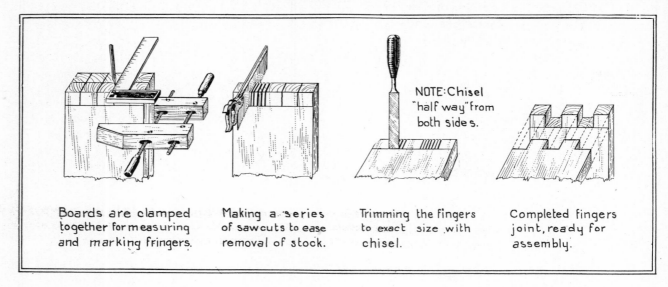

Boards are clamped together for measuring and marking fringers.

Making a series of sawcuts to ease removal of stock.

NOTE: Chisel "half way" from both sides.

Trimming the fingers to exact size with chisel.

Completed fingers joint, ready for assembly.

work. With this equipment it is only necessary to punch out the mortises.

Having completed the mortise we are now ready to cut the tenon. To begin this process, carefully mark off the depth, length, and width of the required tenon. Hold the markings against the mortise and check the accuracy of the proposed cuts. Then with a saw make the necessary cuts, one by one, on each of the two edges and the two surfaces.

Certain types of tenons require less than the usual "four cuts." Obviously, several movements across the bed of a properly adjusted circular saw will remove the required stock in a speedy manner. *Always cut slightly outside the lines* so that the tenon will be slightly over size. Then with chisel, carefully work the tenon down until it slides snugly within the mortise.

Mortise-and-tenon joints may be pinned in either of two ways, that is, the pin may be applied after the assembly, or during assembly by the regular draw-bore pin method. In the former practice, the hole may be bored right through the center of the mortise-and-tenon joint after the project has been assembled and the glue has set. It is then merely a matter of applying glue and driving in the pin. In this case the pin reinforces the glue in maintaining rigid construction.

However, in following the *draw-bore pin* method, the holes must be drilled separately in both the mortise and the tenon, before the joint is assembled.

The hole in the tenon should be approximately one-sixteenth inch nearer the tenon shoulder than the corresponding boring through the mortise. This arrangement causes the tenon to be pulled snugly into the mortise when the pin is driven home, eliminating the need of clamps in the gluing operation. In fact, this type of construction was used long before glue came into use. Round, square, or irregularly shaped pins are used to provide an interesting effect.

For certain types of construction, the tenon is made to extend not only clear through the stock, but to protrude some distance beyond, in order that it may be secured with a decorative wedge. These wedges are made in a variety of interesting styles and are of both the horizontal and vertical types. The hole which is to receive the wedge is really one form of a through mortise. It is made in exactly the same way as the original mortise-and-tenon joint which it secures. The wedge is merely a thin piece of hardwood which is fitted so as to provide maximum strength to the joint. Be sure that the wedge is not too thick or else it will tend to split the extending section of the tenon.

Mortise-and-tenon joints are also secured with *blind* and *open tenon wedges,* just as the tenon wedges described in the article devoted to Peg-Leg Construction (page 75). However, due to the fact that a mortise-and-tenon fitting is usually rectangular in shape, two wedges are generally used; one near each end of the mortise. By slightly lengthening the inner edge of the mortise, the wedges impart a noticeable "fan shape" to the tenon and insure a very strong type of construction.

Finger Joints

Finger joints are frequently employed in corner construction. Sometimes this type of joint is used as a wooden hinge. Its construction resembles, to a certain extent, that of the open dovetail joint. Like the open dovetail, the ends of two adjoining boards overlap.

In making this joint, the ends of the two boards that are to be joined are first marked with a line square across the boards, at a marginal distance from the end corresponding to their thickness. This marking is squared off around the entire end of each board.

Following the initial marking, the width of each "finger" is spotted off on the marginal line of marking. Ordinarily each finger is made of equal width. They are marked with "square" lines from the end of the board. Alternating spaces between the fingers are checked for cutting. After these checked portions have been cut away, the ends of the two boards interlock.

The cutting operation is performed either with a sharp fine-toothed saw, or a backsaw. Of course, the work is simplified when performed on a power saw. Extreme care must be taken not to cut below the depth marking. A number of saw cuts are made between each finger. After the sawing has been completed, the excess material is carefully chiseled away at the depth lines with a sharp chisel. Each finger is evenly cleaned along the cut edges to assure perfect fit. The success of the job is determined by the precision with which the two pieces interlock after the cutting has been completed.

Dovetail Joints

Dovetail joints have long been a favorite of the woodworker. They are strong and dependable and will hold over an indefinite period of time, where all other types of construction might fail.

There is, however, quite a large variety of dovetail joints, and their common resemblance is limited solely to the fact that they all bear the shaping of the "dove's tail." In fact, this family is extended to several common groups which are known individually as *open dovetails, sliding dovetails,* and *dovetail halvings.* Moreover, each of these different types is shaped and fashioned in its own peculiar way.

The *open dovetail*, which is, possibly, the most elementary of the group and the least difficult to make, is fashioned in the following manner. It is first necessary to square lines around the two adjoining pieces, a distance in from the

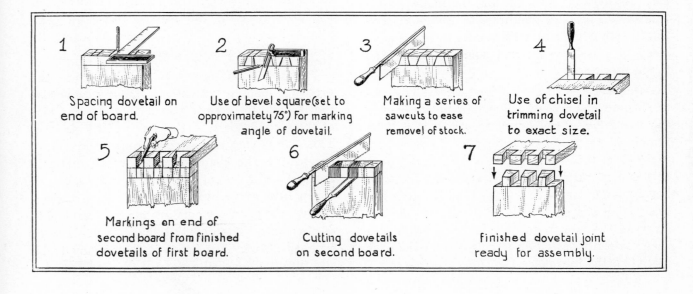

1. Spacing dovetail on end of board.

2. Use of bevel square (set to approximately 75°) for marking angle of dovetail.

3. Making a series of sawcuts to ease removel of stock.

4. Use of chisel in trimming dovetail to exact size.

5. Markings on end of second board from finished dovetails of first board.

6. Cutting dovetails on second board.

7. Finished dovetail joint ready for assembly.

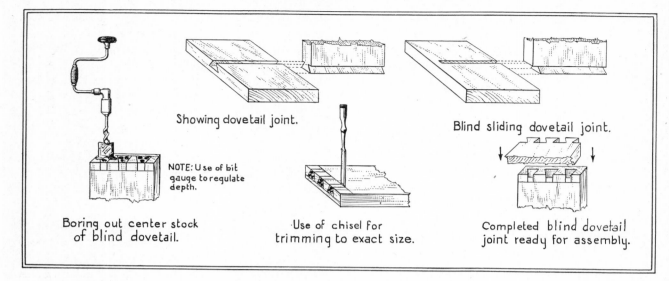

Boring out center stock
of blind dovetail.

NOTE: Use of bit
gauge to regulate
depth.

Showing dovetail joint.

Use of chisel for
trimming to exact size.

Blind sliding dovetail joint.

Completed blind dovetail
joint ready for assembly.

ends equaling the thickness of each piece. This is the *depth line* of the dovetails. This depth line is then marked at intervals, on *one* board to indicate the width of each dovetail. A bevel gauge is then set to an angle of approximately 75 degrees and a series of *alternating* bevel lines are scribed extending from the depth line to the end of the board.

The position of the gauge is then reversed to mark the opposite (alternating) side of each dovetail. Each marking is then squared across the end of the board and scribed with a bevel on the opposite face.

The open portion of the dovetail is checked and sawed with a sharp backsaw or dovetail saw. Additional saw cuts may be made within the waste portion to facilitate the job of removing it with a chisel. Extreme care must be exercised to chisel evenly and squarely along the depth marking.

After the first board has been carefully dovetailed and cleaned, it is held in position over the *end edge* of the board to which it will be attached. Each finished dovetail is carefully marked on this end. For the sake of precision, this end marking should be re-marked with a bevel gauge. A square is then used to carry the lines from the end to the depth lines on both sides of the second piece. These dovetails are then carefully sawed and chiseled and the first piece is fitted into place.

The sliding dovetail functions in much the same manner as a dado joint. It is, however, a much stronger type of construction. In order to make this joint it is first necessary to cut a dovetail groove. A groove of this type is narrow on the surface of the board and spreads, or dovetails, out to a wider width at the depth.

First mark the groove carefully on the board, using a bevel at the edges to mark the angle of the cut. For accuracy of cutting, it is well to clamp a straightedged piece of wood along the marking and with this as a guide, and holding the saw on the proper slant, saw evenly to the depth mark. Sawing is repeated on the second line and a third straight cut is made in between to facilitate chiseling out the inside portion of the groove. After the sawing has been completed the inside of the groove is carefully cleaned with a sharp chisel.

The dovetailed tenon which slides into the groove is made by marking a line square across the board, the same distance in from the end of the second board as the depth of the groove. This line is carried entirely around the end of the board. The shape of the dovetail tenon is marked on this end section. Again, using a sharp saw, and a wooden straightedge for accuracy, the shoulder cuts are made on each side of the tenon. The dovetail shape is made with a sharp chisel. This tenon is then ready to be slid into the dovetail groove.

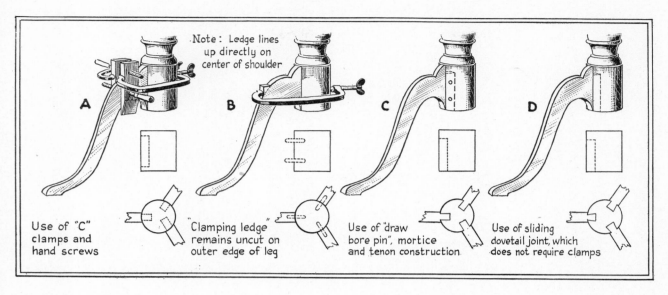

A Use of "C" clamps and hand screws

Note: Ledge lines up directly on center of shoulder

B "Clamping ledge" remains uncut on outer edge of leg

C Use of "draw bore pin", mortice and tenon construction.

D Use of sliding dovetail joint, which does not require clamps

Blind Dovetail Joints

The blind dovetail joint is commonly used in drawer construction where the sides of the drawer are dovetailed into the front. It differs from the open dovetail joint in that the connecting parts do not entirely overlap each other. In fact, only one piece is openly dovetailed, and this laps part way across the edge of the piece to which it is connected.

The part of the joint on which the open dovetail is cut (in drawer construction the side) is first marked and cut in the manner already described, for the primary cutting of open dovetail joints. When this piece has been cut, the dovetails are held in place over the edge of the front piece. This permits marking on the second piece. The dovetails should lap about three-fourths of the way across the edge. The edge of the front piece is marked from the side piece and the cut-out portions are removed. This operation is most easily performed with a boring bit and sharp chisel. The dovetailed pieces are then ready to be joined together with glue.

Stem-Leg Assembly

At first glance it appears quite difficult to assemble a cluster of curved legs to a central table stem. As a matter of fact, this process is by no means simple, but, like many another complicated process, it may be accomplished by careful adherence to a few fundamental directions.

When the mortise-and-tenon joint is employed for this construction, very little pressure is needed to hold the members together. One method of obtaining this necessary pressure is provided with the use of an ordinary hand screw applied to the leg in a parallel position to the stem. The two jaws of the hand clamp, as shown at A, will serve as ledges for pressure clamping. Another method is to leave a small shoulder, cut square and parallel to the tenon, and in line with the center of the tenon, on the otherwise shaped leg. This shoulder serves as a clamping jig and after the leg has been glued into place it may be easily removed with a coping saw. When either of these methods are employed by the amateur in assembling tripod legs, each leg in turn should be glued, clamped, and allowed to dry.

The use of clamps in assembling stem legs may be eliminated by following through with the drawbore-pin-and-tenon assembly, or by using a sliding dovetail joint. The sliding dovetail joint, shown at D, requires some degree of craftsmanship in its execution, but provides a splendid method of construction.

V

Woodworking Machinery

Circular Saw

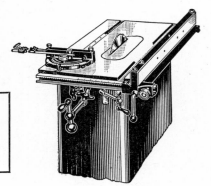

Guards omitted to better illustrate use. However, safe usage *always* calls for guards.

The circular saw is one of the most important power machines used in woodworking. It is used for ripping, cross-cutting, shaping edges, cutting moldings, cutting dadoes, grooves, tenons, and various other woodworking processes.

There are many different types and sizes of circular saws, ranging from the small bench models to the large industrial, heavy-duty machines. However, the working parts common to all types are (1) a circular blade, (2) a flat table (3) a cross-cutting fence, and (4) a ripping fence.

Circular saws are adjusted in various ways. Some types are made so that the cutting blade itself may be raised or lowered, while with others the blade remains stationary and the table is moved up and down. Likewise, with one type of saw, the table is tilted on an angle for slanted or beveled cutting, while on other types, such cutting is performed by tilting the blade.

Some very excellent circular saws have been introduced during the past few years. Most of these are light in construction, yet may be accurately adjusted for the many cutting operations. They serve the needs of the average woodworker; performing all the jobs of heavy duty equipment, lacking only its ponderous size. Moreover, these light machines are very easy to set and to adjust for various wood-working operations.

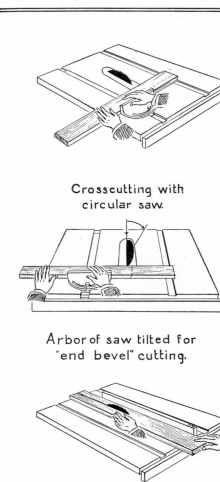

Crosscutting with circular saw.

Arbor of saw tilted for "end bevel" cutting.

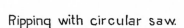

Ripping with circular saw.

Arbor of saw tilted for ripping edge bevel.

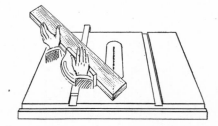

Crosscut feed set for cutting miter.

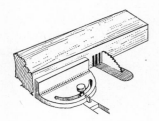

Cutting dado by making several trips across revolving blade.

outside cutter - inside cutter - assembled
DADO HEAD

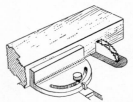

Using dado head which has been assembled for cutting to desired width. NOTE: Dado head also used for ploughing groove.

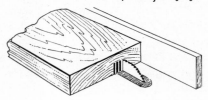

Cutting grooves by adusting ripping fence for each successive cut.

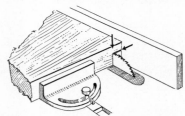

Rabbeting a board by sawing edge and surface to required depth.

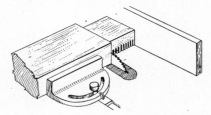

Cutting a tenon by making several trips across revolving blade.

The principal uses of the circular saw are outlined in the following paragraphs.

Cross-cutting. The blade of the circular saw is set slightly deeper than the thickness of the wood to be cross-cut. Press the wood firmly against the cross-cut fence and slide it with even pressure through the revolving blade. The ripping fence should never be used as a measuring gauge during cross-cutting operations. Otherwise the cut-off section may bind between the revolving blade and fence, causing a "kick back." Be sure to follow through evenly and avoid jerky motions.

Ripping. When ripping boards to width, the ripping fence should be set so that the distance between the ripping fence and the revolving blade will correspond to the width of the desired board. With the fence accurately set, the wood is driven into the blade, pressing it against both the table and the ripping fence. In ripping narrow strips, a small notched stick is generally employed to push the final end of the stock through the blade.

Beveling and Mitering. In order to cross-cut the end of a board at a prescribed angle or miter, the cross-cutting fence is adjusted to this angle.

End Bevels. Chamfers and bevel cuts which extend across the end of a board, are cut by adjusting the saw blade so that it forms the desired cutting angle to the saw table. If the saw has a stationary blade, the table is tilted to form the necessary angle.

In order to cut a bevel, miter, or chamfer along the length of a board, the saw is again adjusted so that the blade and table form the desired angle. The work is then fed along the ripping fence.

Dadoes. For an open dado, the board is first marked for the dado, care being taken to square the lines across the edges as well as the faces of the wood. The saw blade is then set for the required depth of cut and the wood is fed across the blade so that the actual cutting is performed *inside* the dado lines. Ordinarily several inside cuts are made between the outer dado cuts. This method makes it much easier to remove the remaining stock within the dado. Special dado cutters, dado heads, which cut the entire dado in one operation do away with the necessity of making a series of saw cuts.

Blind Dadoes. After the dado has been marked, the work is held above the revolving blade. It is then carefully pressed down on the blade and fed across the wood as far as the

marked width of the dado. Then it is carefully lifted off the revolving blade. Care must be exercised not to go too far across the wood and thus exceed the marked bounds of the blind dado. This mistake may be avoided by marking lightly with pencil or crayon, the "span" of the dado, on the saw table, and using these markings as a gauge when cutting.

Grooves. After marking the groove along the face of the board, the ripping fence is set so that the blade will make a *primary* cut of the required depth, just inside the marking of the groove. Then the ripping fence is adjusted for the other side of the groove. It is good practice to make additional cuts inside the marking if the width of the groove makes it necessary. The cut portions of wood, inside the groove, are then removed with a sharp chisel, that is, if all the waste stock has not already been removed by additional trips through the saw.

Tenons. After the tenon has been carefully marked, the cutting is performed in either of two ways, namely (1) the saw is set to the side depth of the tenon and an initial cut is made across the wood at this required depth to form the shoulder. The ripping fence is then adjusted and the piece is fed across the saw blade *end down* for the side cut.

A far safer and more practical method (2) is to make a series of cross-cuts, closely together at the required depth of the tenon. The waste stock is then easily removed with a sharp chisel.

Blades. There are three distinct kinds of blades used with the circular saw, namely, (1) the cross-cut blade, (2) the ripping blade, and

(3) the miter blade. A utility blade has recently been introduced which can be used successfully to perform a variety of operations. Blades of varying types for special cutting may also be obtained.

Cut-Off Saw

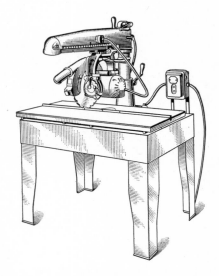

While the average small shop does not require a cut-off saw, its use in the general field of woodworking warrants mention. There are many different types of cut-off saws, but their purpose is generally the same: They are used to cut large pieces of lumber to length, and also for dadoing and tenoning. The types of cut-off saws are classified as follows:

(1) Swing saws; mounted to the ceiling or overhead structure and swinging in pendulum fashion over a bench.

(2) Slide saw; mounted to bench. In operation the saw slides on a projecting arm. It can also be used for mitering, beveling, chamfering, dadoing, rabbeting, tenoning, ripping, etc.

(3) Under-swing saw; blade mounted beneath saw table, swings with pressure of foot treadle.

Cross-cutting is performed by placing the board on the cutting counter, pressing it against the back rest and pulling the revolving saw blade evenly through it. In performing this operation, the worker should be careful not to "rush the job" because if the blade is pulled too hurriedly, it will bind and cut in jagged fashion.

Ripping. The slide saw can be used for a number of processes. It is so constructed that the cutting head can be adjusted for ripping as well as cross-cutting. With this type of saw, the cutting head slides out along a projecting arm when cross-cutting operations are being performed. However, when being used for ripping, the head is turned so that the blade is in a parallel position to the stationary back rest. Thus the blade is adjusted on the slide arm at the desired distance from the back rest (which now serves as a ripping fence) and clamped securely in place. When a board is being ripped, it is fed along the counter and into the revolving blade in much the same fashion as it would be fed into a circular saw. The difference, however, is that the blade is above the work, rather than underneath it.

Band Saw

After the circular saw, the most important power machine used in woodworking is perhaps the band saw. The working parts of this machine consist of a flexible blade which moves with the same action as an endless belt, around two revolving wheels. The work is placed on a flat table which may be tilted for bevel cutting. While the band saw is designed primarily for curved cutting, it may also be used for straight cross-cutting and ripping. Most band saws are equipped with a cross-cut and ripping fence to guide accurate operation.

OPERATING THE BAND SAW. To obtain the best results in operating the band saw, the worker should first determine that the saw itself is properly adjusted and that the blade is adequately sharp. The guard should be lowered as far as possible so that only a slight clearance is allowed for the stock to pass through. Actually there is no more difficulty involved in using a band saw than there is in cutting out a paper design with a pair of scissors.

At first the worker should proceed slowly; feeding the work toward the blade so that the saw skirts the outside of the marked line. Don't be afraid to steer the work gently at the curves, avoiding undue strain on the blade. Hold it flat and steady on the cutting table. Feed it along evenly and avoid jerky moves which might cause an uneven cut.

There is often an advantage in making a series of cuts leading into the curve, in order to keep the work clear of cut portions and to permit the cutting of sharp curves. Blades of varying widths are used with the band saw; the wider widths being used for heavy-duty work where sharp curves do not appear, while the narrower widths are kept for fine work where abrupt curves must be cut.

Some band saws are equipped with a cross-feeding device to help in accurate cross-cutting, and a ripping fence which may be attached to the table to facilitate accurate ripping. Likewise, the table of the band saw may be tilted for cutting bevels, miters, and large chamfers.

The band saw is an awkward tool when it is off the machine. To save the saw from damage and to save space it is rolled into a threefold circle. This can be done without injury to the saw.

To fold the saw, the operator stands with the saw in front of him, one hand on each side of the saw about one-third the distance from the top, as it stands in an oval position, as in the machine, the lower edge resting on the floor. The top is bent forward by twisting both hands so that the top bends out. One side of the saw is brought in back of the other, and the top continued down until it nearly meets the lower end of the saw about a foot off the floor. The saw then will naturally fall to the floor with a perfect roll or fold, and without a twist in it. The saw can then be hung on a hook, as it makes only a 16- or 18-inch circle.

Scroll Saw or Jig Saw

This type of saw is also designed for curved cutting. The fine blade of the jig saw with its up and down action makes possible the cutting of sharper curves than would ordinarily be attempted on a band saw. An added feature is the ability of the scroll saw to cut *inside* curves.

This is done by threading the blade through a hole inside the marking.

OPERATING THE SCROLL SAW. The scroll saw is operated in much the same fashion as the band saw. The work is held flat on the table and fed evenly into the cutting blade, the action of which is up and down rather than in continuous revolutions as in the case of the band saw. The action of the saw, together with the fineness of its blades, permits more delicate and precise cutting.

When the inside portions of a piece of work are being cut on the scroll saw, a hole is first bored along the inner edge and the saw blade *threaded* through this hole. After the blade has been re-attached the sawing is continued and, when finished, the blade is detached and the work removed from the table.

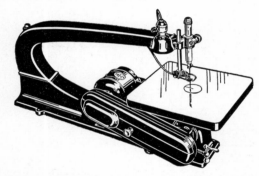

Blades of varying sizes may be purchased for the scroll saw. This saw, like the band saw, may be used for different purposes; including tenoning, cross-cutting, and ripping.

Jointer

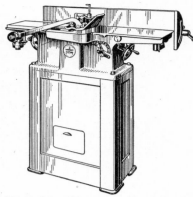

The labor of squaring the edges of boards is largely eliminated with the use of the jointer. The working parts of this machine consist of a *revolving cutter*, *adjustable fence*, and *table*. In operation, the work is pressed against the fence and driven across the cutter. Thus the work is planed square along the edge. Like most of the other machines mentioned in this text, the jointer is manufactured in both light- and heavy-duty types.

A variety of small bench jointers which mount on the regular work bench are becoming increasingly popular in small woodworking shops. It should be noted that the jointer is considered one of the most dangerous woodworking machines. Extreme caution should, therefore, be observed in its operation. At no time should small boards or blocks be processed on the jointer because of the immediate danger of their being "kicked," thus bringing the hand in contact with the revolving cutter.

OPERATING THE JOINTER. In operating the jointer, the worker must at all times be ex-

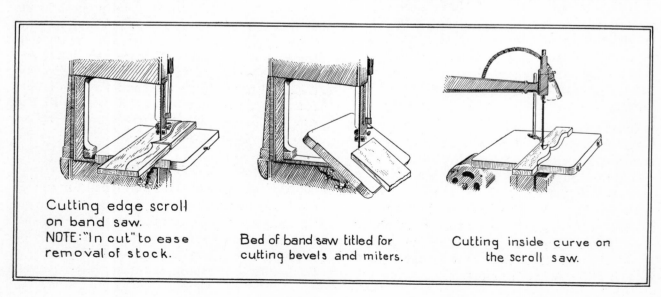

Cutting edge scroll on band saw.
NOTE:"In cut" to ease removal of stock.

Bed of band saw titled for cutting bevels and miters.

Cutting inside curve on the scroll saw.

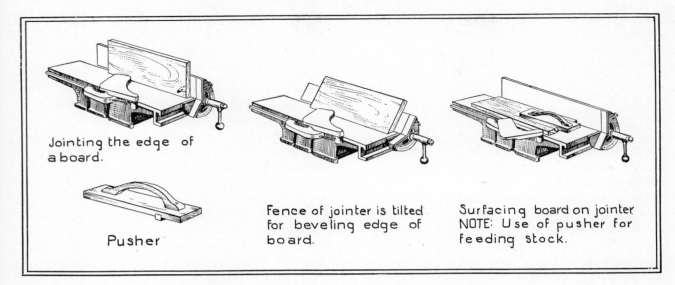

Jointing the edge of a board.

Pusher

Fence of jointer is tilted for beveling edge of board.

Surfacing board on jointer NOTE: Use of pusher for feeding stock.

tremely careful to keep his hands and body clear of the moving parts. The board that is to be jointed, that is, squared along the edge, is pressed evenly on the table and against the back rest, while the edge moves at right angles along the revolving cutter. The work should not be hurried, but should be pushed evenly and firmly across the cutter, the same amount of pressure being maintained throughout.

Ordinarily, two or more trips across the cutter are required to bring the edge to perfect straightness and squareness. The accuracy of the edge may be checked with a straightedge and square. It should be noted that the jointer can be adjusted for cuts of varying depths. It is well to remember that the deeper the cut, the greater the danger of a "kick back" and the rougher the finished edge will be.

As shown in the illustration, the fence of the jointer may be tilted so that the edges of boards may be beveled to any desired angle.

Planer

In the larger woodworking shops, where lumber is bought unsurfaced, a machine planer may be used to smooth the rough stock. Each piece of stock is fed flat into this machine and is automatically carried through a set of revolving cutters. Most planers surface both sides of the board in a single operation. They may be adjusted so as to plane a piece of wood down to any required thickness.

Combination Machine

This type of machine is ideally adapted to the needs of the small shop owner who cannot afford the many individual machines associated with woodworking. A variety of excellent combination machines, operating on a single motor, may be purchased. The most common combination includes the lathe, circular saw, and sanding disk. More elaborate combinations go on to include band saws, scroll saws, drill presses and mortisers. These machines are being developed for greater safety, to render them ideal for the school shop.

While the combination machine ordinarily is not suited for heavy-duty work, the all-in-one feature is certainly a boon to the woodworking hobbyist.

Shaper

While designed primarily for shaping wooden edges, the machine shaper can be adjusted for rabbeting, grooving, beading, and shaping various types of moldings. The action of the machine is provided by revolving knives, or cutters, which

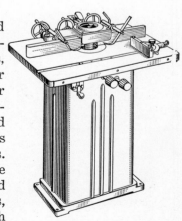

are shaped for desired types of cuts. The work is fed along a table which is equipped with an adjustable fence. The cutter is adjusted so that the blades revolve at the required distance *outside* of the fence. Cutting knives revolve at very great speed and trim the edges of the wood, as it is fed into them. Even end grain portions of the wood become smoothly shaped because of the high speed of the sharp cutter.

A portable shaper, of recent manufacture, while small in size, performs a variety of the processes ordinarily performed by the regular heavy duty machine. The portable type may be removed from its regular mounting and taken to the job when necessary. It need hardly be emphasized that a shaper revolving at fast speed is an extremely dangerous machine. Every precaution should be observed in its operation.

OPERATING THE SHAPER. "Keep your fingers away from the cutter," are the key words of advice in regard to the operation of the shaper. The cutter on this machine revolves at very great speed and if the fingers get in the way, a most serious accident will result.

However, with due caution the shaper may be easily operated. After the cutter has been locked securely in place, and the feeding fence adjusted for the proper depth of cut, the work is simply rested on the table, pressed firmly against the fence and fed evenly across the cutter.

The shaping of end-grain portions is somewhat more difficult than with the grain. Unless the cutter is absolutely sharp, there will be a tendency for the work to vibrate or for the edge to burn as it is being fed.

The portable shaper, when it is mounted in its arbor, is operated in the manner already described. However, when it is removed from the arbor and used by hand, the technique is a trifle more difficult. While the cutter revolves at very high speed, the operator will feel the gyroscopic action of the little shaper as he holds it freely in his hand. Extreme care must be exercised to hold it *evenly* along the edge which is being shaped. Otherwise a wavering shape will result. Obviously, the shaper held free is an exceedingly dangerous tool.

Machine Router

Like the hand router, this machine is used principally for cutting grooves and dadoes. It is manufactured with a motor-in-head which drives the cutter in shaper fashion at very high speed. It is guided by two handles and may be set for varying depths of cuts. Cutters are obtainable in different widths and shapes.

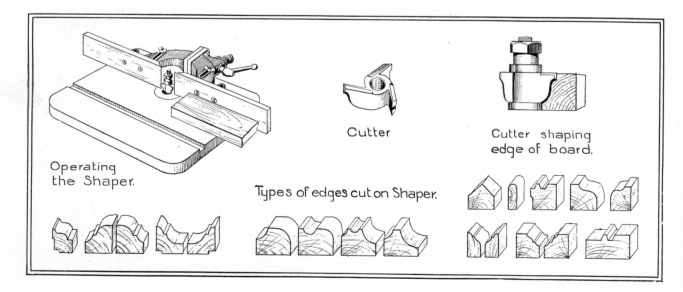

Operating the Shaper.

Cutter

Cutter shaping edge of board.

Types of edges cut on Shaper.

Spur bit

Boring wood with spur bit.

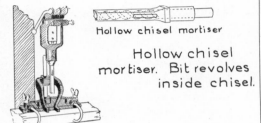

Hollow chisel mortiser

Hollow chisel mortiser. Bit revolves inside chisel.

Drill press used for mortising

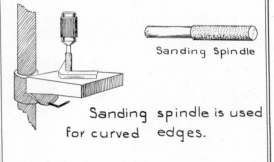

Sanding Spindle

Sanding spindle is used for curved edges.

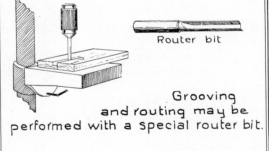

Router bit

Grooving and routing may be performed with a special router bit.

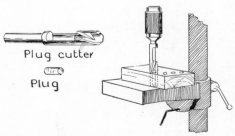

Plug cutter

Plug

Plugs and short dowels may be cut on drill press.

Bench Shaper

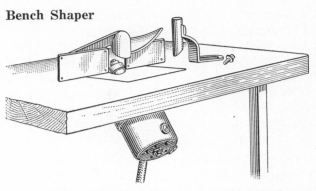

The bench shaper has a tilting spindle by which an endless variety of molding cuts can be produced. Since the guard covers the small high speed knives, this machine can be safely operated in the school shop.

Drill Press—Mortiser

The drill press is another important piece of power machinery. It is designed for boring holes. In line with this performance it can be used, with special equipment, for mortising. There are several different types and sizes of drill presses; some for heavy-duty work and others of lighter variety. The portable power drill is included in this group.

While the drill press cannot be classed as an absolute necessity, still it is a very handy machine to own. The task of drilling holes, with exact precision, is accomplished with relative ease through use of this machine. Moreover the job of mortising, a somewhat difficult operation which requires a degree of skill, is greatly facilitated through the use of the hollow chisel and mortising bit.

OPERATING THE DRILL PRESS—MORTISER.
The standard types of drill presses may be
fitted with a hollow-ground chisel for mortising. They are operated with a lever which
pulls the cutter and chisel directly *down* into
the work. The mortising bit in this case revolves
within the hollow chisel. As this assembly is
pressed into the work, a square hole results.
In mortising, however, it is first necessary to
carefully mark the area to be mortised, on the
stock. The work is then adjusted on the table
of the drill press, so that the chisel drops into
direct contact with the marked area. An elongated mortise is made by making a series of
cuts with the mortising chisel.

Some drill presses are equipped with a foot
lever controlling the up and down action of
the drill. There is an advantage in this arrangement, because the operator is left with two
hands free to hold the work. Still another type
of mortiser is operated in horizontal position,
the work being fed *against* the cutter, through
lever action.

Power Grinder

While the hand-oper-
ated emery wheel meets
the need for a grinding
machine in the smaller
woodworking shop, the
electric grinder, com-
plete with interchange-
able abrasive wheels of
varying coarseness, is by
far the more useful
sharpening device. Many
electric grinders are so
constructed that the re-
volving wheels are lubri-
cated from an oil reser-
voir for constant and
uniform oiling of the
abrasive stone. The speed of operation of the
wheel is also variable. For the craftsman who
insists on sharp tools (and what craftsman
doesn't), the electric grinder is the answer.

OPERATING THE POWER GRINDER. The correct method of operating the power grinder will
be described in the chapter devoted to Sharpen-

ing Tools. Most types of grinders, like the one
illustrated, are equipped with automatic oiling
devices and with an adjustable rest for holding tools. Unless the machine is also equipped
with a glass plate, through which the worker
looks while sharpening a tool, glasses should
be worn while the work is in operation. Otherwise small fragments of ground metal or small
chips from the stone, which are sometimes
thrown from the revolving wheel, might prove
injurious to the eyes.

Sanding Machine

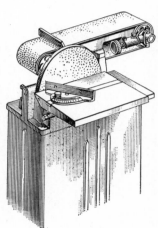

Sanding is, of
course, a common
operation in wood-
working. For this rea-
son the craftsman is
always looking for
new and better ways
of doing the job.

Several different
types of sanding ma-
chines have been de-
veloped. The *belt
sander,* consisting of a long endless belt of sanding abrasive which passes over two large parallel wheels, set a number of feet apart, is one of
the pioneer forms. This type of sanding device
still retains much of its popularity, particularly
in woodworking factories. In operating the
belt sander, the work is placed beneath the middle slack part of the belt and as the belt moves,
revolving about the wheel, the abrasive is
pressed down upon the work. The work, placed
upon a movable carriage, may be moved back
and forth so as to produce a uniformly sanded
surface.

Another type of sander, the *circular disk
plate,* is likewise very popular. This sander is
made by simply gluing a circular sheet of sandpaper to a disk. It may then be mounted in a
lathe. As it revolves, the work is pressed against
the plate.

Of comparatively recent origin, the *portable
sander* is fast becoming one of the most popular
types yet originated. As the name implies, the
portable sander may be carried to the work and
is, therefore, useful for types of sanding where

Sanding surface of board
with portable sander.

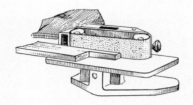

Portable sander mounted in
"arbor" for stationary sanding.

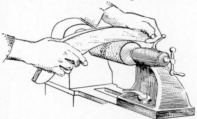

Sanding cylinder
may be mounted in lathe
for "drum sanding".

Disc sander is
attached to face plate
of lathe.

Final shaping of curved edges
may be finished on spindle
sander.

other machines could not easily be used. The portable sander is usually equipped with a frame to which it can be attached for stationary use. Home-craftsmen, weary of the job of hand sanding, have promptly yielded to the practicality of the portable sander and they have found their interest well rewarded.

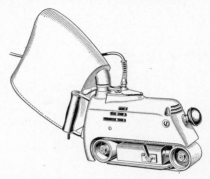

OPERATING THE SANDING MACHINE. In order to operate the sanding machine successfully, it is necessary, first of all, to be careful to select the proper grade of sanding belt. Coarse abrasive belts are intended for use where rough sanding is required. They cut quickly into the surface of the wood and, because of their rough texture, will wear down the thickness of a board in short order. On the other hand, the fine-textured belt does not leave any marks and serves only to smooth the surface of the work.

The worker should at all times be careful to handle the sander carefully. If it is of the portable type, it should be guided evenly along the surface. If it is tilted so that the edge of the belt comes in direct contact with the wood, it will leave deep ridges and scratches on the surface. It must, moreover, always be operated with the grain of the wood.

Drum Sanders

The drum sander consists of a cylinder to which abrasive has been attached. It is a stationary unit and the work is fed against the cylinder as it revolves. This type of sander is often used for shaping as well as for sanding. Small drum sanders of varying diameters may be made by attaching sandpaper to plain wooden cylinders. These abrasive cylinders may then be mounted on the lathe and used in much the same way as one would use a regular drum sander.

The Disk Sander

The disk sander is likewise a stationary machine. It consists of a disk of abrasive attached to a face plate. As previously stated, this type of sander is often improvised on the face plate of the lathe. Like the drum sander, the disk type is used largely for the shaping and smoothing of small pieces of work.

Lathe

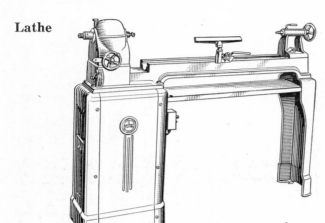

The lathe is undoubtedly the most interesting machine used in the woodworking shop. Most amateur and professional craftsmen enjoy working on it. The lathe, of course, dates back many centuries. In its earliest form, it consisted of a crude mechanism operated by a treadle. Its function, then, as now, was to cause pieces of wood to revolve so that in the process the edges could be cut to form a round piece of varying diameters and shapes.

The modern wood-turning lathe is essentially a very simple and easily understood machine. It consists of two centers between which the piece of wood being turned is mounted. One of these centers is attached to a motor and causes the work to revolve. This is the *live* center. The other center serves as a stationary bearing on which the work revolves. This is the *dead* center. As the work revolves between these centers it is cut with one of a variety of chisels or gouge-shaped turning tools. The tools are rested on a stationary tool rest which is adjusted to maintain proper clearance and position to the work.

OPERATING THE LATHE. Probably the best way to learn to operate a lathe—always bearing in mind a few simple rules of safety—is

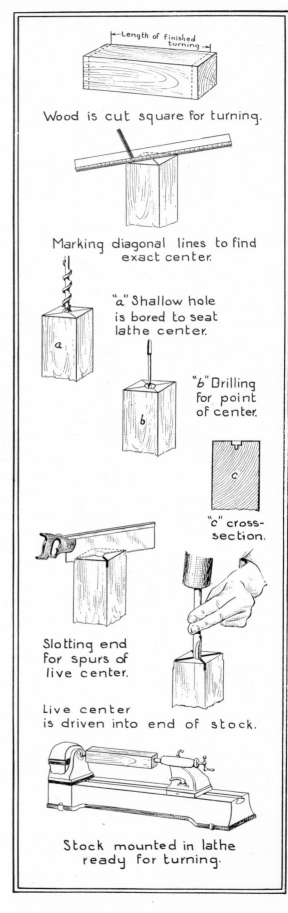

Wood is cut square for turning.

Marking diagonal lines to find exact center.

"a" Shallow hole is bored to seat lathe center.

"b" Drilling for point of center.

"c" cross-section.

Slotting end for spurs of live center.

Live center is driven into end of stock.

Stock mounted in lathe ready for turning.

actually to operate a lathe. Just as you can best learn to ice skate by ice skating, in like manner, correct practice leads to precision in the art of wood turning.

At the start, however, it might be well to practise lathe work by actually turning a small spindle. Start off by selecting a square piece of soft wood which is slightly larger in size than the finished dimensions of the piece you intend to turn. An allowance is made on the length for the turning centers, the ends of the piece being frequently cut away after the turning is finished.

It is then necessary to find the centers of both ends, in order that the square stock may be spun with a minimum of vibration. Drawing diagonal lines from corner to corner, on each end, usually provides a fairly accurate center.

To safeguard against any danger that the shaft of wood may be thrown from the lathe, it is well to recess both the live center and the dead center. To do this, merely drill a hole to a depth of about $\frac{1}{4}$ inch into the center of both ends with a $\frac{1}{2}$-inch or $\frac{3}{4}$-inch bit, depending upon the size required for the centers. On hardwood, it is well to drill a very small pilot hole in the center of both ends of the cylinder, so that the center spurs will not be damaged. Also, make diagonal saw cuts on the live-center end of the cylinder to admit the spurs of the live center. The spurs of the live centers may then be driven into the saw cuts of one end, so as to prevent "slippage."

After placing a drop of two of oil upon the dead center, to prevent unnecessary friction, the square piece of wood may be secured in the lathe.

The tool rest may then be adjusted so as to be slightly above the height of the turning centers and, if everything spins freely, we are now ready to operate the lathe.

Wood Turning Tools

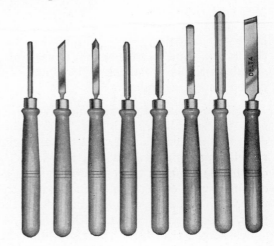

The art of wood turning makes necessary the use of a variety of wood-turning tools. Like the wood carver who requires a separate tool for each type of cut, the wood turner also requires separate types of tools for each of the various turning operations. There are six distinct types of wood-turning tools. These are: gouge, skew,

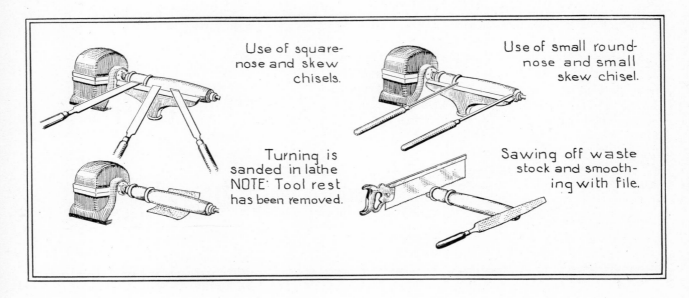

Use of square-nose and skew chisels.

Turning is sanded in lathe NOTE: Tool rest has been removed.

Use of small round-nose and small skew chisel.

Sawing off waste stock and smoothing with file.

spear, round nose, square nose, and parting tool. Each of these tools serves its own distinctive purpose and most of them are manufactured in various sizes.

The large gouge seems to be best adapted for "roughing down" the square stock so as to form a rough cylinder. Grasp a large sharp gouge firmly in both hands and allow it to just touch the slowly revolving stock. The chips fly with amazing ease. By moving the gouge back and forth, the diameter of the spinning member gradually diminishes. Stop the lathe periodically, move the tool rest nearer the stock, and continue at increasing lathe speeds until the wood takes the shape of a completed rough cylinder.

To turn a plane cylinder to a given diameter, adjust the calipers slightly larger than the desired finished diameter. As the stock spins and the parting tool (which is usually held in one hand) touches the cylinder, it cuts a small channel wide enough to accommodate the calipers. The lathe is stopped, and when the calipers, usually held in the other hand, snugly slides across the stock, the right diameter has been reached. It is well to cut a series of these channels across the length of the stock, spaced approximately an inch apart. The depth of these tiny channels then serves as a guide for carefully reducing the entire cylinder, with the tool you find most efficient, the square-nose chisel, skew, or the gouge.

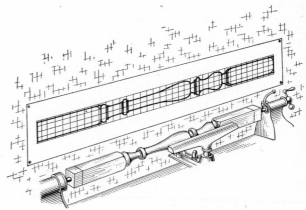

TURNING FROM FULL SIZE PATTERN

Now, if a pattern is to be cut upon the plain cylinder, simply touch a pencil so as to mark the lengthwise measurements for each major change in diameter, while the cylinder is spinning rapidly. Then with a parting tool cut a channel to the required depth at each marking. These various spacings and diameters then serve as guides for producing each of the various shapes. Sanding is best performed while the stock is revolving, always being careful to first remove the tool rest from the lathe. This is done so as to prevent the possibility of accidents in catching the hands between the revolving work and the tool rest.

Turning a disk upon a faceplate follows much the same technique as that used for spindle turning. In this case the stock should obviously

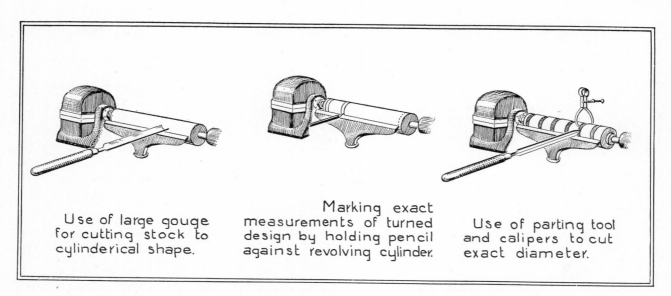

Use of large gouge for cutting stock to cylinderical shape.

Marking exact measurements of turned design by holding pencil against revolving cylinder.

Use of parting tool and calipers to cut exact diameter.

be cut to a circular shape and should then be mounted carefully and securely upon the face-plate. Due to the increased vibrations of large disks, make sure that the stock is accurately centered and turns at a relatively slow speed. Square-nose chisels and round-nose chisels of various sizes are used as the basic process tools. The measurements, shapings, and sanding operations are performed just as in spindle turning.

One danger found in large disk turning is that presented by the possibility that the face-plate will unscrew itself from the lathe thereby releasing the combined disk and faceplate and permitting them to be hurled across the room with great force. This frequently occurs when shifting from a higher to a lower speed. The sudden reduction in speed causes the momentum of the heavy disk to exert pressure in the direction which tends to unscrew the faceplate. Unless the lathe is equipped with a locking device, it is a sensible precaution to turn off the switch, thereby permitting the speed to slow down gradually.

There is also the interesting problem of split turning a column or spindle which separates

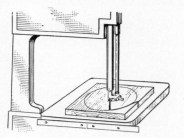

Band saw is used to cut disc.

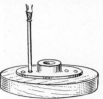

Disc, carefully centered, is mounted on face plate.

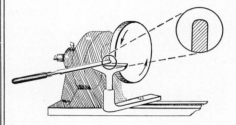

Cutting edge of disc to form perfect circle.

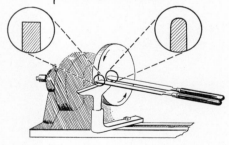

Face of disc is worked to exact thickness.

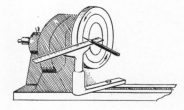

Pencil is touched against revolving disc to mark design.

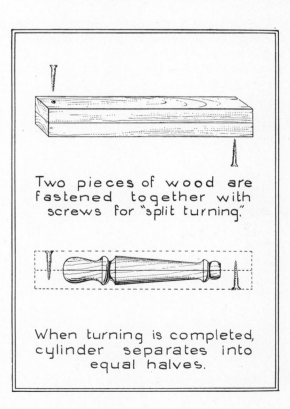

Two pieces of wood are fastened together with screws for "split turning."

When turning is completed, cylinder separates into equal halves.

so as to form duplicating halves. To perform this operation, it is merely a matter of securing two perfectly fitting strips of wood together so as to form one square strip. These two strips are usually held together during the turning process with screws, driven through stock which extends beyond the required turning, at both ends. When the turning has been completed, the two temporary ends may be cut off, causing the finished spindle to fall into halves.

In preparing small split turnings, many workers prefer to place a piece of wrapping paper between the two strips of wood, before gluing up the stock. In this way the two halves may readily be separated after the turning has been completed.

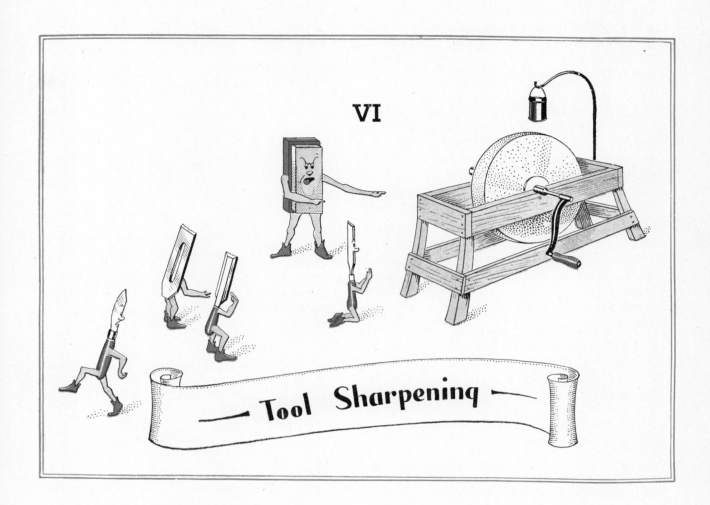

How to Sharpen Hand Tools

Every one has heard the statement that "a good workman cannot succeed with dull tools." Certainly this statement strikes directly home when applied to woodworking. In fact, it might be added that the sharpness of the tools and the condition in which they are kept, determines the final measure of the quality of the finished work.

All cutting tools should be re-sharpened from time to time. Chisels, plane blades, saws, boring bits, and other types of cutters should be examined at regular intervals and their condition checked. It should become second nature for the worker to examine the cutting edges of all the necessary tools before starting a job.

One of the first essentials in a well-equipped shop is a hand or power grindstone. This machine is an absolute *must* in shop equipment. As tools are used, they are bound to become worn, nicked, and damaged. In order to recondition them, the edges must be ground.

Together with the grindstone, it is necessary to have on hand one or more flat and rounded sharpening stones. The flat stone many be obtained in convenient boxes which serve as holders during the sharpening process. They are manufactured with two sharpening surfaces; the coarser surface for sharpening and the finer for honing.

Nor does the sharpening equipment stop at this point. The skilled craftsman is determined that his edge tools be every bit as sharp as a razor. In order to bring them to this degree of sharpness, he not only *hones* the cutting edge, but likewise *strops* it in razor fashion on a regular leather strop.

Common shop tools, such as chisels, plane blades, and spokeshave blades, are all sharpened in practically the same manner. These tools have a single beveled cutting edge and the actual sharpening is performed mostly on this edge alone. The thing to remember is to always keep the *same degree of bevel* along the cutting edge, when the tool is being sharpened.

Take the chisel as an example. Unless the edge is nicked or rounded from too frequent rubbing on the sharpening stone, it may be re-

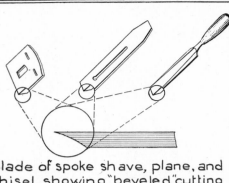

Blade of spoke shave, plane, and chisel, showing "beveled" cutting edges.

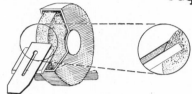

Tool rest of grinder is adjusted to proper bevel.

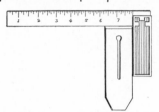

Edge is checked for squareness.

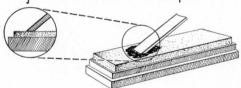

Circular motion is used to "whet" bevel on oilstone. NOTE: Blade is held on <u>exact</u> slant of bevel.

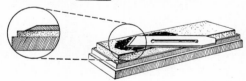

Straight edge of blade must be kept <u>flat</u> on oilstone.

Leather strop is used for final sharpening.

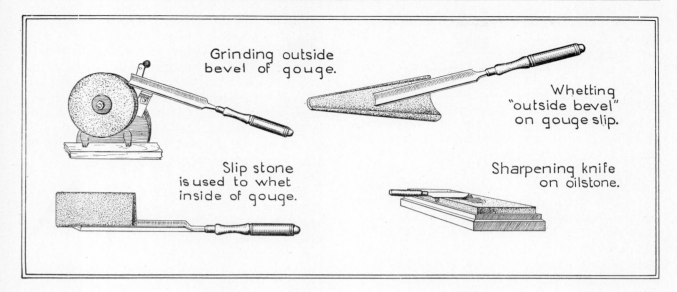

Grinding outside bevel of gouge.

Whetting "outside bevel" on gouge slip.

Slip stone is used to whet inside of gouge.

Sharpening knife on oilstone.

sharpened without using a grindstone. This sharpening is performed by spreading a few drops of thin oil on the surface of the stone and then holding the chisel so that it rests evenly on its cutting bevel. Then it is rubbed backward and forward, or with a circular motion on the surface of the stone. However, it must be remembered that the blade should at all times be rubbed on the slant of its cutting bevel. During the sharpening process, the position of the blade is alternated on the stone, the opposite straight side being held flat on the sharpening surface. After the cutting edge has been carefully sharpened, it is ready to be honed and stropped to final razor sharpness.

However, if the cutting edge happens to be worn or damaged, it will be necessary to re-grind it. This is done by holding the blade against the grindstone, on the correct beveled slant, and sliding it back and forth evenly on the revolving wheel. For this operation certain power grindstones have an automatic oiling device, to keep the wheels oiled while they revolve.

To prevent burning the blade, certain types of hand-operated stone should likewise be oiled. After the grinding has been performed and the cutting edge of the blade properly reshaped, it should be carefully sharpened, honed, and stropped in the manner outlined in the preceding paragraph.

Before leaving the power grindstone it should be mentioned that the business of grinding a beveled edge accurately is greatly simplified when a special tool holder is attached to the grinder. The blade is then simply clamped in the holder so that it may be pushed back and forth across the wheel at the exact slant of the cutting bevel.

Gouge chisels and wood-turning tools require a special sharpening technique. Some gouges are beveled on the outside or *convex* edge, while others are beveled on the inside or *concave* edge. Those that are ground from the outside must be held at the required beveled slant against the grindstone and turned in such a manner that the proper bevel is uniformly maintained along the curved edge.

The final sharpening of the inside and outside gouge is performed with a special round edge, wedge-shaped oilstone (gouge slip). The straight edge of the blade is honed perfectly flat. Many of the turning tools, as well as the carving tools, belong to the gouge family and are sharpened, therefore, in the manner suggested.

How to Sharpen a Saw

The sharpening of saws is a rather special job. Unless the worker happens to be interested in the experience, it might be advisable to send any dull saws to a professional saw sharpener who will do the job expertly for a nominal fee.

A saw that has been used over an extended period of time, and as a result has become dull and worn, should first be *jointed*. This term means that the tips of the teeth must be leveled off so as to provide an absolutely straight cutting edge.

In the jointing process, the saw is held in place either with a special clamping device or between two strips of wood in the regular vise, at the work bench. A file or flat emery stone is then rubbed across the points of the teeth, along the entire length of the blade. During this process the teeth are checked with a straightedge until they are found to be perfectly straight and level. It should be noted that if an emery stone is used, extreme care must be observed to avoid spoiling the stone by creasing it in a single groove.

When the blade has been properly jointed, each tooth is filed to a uniform shape. This filing is usually done with a triangular seven-inch file. In the case of the cross-cut saw, each tooth is shaped to a perfect triangular point, the filing being performed on the inside edges of the teeth. The file is held at a 60-degree angle thus making a bevel on the front edge of one tooth and at the same time making a similar bevel on the back edge of an adjoining tooth.

It will be noted, however, that the teeth of ripsaws are sharpened to an even chisel edge at the point. The front edge of each tooth forms a perfect right angle to the blade.

Before the saw teeth have been properly filed, it is necessary to set each tooth so that it staggers, or bends in an opposite direction to its neighbor. This set is attained by using a tool which resembles a pair of pliers, called a *saw set*. All teeth should be bent to a uniform *set;* those which spread out too far being brought in while others are spread out to the desired amount of set. The proper amount of bend, or set, is frequently marked on the saw blade, and the saw set may be adjusted to this amount.

Saw Set

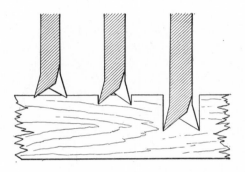

The teeth of a saw are set to clear the blade and prevent it from binding. It is interesting to note that soft and wet woods require more set to cut them properly than hard and dry woods.

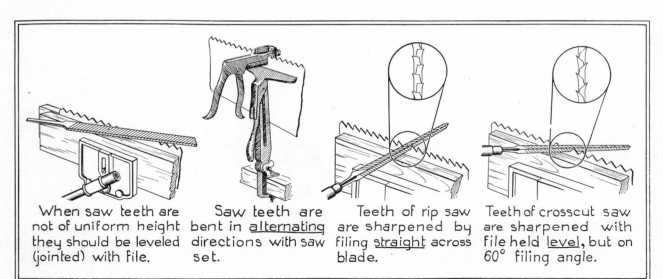

When saw teeth are not of uniform height they should be leveled (jointed) with file.

Saw teeth are bent in <u>alternating</u> directions with saw set.

Teeth of rip saw are sharpened by filing <u>straight</u> across blade.

Teeth of crosscut saw are sharpened with file held <u>level</u>, but on 60° filing angle.

Point of drill is ground to correct slant.

Drill point is sharpered on oilstone.

Auger bit file.

Using bit file to sharpen "nibs" of auger bit.

Sharpening "lips" of bit.

How to Sharpen Drill Bits

Bits that are used with the various types of drills are sharpened at the cutting point. The push drill bit, which must move in reverse directions while it actually drills only on the drive stroke, is fluted on both sides. At the slightly pointed tip, each flute forms the edge of a cutter. On the other hand, the drill bit used with the hand automatic and machine drill revolves in a single direction. Its two spiraled cutting flanges form individual cutters at the slightly sloping point.

When sharpening these bits, it should be kept in mind that each type is shaped at the point with two cutters, and that each cutter is slightly slanted to provide a sharp cutting edge. Both types may be sharpened on a grinding wheel. A sharpening stone, or oilstone, may be used to improve their condition.

How to Sharpen Auger Bits

The sharpening of an auger bit is really not a very difficult job. In fact, it only requires the careful use of a small bit file in reshaping the cutting parts.

The cutting, or boring, parts of an auger bit are the *nibs* and the *lips*. The lips consist of the two cutting knives which terminate the spiral above the pointed tip, or tang, of the bit. Each lip should be filed to an even slanted

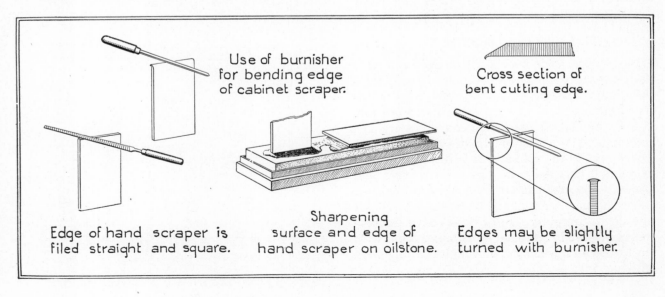

Use of burnisher for bending edge of cabinet scraper.

Cross section of bent cutting edge.

Edge of hand scraper is filed straight and square.

Sharpening surface and edge of hand scraper on oilstone.

Edges may be slightly turned with burnisher.

cutting edge on the upper sides. The nibs which project on both sides, on the rim of the spiral, serve to cut the outside circumference of the hole. In sharpening, they should be filed from the inside. If a burr appears outside of the nibs, it should be filed off flush to the circumference of the bit.

How to Sharpen a Scraper

The edge of a cabinet scraper, is first bevel-ground in the same manner as a plane blade, and may be sharpened, and honed in somewhat similar fashion. After this treatment, however, the sharp edge must be bent over so as to form a shallow lip. Ordinarily it is necessary for this lip to project only about $\frac{1}{32}$ of an inch over the edge. The delicate job of bending the sharpened lips is most easily preformed with an oval-shaped burnishing tool. The burnisher is pressed gently back and forth against the beveled edge. By slow degrees this edge is then bent over to provide the necessary lip. A suitable burnishing tool can be made by grinding the teeth off an old half-round or rat-tail file.

The straightedge hand scraper is not as difficult to sharpen. It is only necessary to file the edges until they become perfectly straight and square. Each edge is then rubbed on the surface of an oilstone, the blade being held at a perfect right angle to the surface. The blade is then placed flat on the surface of the stone and rubbed in this position to remove the burr which has collected along the edge. It will be noted that in the case of the hand scraper, a perfectly sharp and square cutting edge is required.

Keeping Tools in Good Condition

Despite the very best of care, tools and shop equipment are bound to become damaged occasionally. The ends of screwdrivers may become chipped or misshapen, chisels broken, a saw may fall off the bench causing a cracked handle, and working parts of vises and machines may bind and balk. It is usually possible to regrind chipped points of screwdrivers and broken ends of chisels to their original shape. Loose hammer and mallet heads should be tightened promptly. Tools that have become rusted may be brightened by rubbing them with steel wool, followed by a thorough rubbing with anti-rust oil.

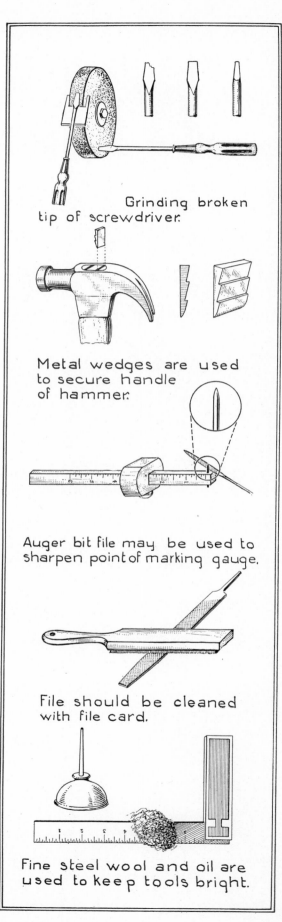

Grinding broken tip of screwdriver.

Metal wedges are used to secure handle of hammer.

Auger bit file may be used to sharpen point of marking gauge.

File should be cleaned with file card.

Fine steel wool and oil are used to keep tools bright.

VII

— Wood Finishing —

Wood finishing is a broad subject in itself and one which requires special treatment. In general, there are many ways of finishing wood. All those who show interest in the subject present their own special methods and, with the exception of a few basic steps, on which all agree, there is little in common in the way different people go about the job.

Excellent and highly effective finishes are often obtained through methods which might strike the professional as being quite unusual. Different finishing agents are used in various parts of the world. Some favor methods of procedure at which others scoff.

Yet all are agreed that the good finish, regardless of the methods or finishing agents employed, should by all means enhance the final appearance of the article on which it is used. Moreover, if it is a transparent finish, it should bring out to the fullest extent the beauty of the grain and the surface characteristics of the wood.

For this reason it is generally agreed that before any type of finish is applied to an article, the article itself should be carefully prepared for the finishing agents. Indeed, the final appearance of the work is largely dependent on the thoroughness with which these basic steps have been taken.

Preparing the Work for Finishing

Before any of the finishing steps are undertaken, the work should be carefully examined for scratches, mars, grain irregularities, dents, glue spots, and kindred imperfections.

Glue which has adhered at places of joining will not absorb stain and must, therefore, be carefully removed before any further steps are taken. Ordinarily, it can be scraped or peeled off with a sharp knife, chisel, or cabinet scraper.

Dents and depressions may often be lifted by placing a wet piece of blotting paper directly over the spot and pressing it with a hot flatiron. Cracks, unless they are large ones, can ordinarily be filled with wood filler, and toned to the same color as the desired final finish. Stick shellac may be bought in colors which blend exactly with most standard tones of finished

"Limbering" a piece of sandpaper.

Dividing the sandpaper.

Saw may be used for cutting. *NOTE:* Blade lies on smooth side.

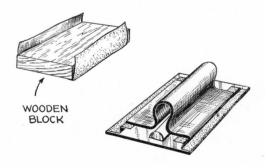

WOODEN BLOCK

Sandpaper is often held on small blocks or special holder.

Sanding is performed with the grain.

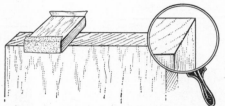

Sanding end grain. *NOTE:* Fine sandpaper produces interesting graining.

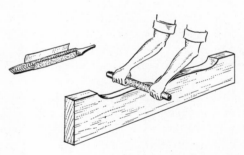

Spindle or file, wrapped in sandpaper is used for curved work.

Sandpaper is held loosely for dulling edges.

wood. This shellac may be used to fill larger cracks or openings. All other imperfections will generally be overcome by the final and thorough use of sandpaper.

Too much emphasis cannot be placed on the importance of thorough sanding. Much of the basic sanding should be taken care of even before the work has been put together. The parts are easier to get at in this way. Two grades of sandpaper should be used; first a medium grade and then, for final sanding, a fine grade.

All sanding should be performed with the grain of the wood. To insure an even and thorough job a sandpaper block should be used wherever possible. End grain portions must be especially well sanded so that the natural grain appears hard and clean. The end grain is especially porous and unless the sanding is very thorough, these portions will absorb the stain and turn a darker color than the rest of the work.

Choice of Stain

Choosing the right stain provides the first point of discussion in the art of wood finishing. There are many different types of stain and each type has its own particular group of followers. In fact, many insist that the richer woods are better off without any stain. However, most people do have occasion to use wood stains at one time or another and it will be well, therefore, to discuss a few of the more common types.

Water Stain is extremely popular because it is easily mixed and does not fade very readily. Pure aniline colors are mixed in hot water and are applied directly and permitted to penetrate and dry on the wood. The water stain is not rubbed. The only objection to stains of this character is that they are apt to raise the grain of the wood, after application. This fault, however, can be overcome by sponging the wood with water and permitting it to dry. The grain, which has been raised during this initial sponging, is then carefully sanded with fine sandpaper, thus providing a protected surface for the water stain.

Spirit Stains, like water stains are mixed with pure aniline colors. However, the liquid agent is alcohol. Spirit strains must be applied carefully because they dry very quickly. When they are applied with a brush, a degree of skill is necessary in order to avoid streaks where brush strokes overlap. In large furniture factories, stains of this kind are generally applied with an air brush.

Oil Stains are favored by many people because they are very easy to apply, and because they enable the worker to develop many interesting effects of tone and color, which would be difficult to attain with stains of other types. The oil stain is mixed from aniline colors compounded in oil and turpentine. Sometimes a small amount of linseed oil is added to give additional body to the stain. Stains of this type which are sold already mixed may contain benzol, benzine, or naphtha as their mixing ingredient.

The oil stain is a common favorite because it does not dry quickly and may be worked over with a rubbing rag after it has been applied. Moreover, it can be worked for tones and contrasts which cannot be obtained with any of the other varieties.

Other Common Methods of Staining and Coloring Wood

Distinctive colors are often obtained on wood through the use of various types of acids and other preparations which bring about a chemical reaction in the wood itself. This reaction produces the distinctive color. The variety of these chemical solutions is almost limitless, so it will be advisable to discuss only two or three of the most popular kinds.

Attractive colors and tones may be obtained on oak through the use of ammonia, potash, and bichromate of potassium. When ammonia is used, the work is exposed to the fumes and as a result takes on a dark tone.

Mahogany may be given a rich color through the use of quicklime. This material is applied and later rubbed off with linseed oil. If the quicklime is permitted to stay on, it discolors the work. However, when it is quickly removed with linseed oil, the result is exceedingly rich.

The Use of Wood Filler

In order to obtain an effective finish on wood, it is not only necessary to color it, but, in the case of open-grained woods, it is necessary as well to *fill* those portions which are to be finished. Close-grained woods, on the other hand, do not require a filler because the texture of the wood is not porous or open, and for this reason the ordinary finishing agents, such as shellac, varnish, or lacquer, will provide whatever filling may be necessary.

Wood filler can be purchased in paste form. It consists of silica, a white powder, mixed in linseed oil, turpentine, and japan. The so-called transparent finish is cream-colored and may be tinted to any desired tone or shade through the introduction of oil colors.

Filler should be thoroughly mixed and diluted with turpentine until it is of the consistency of heavy cream. Generally speaking, it is good practice to stain the work before applying the filler. The latter is applied to the work with a stiff brush. It dries and hardens in a relatively short time and for this reason, on large projects it should be brushed on portions at a time, in separate applications. After each portion has been treated and allowed to dry for a few minutes, it is rubbed vigorously across the grain with a coarse rag or piece of burlap. The idea is to work the paste well into the open and porous grain. After the initial cross-grain rubbing has been performed, the filled portions are again rubbed with the grain, this time with a finer piece of cloth.

If the filler adheres and hardens in places on the surface of the work, it should be carefully removed with a rag moistened with turpentine. Excess filler should be removed at intersections and places of joining, with a sharpened stick or knife blade covered with a rag.

While it is not always necessary to do so, sometimes the idea of re-staining the article after the filler has been applied is a worth-while practice. Frequently this operation improves the appearance of the finished product. Naturally, it is rather difficult to color the wood filler to the exact desired shade, and thus when the work is re-stained, the color may be adjusted and brought to the shade desired.

Stain is applied evenly from center area.

Soft cloth is used to rub stain, with the grain.

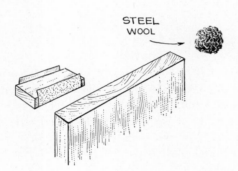

Fine sandpaper or steel wool is used to "brighten" end grain.

Center areas and edges are thoroughly rubbed to produce high lights.

Wood filler should be given at least twenty-four hours to dry and harden before continuing with further steps of finishing.

How to Apply Stain

The application of water or spirit stains is relatively simple, as both of these types of stain are merely brushed on the well-sanded wood and permitted to penetrate into the surface. Sometimes, however, it is necessary to remove carefully with a rag any excess stain from portions of the wood, especially on the end grain. The main idea is to let the stain penetrate and dye the wood.

Likewise, in the application of chemicals and acids which are used to change the color of the wood, it is only necessary to apply them in the regular manner, and remove the excess with a rag.

However, in the application of oil stains, especially where a special effect is desired, the technique is somewhat different. For example, let us say that a small table is being stained. The stain is first brushed freely and quickly on the four legs and the underneath structure. While it remains wet on these portions, it is rubbed carefully with a rag until the grain and surface characteristics of the wood show through. Moreover, in the rubbing process, it is possible to *tone out* certain portions of the wood to obtain either uniform or contrasting effects. Light rubbing with very fine steel wool will help in this process.

With certain types of close-grained woods, notably pine and maple, there is a definite advantage in mixing the oil stain to a fairly heavy consistency. Maple is not very absorbent, while pine is porous and generally absorbs the stain in patches. Unfortunately, these patches cannot be detected until after the stain has been applied. The heavy oil stain, because it permits an opportunity for extra rubbing with cloth or fine steel wool, is excellent for obtaining tone effects. Its use allows the worker a greater margin of control in obtaining the desired tones and uniformity of color.

High Lighting

Oil stains, especially when they are mixed heavy, lend themselves well to the process of high lighting, or toning an article for contrasting tonal effects. In the finishing of furniture made of pine, maple, oak, chestnut, and certain other woods, it is often desirable to produce varying tones in the finished color. Table tops assume a richer and more vital appearance when the mid-portions and corners are a few shades lighter in tone than other portions. The central area of legs, rails, and aprons should be in contrast, remaining somewhat lighter in tone than the darker sections at the points of joinery. These effects may be obtained by rubbing off the oil stain with additional vigor where the lighter shades are desired. Fine steel wool also helps to remove excessive stain. Indeed, the final appearance of the work will warrant the additional effort involved.

The Shellac Finish

Shellac, as it is prepared commercially, is usually composed of four pounds of shellac gum mixed in one gallon of alcohol. This mixture is referred to as a "4-lb cut." However, it is not wise to apply the shellac directly to the work in this consistency. It should be diluted.

Before proceeding with any of the steps of shellacking, the worker should be sure that the article to be covered is thoroughly dry and clean, that no dust or dirt is adhering to the surfaces, and that it is altogether ready for the final finishing steps.

For the first coat, the regular commercial shellac should be cut with alcohol in any amount varying from one-third to one-half. It should be almost *water thin*. As shellac dries quickly when it is being applied, the worker should proceed briskly and evenly, working with the grain of the wood to avoid over brushing. The first thin coat is absorbed into the wood and provides a base for further coats.

After each coat of shellac, the work should be carefully rubbed with fine steel wool. Ordinarily, three or four coats of shellac will provide an excellent finish. The final coat may be sprinkled with fine pumice stone and rubbed with an oil-soaked felt pad to obtain perfect smoothness. Afterward the work should be thoroughly waxed, both to protect the finish and to bring it to a beautiful luster.

It is generally agreed that the shellac finish should not be applied over a stain that has been mixed in alcohol; or for that matter, over any other type of spirit stain. The alcohol in the shellac is apt to cut and fade stains of this type.

The Varnish Finish

Varnish has many advantages over other types of finishing agents in that it may be applied more easily and provides an excellent luster. However, it is by no means impervious to damage and, unless a specially fine quality of varnish is used, it will, in time, crack and check, and require refinishing.

One of the first requisites in varnishing is to find a dust-free work room. The very fact that varnish dries slowly, makes it vulnerable to any dust or dirt which may come in contact with it during the drying period.

However, after the varnish has been suitably cut with turpentine, the worker will delight in the fine free fashion in which it flows from the brush. Indeed, as the work is being brushed, ample time can be taken to smooth out the brush strokes, pick up drips, and examine and re-touch all parts of the article.

Although there are a number of quick-drying varnishes on the market, and while most of these are excellent, still the worker should allow ample time for each coat of varnish to become thoroughly dry. When this time arrives, each coat in turn is carefully rubbed and smoothed with fine garnet paper, before the next coat is applied. This provides an even binding surface for the succeeding coat.

Three good coats of varnish generally suffice. The final coat, which should be rubbed to a smooth luster, is polished thoroughly with a mixture of fine pumice stone and rottenstone, or with rottenstone alone. The rubbing is performed with an oil-soaked felt pad. After all parts have been carefully polished, the finished article may be waxed, both for extra luster and to protect the finish.

The Lacquer Finish

Lacquer is a comparatively new commercial finishing product. However, a product bearing this name has been used in the Orient since the beginning of civilization. Because of its many excellent qualities it has been greeted with much enthusiasm by manufacturers. It is used to a great extent by the furniture industry.

Lacquer provides an exceptionally durable finish. It does not crack or mar very readily and it resists the action of liquids, as well as changing climatic conditions. Moreover, it dries quickly and with the proper equipment is not difficult to apply.

Although lacquer may be obtained in various shades and colors, we are concerned at present with its use in clear form, that is, like shellac and varnish. The ingredients of lacquer (it contains a high percentage of lead acetate, or "banana oil") cause it to be injurious to a stained surface. For this reason, it is wise to first cover the stain with one or more sealing coats of shellac, before any lacquer is applied.

Because it is extremely quick in drying, the most satisfactory way of applying lacquer is with an air brush. When skillfully sprayed on the work it dries uniformly and evenly. However, if it is properly diluted with its exclusive thinner (lacquer thinner) it may be brushed on, providing, of course, that the worker proceeds with due caution and takes care not to repeat brush strokes.

There are two schools of thought regarding the treatment of lacquer after it has been applied. Some assert that each coat should be sanded or steel-wooled in the manner of varnish and shellac, while others maintain that the dull even luster of the untouched lacquer should provide the final finish. However, if the final coat is carefully rubbed with either fine steel wool or pumice, no harm will result and, indeed, the beauty of the surface may be enhanced.

Natural Finishes—Oil Finish

For bringing out the inherent characteristics of wood, for the beautification of fine graining, and for the development of a lovely natural luster, no type of finish can excel that which is obtained with boiled linseed oil. The luxurious, rich tones which oil produces in natural walnut, gumwood, teak, mahogany, and similar hardwoods, causes this type of finish to be especially desirable. Moreover, the surface which is treated with oil is amply protected against ordinary damage, and it may be freshened up at any time with new applications of oil.

To produce this finish, it is first necessary to thin the boiled linseed oil with an equal quantity of turpentine. It is applied with a brush, excess oil being removed with an absorbent rag. Successive coats of oil are applied, up to three or four, allowing each coat to dry before applying the next. The final coat is carefully rubbed with a clean cloth until a warm luster has been produced. The oil penetrates the wood, and once it has hardened, there is little likelihood of it coming off and soiling covers or clothing.

Orange Shellac Finish

To obtain a beautiful natural finish on light colored woods, pine especially, the work should be left unstained and finished with a mixture of orange and white shellac. The two colors of shellac are mixed to a light orange tone and diluted from one-third to one-half, with alcohol.

Ordinarily three coats of shellac will suffice; each coat, after it has dried, being carefully rubbed with fine steel wool. After the final rubbing, the work is thoroughly waxed.

This natural finish is especially recommended for pine, maple, birch, and cherry, as it permits the wood to age and darken to its own excellent tone.

Wax Finish

It has already been noted that waxing plays an important part in the proper finishing of wood. Indeed, some very effective finishes have been accomplished with stain and wax alone. If the worker so chooses, he may proceed to wax his work immediately after the stain has become thoroughly dry. Let him be reminded, however, that the plain wax finish is absolutely dependent upon perfectly smooth initial sanding. It is not well to attempt such a finish on any woods other than those of the close-grained varieties.

The principal idea in waxing is to obtain and to keep the finished beauty and luster of the wood. As furniture becomes older, it may, from time to time, be waxed again. This process protects its original freshness of finish and also enhances the more mature tones which age produces in wood.

There are several types of wax which may be used in this work. Many wood finishers employ a wax which is obtained by mixing beeswax and turpentine. It is prepared by dissolving beeswax in turpentine for at least two days. To this heavy wax solution is added a small amount of burnt umber for coloring purposes.

The better varieties of commercial paste wax also serve excellently for this work. Burnt umber or a blending of colors in oil should be added to any wax so as to tint it to match the finish. This treatment prevents the possibility of conspicuous smudges where wax is likely to dry. Wax, of natural color, may otherwise adhere in places of joining, leaving such places noticeably off color.

It is well to apply the wax evenly with a small, soft, cloth pad. While usually it is proper to let the wax remain on all parts for an extended period of time before rubbing, it is only advisable to do so when the temperature of the room in which the work is being performed, is sufficiently high to prevent hard setting. The object in letting wax stand is to help the worker in obtaining a proper luster, but in a cold room the wax may become so hard that it will be difficult to remove it successfully. Under such conditions, the wax should be rubbed with a soft lintless cloth shortly after it has been applied. Subsequent waxing will further develop the luster.

A new commercial product has lately appeared on the market which combines stain and wax. It may be applied directly to the work, which is later rubbed to a dull luster.

How to Paint

The same basic rules carry through in painting that apply in preparing work for a natural finish. Naturally, however, painting is not quite as precise an operation as shellacking or varnishing. In most cases, paint will serve to conceal many of the blemishes which might mar

Small dents and depressions are lifted with wet blotting paper and hot iron.

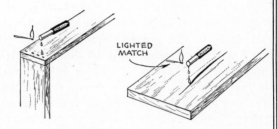

Stick shellac may be used to fill nail depressions and cracks.

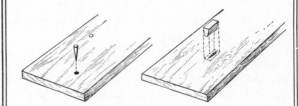

Pegs and wedges are used to repair small holes and damaged areas.

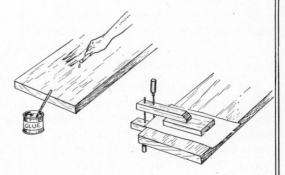

Grain splinters should be carefully glued and clamped.

or damage the appearance of work which is finished naturally. But it is a good idea to prepare carefully the surface on which paint is to be applied.

Surfaces should be well sanded and free of grease spots, dirt, cracks, or nail holes. Nail holes and cracks can be filled with putty or with a similar filling substance, after the priming coat of paint has dried, and sanded flush to the surface of adjoining parts. Porous, open-grained woods should be carefully filled.

It is always wise to give the work a priming coat of paint before proceeding with additional coats. The priming coat is absorbed by the wood and provides a base for the coats which follow. Where several successive coats are to be applied, each coat, in turn, should be carefully sanded to perfect smoothness. The final coat is then evenly applied and permitted to remain unsanded.

One or more priming coats should always be applied as a base for enamel. One coat of enamel will suffice. Of late, there has appeared on the market a new type of enamel which covers the work thoroughly with a single coat. On new work, however, even with enamel of this character, at least one priming coat of paint should be used.

Lacquer is popularly used where bright color effects are desired. It is especially demanded for both indoor and outdoor furniture. As previously explained, lacquer is exceedingly fast in drying and as a result it must be applied quickly. Best results are obtained by spraying it on the work. However, if it is properly thinned with lacquer thinner it may be applied by brush. The worker must proceed alertly and *must not repeat brush strokes*. Two or three coats of colored lacquer are usually sufficient.

Care of Brushes and Finishing Equipment

It almost goes without saying that paints, shellacs, varnishes, stains, and so forth, should always be kept in air-tight containers when they are not in actual use. White shellac is subject to a degree of damage if it is kept in the light. For this reason it should be kept in an earthenware light-proof container. It will corrode the ordinary metal can and leak away, if kept over an extended period.

A sealed metal container should be kept handy for storing steel wool, rags, pumice stone, and associated materials.

It is a good idea to wash brushes out in a brush-cleaning solution, various brands of which may be purchased in hardware stores, after they have been used. In this way the bristles are kept clean and soft. They may be left in water to which a small amount of the cleaning powder has been added, but they should never be permitted to rest on their bristles. This causes the bristles to bend and in time renders the brush worthless. To avoid this damage, it is a good idea to hammer a tack in the mid part of the brush handle and suspend the brush on the rim of the can so that its bristles, while they are immersed in the liquid, do not rest on the bottom of the can.

VIII

Safety First in the Shop

We have all heard the slogans: "Watch your Step!—Look Before You Leap!—Take It Easy!" and dozens of others meaning the same thing. We have also heard that very important slogan *"Safety First!"*

Safety First is a law that should be observed at all times. It is not restricted to any single type of activity but carries over to all activities and works its way into our general method of living.

Each year thousands of accidents occur which might have been avoided. Carelessness is the cause of most accidents. The classic example of "The Man who didn't know the gun was loaded" demonstrates the exact manner in which many of these accidents occur. Let us also remember that the shop is a place where accidents *can* and *do* occur. So is the bathtub. But this circumstance does not prevent us from taking a bath.

When working in the shop, however, we should become acquainted with the things that *may* cause trouble. If we know about them we can avoid them. So, let us review some of these shop hazards and see what can be done to prevent accidents.

Undoubtedly there are more *safe ways* of doing a job than there are *unsafe ways*. Being in a hurry or trying to take short-cuts to gain speed, frequently ends up in a serious accident. You may be able to get away with a few occasional short-cuts, but according to the law of averages you will get hurt sooner or later.

Don't take chances! We hear lots of talk these days about different types of machines being "fool-proof." Unfortunately there is generally a fool who will come along to challenge this claim. Most of our woodworking machinery, properly equipped with guards and safety devices, may be considered practically fool-proof. Still, if it is not used the right way, accidents may occur that could have been prevented.

There are a number of safety suggestions that we should consider. First of all it is not a good thing to let the shop floor become strewed with scraps and debris. Under such conditions the worker may slip and fall, the chances of serious accidents being magnified with the presence of

sharp-edged tools and machinery. If nails are not removed from boards the unwary person may step on them. Don't leave boards lying around that have nail points sticking out beyond the surface.

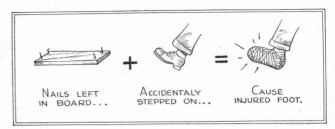

NAILS LEFT IN BOARD... + ACCIDENTALY STEPPED ON... = CAUSE INJURED FOOT.

Sharp edges and rough edges of boards are the cause of many cuts and sliver wounds. Handle rough lumber carefully. You won't be considered effeminate if you wear gloves!

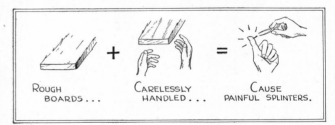

ROUGH BOARDS... + CARELESSLY HANDLED... = CAUSE PAINFUL SPLINTERS.

Certainly the shop is not a place for horseplay or fooling around. Many tragic accidents have resulted from practical jokes and silly activity. In most cases the trouble was started by levity on the part of an individual.

We all know that the live current in the electric light socket, or floor outlet, is just waiting for a contact in order to produce active electricity. When this contact is made by a misguided person who inserts a nail, or metal object, into the socket, a severe shock will follow. We can

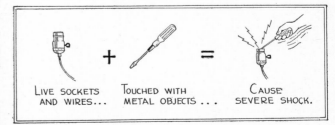

LIVE SOCKETS AND WIRES... + TOUCHED WITH METAL OBJECTS... = CAUSE SEVERE SHOCK.

imagine the dreadful result if this experiment is made on a high voltage power line! It is a good idea to snap off the main switch before making repairs on electrical equipment. In his repair work the electrician uses rubber gloves and tools that have insulated handles.

Never put brads, tacks, or screws in your mouth. Should you cough or stumble while they

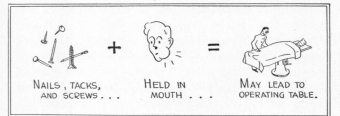

NAILS, TACKS, AND SCREWS... + HELD IN MOUTH... = MAY LEAD TO OPERATING TABLE.

are in your mouth, you may swallow a few. Aside from this possibility you are apt to irritate your mouth. Screws and nails are also germ carriers. There are many cases reported where acute infection has resulted from this practice.

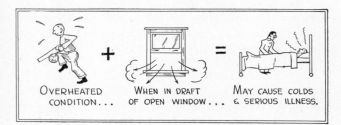

OVERHEATED CONDITION... + WHEN IN DRAFT OF OPEN WINDOW... = MAY CAUSE COLDS & SERIOUS ILLNESS.

You may get yourself overheated while you are working and be tempted to open wide a window, in order to cool off. With your pores open and perspiration flowing freely, this is a fine way to get pneumonia. Don't do it.

Avoid the practice of throwing tools and articles to another person. This game may work out all right in a grocery store or on a skyscraper construction job, where riveters are practiced in

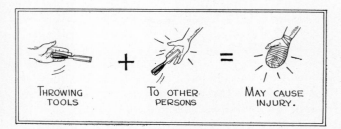

THROWING TOOLS + TO OTHER PERSONS = MAY CAUSE INJURY.

the job of throwing hot rivets. In the shop, however, there is a possibility of your catching the sharpened edge of the tool and thus getting an ugly cut.

Get Acquainted With Your First-Aid Kit

It goes without saying that every shop should be equipped with a complete first-aid kit. Handy kits are available containing the various items that are necessary for first aid. They should be kept within easy reach.

A WOODWORKING SHOP... + WITH A FIRST AID KIT... = IS PREPARED FOR EMERGENCIES.

Regardless of how trivial you may consider a cut, be on the safe side and have it looked after. In so doing you may avoid blood poisoning.

Small cuts and scratches may be cleansed with antiseptic soap and warm water. They should be treated with an antiseptic solution such as iodine or mercurochrome. A sterilized bandage or covering placed directly over the wound prevents exposure to dust and dirt. Various types of small prepared bandages are now on the market. They are very easily applied.

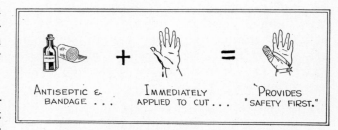

ANTISEPTIC & BANDAGE... + IMMEDIATELY APPLIED TO CUT... = PROVIDES "SAFETY FIRST."

If the cut is large and bleeding freely it is wise to see a doctor or nurse immediately. Cuts which enter veins or arteries must be given first aid with tourniquet treatment. This means that the flow of blood must be stemmed at a point above the cut. For such treatment improvise a loose sling, inserting a stick to twist and tighten. Pressure may be applied directly by pressing the fingers against the blood vessel leading to the wound, thereby stopping the flow of blood. Then take the patient to the hospital.

The layman is not qualified, except in extreme emergencies, and where a doctor is not available, to treat cuts and injuries that are of a serious nature. Nor should the layman experiment with the job in amateur fashion.

Bruises and burns require special treatment. A bruise is a type of injury in which the skin itself has not been broken, but the tissues beneath have been torn, thereby allowing blood to

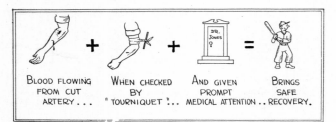

BLOOD FLOWING FROM CUT ARTERY . . . WHEN CHECKED BY "TOURNIQUET" . . . AND GIVEN PROMPT MEDICAL ATTENTION . . BRINGS SAFE RECOVERY.

ooze into this area without coming to the surface. A pad of gauze should be bandaged tightly over the injury as soon as possible in order to check excessive spread of the bruised area. You may be tempted to open the bruise and release the "bad blood," *but don't do it.* This blunder may result in the formation of pus and even cause blood poisoning. When severe bruises must be opened, this is a job for a doctor.

Safety First and Power Machinery

Power machinery does, of course, present the greatest amount of risk. Circular saws, band saws, jointers, lathes, shapers—all of them—with their sharp cutting parts exposed and turning at very high speed, must at all times be watched. The error of a single second may result in a serious accident.

Fortunately, most of these machines are being manufactured with adequate guards so that their danger of operation is reduced to a minimum. Even so, they are not entirely fool-proof, and if they are not operated correctly accidents may result.

Get into the habit of paying strict attention to your work while operating a machine. The

REVOLVING BLADES AND CUTTERS . . . PROPERLY GUARDED . . . PREVENTS INJURY TO HANDS.

old trolley cars displayed a large sign which read "Don't Talk to the Motorman." This precaution should likewise be observed when a person is operating a machine.

The student or amateur should, of course, be thoroughly instructed before attempting to use a machine. There are certain definite *do's* and *don't's* which should be followed, many of which may be demonstrated. This writer recalls the instance of an instructor who was so conscientious in his demonstration of the *do's* and *don't's* that he cut off his own index finger while demonstrating a *don't.*

We all like to be helpful and it is a common thing to see amateur woodworkers trying to help each other in the operation of a machine. This should be avoided, excepting when long planks are being cut which virtually require two people for handling. Even then one person should take care of the operation of the machine while the other person walks along slowly to guide and support the extremity of the plank.

In most instances the operating of woodworking machinery is strictly a one-man job. After all, no two persons can safely operate a car at the same time. In carrying this idea over to woodworking, the would-be helpful "back-seat driver" is generally the one who causes the accidents.

Frequently we see one person snap the switch, to start a machine for another person. This practice, of course, is extremely dangerous. Suppose

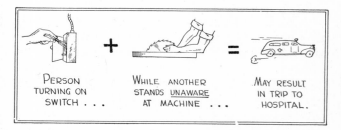

PERSON TURNING ON SWITCH . . . WHILE ANOTHER STANDS UNAWARE AT MACHINE . . . MAY RESULT IN TRIP TO HOSPITAL.

the worker has his hand, or a part of his body, in the vicinity of the moving parts of the machine when the switch is snapped on!

Get into the habit of staying at your post, at the machine, even after the switch has been turned off. Modern machinery operates so quietly that it is often difficult to tell whether or not the machine is running. If you leave the machine while it is still running under full power, or while it is coasting to a stop, another person may accidentally come in contact with the moving parts and be seriously injured.

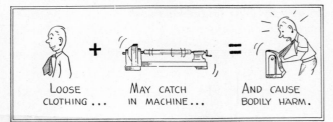

LOOSE CLOTHING . . . + MAY CATCH IN MACHINE . . . = AND CAUSE BODILY HARM.

Even your clothing may provide a cause of accidents. Loose neckties and cuffs may get caught in the moving parts of the machine. It is a good idea to roll up your sleeves and tuck in your necktie before starting to work. In this way you are ready for action and thus you minimize the risk of accident.

Most of our modern machinery is equipped with guards which cover the belts, gears, pulleys, and shafts. If your machinery is not safely equipped you can probably obtain guard attachments. They are a very good investment.

SLIPPERY FLOORS . . . + AND RESULTING FALLS . . . = MAY CAUSE SERIOUS INJURY.

A basic precaution in safeguarding the operation of a power machine is to be sure that at all times the floor in the immediate vicinity of the machine is free of any obstructions. Moreover, the area where the operator stands should afford firm and solid footing, and should be kept free of anything which might cause it to become smooth or slippery. Wide mats of corrugated rubber are often attached to the floor around the machines, which seems to be a very sensible precaution. Also, wet paint is sometimes sprinkled with fine sand, providing a non-skid footing as soon as the paint has thoroughly dried.

Then too, the person operating the circular saw must always be careful to keep his hands a good distance from the blade. If small pieces of

wood are to be cut, special sticks and feeders should be introduced to safeguard the work.

Generally speaking, it is unwise to attempt to cross-cut pieces to a required length by feeding with the material against the ripping fence. The pieces are apt to bind momentarily between the revolving blade and the ripping fence and then

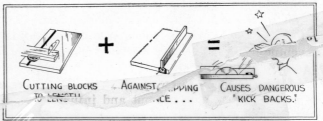

CUTTING BLOCKS TO LENGTH + AGAINST RIPPING FENCE . . . = CAUSES DANGEROUS "KICK BACKS."

"kick back" in the direction of the operator at terrific speed. It is risky too, to attempt to rip very small pieces of wood. Here again lurks the danger of a kick back.

OPERATING GRINDER . . . − WITHOUT EYE "PROTECTORS" . . . = MAY CAUSE EYE INJURIES.

The power grinder is usually equipped with a wide lens through which you look when a tool is being sharpened. This lens is put there so that you will not get fragments of steel or abrasive in your eyes. If the grinder is not equipped in this way, a pair of goggles should be used.

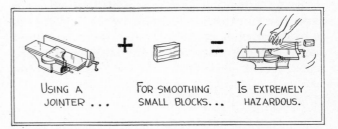

USING A JOINTER . . . + FOR SMOOTHING SMALL BLOCKS . . . = IS EXTREMELY HAZARDOUS.

The jointer is considered by many to be one of the most dangerous machines in the shop. Indeed, there is good reason for its evil reputation, for as the cutting blades revolve at a tremendous speed there is very little hope for anything which might get in the way. Ordinarily the operator is able to keep his hands a good distance from the revolving blade as the work is being fed into the machine. It is both wise and sensible to avoid using the jointer for surfacing small pieces of wood.

Even the ordinary wood-turning lathe has several risks attached to its operation. Primarily, of course, the operator must be careful to secure all loose clothing. Then too, the various working tools must be correctly held so that they do not catch in the work and cause an accident. The lathe can be a really vicious and dangerous machine when not used in a sensible manner, and so above all—*safety first*! First and foremost, be sure the stock is securely fastened so that there is no danger of it flying out and injuring some one. This rule holds true for work mounted upon the face plate as well as for stock which is being spun between the two centers. It is always well

LATHE TOOLS... + LIGHTLY AND IMPROPERLY HELD... = MAY BE WRENCHED FROM HANDS.

to test the final adjustments by "spinning" the lathe by hand before turning on the mechanical power. And by all means always practise on small pieces of softwood.

Be sure the stock is well balanced so as to avoid excessive vibration which, in itself, creates a tendency to tear the stock out of the lathe. Also, the extent of vibration increases with the increased speed; so run the lathe at slow or medium speeds until the stock is perfectly round. Be sure the tool rest is securely fastened so that it does not slip, which might cause either the cutting tool or the tool rest itself to get caught by the edges of the rough stock.

A necktie or any other flowing bits of one's clothing can easily get caught in the lathe. More than one person with long hair has had a great deal of it painfully torn from his scalp when stooping before a spinning lathe, as it became wrapped upon the fast moving cylinder. The answer to the lurking of this danger is: *Avoid wearing anything which may be grabbed by the spinning parts.*

Another sane caution is to refrain from touching the stock while it is in motion. A piece of wood with splinters, or edge breaks, may look perfectly smooth when spinning at high speeds. The eye, as you know, is much too slow to be able to detect these dangerous spots on rapidly turning stock and thus many a hand has been injured.

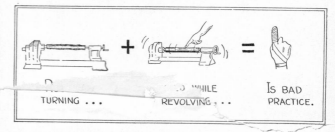

... TURNING ... + ... WHILE REVOLVING ... = IS BAD PRACTICE.

Safety First With Hand Tools

Nor are these risks limited to the operation of power machinery. Indeed, hand tools may cause severe injury if they are not used with the right amount of care. Chisels especially, are dangerous if not properly handled. The worker should always take care to use the chisel in such a way that the cutting is performed in the direction *away* from the parts of his body. Clamping the stock firmly in place and using *two hands* to operate a chisel, obviously eliminates the danger of cutting the one hand which might otherwise be used as the clamping agent.

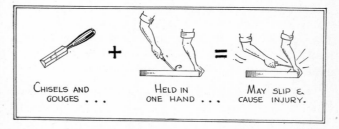

CHISELS AND GOUGES ... + HELD IN ONE HAND ... = MAY SLIP & CAUSE INJURY.

Automatic screwdrivers should be carried about and used in such a way as to avoid the chance of the screwdriver point snapping out to full extension and injuring oneself or neighbor. Knives, and even saws, must be watched. Fortunately, in the case of hand tools, when the tool is correctly used the possible risk remains at a minimum. It is usually the careless individual who injures himself.

More accidents are caused by dull cutting tools than by those which have keen cutting edges. The sharp tool does a fine job with very little effort. On the other hand, when using a dull cutting tool such as a knife, hatchet, chisel, or saw, the work may slip or the dull tool may glance off, causing injury. After the worker has exerted and fatigued himself trying to cut with a dull tool he is apt to become careless and at this point the tool may slip and a serious cut result. Keep your tools sharp!

When handing an edged tool to another person, extend the handle first. This is both courtesy and sound practice toward accident prevention.

Even when you are carrying tools, there is a safe way of going about it. Hold the sharp edges down so that they will not come in contact with any one who is standing or walking nearby.

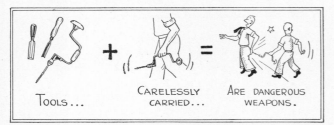

Accidents are avoided when tools are used in the proper way. Even the plain, old-fashioned hammer, may in its blunt, unintentional way, cause trouble. Think of the number of times that people have missed the nail and bruised their thumb!

Be sure that your tools are in good condition. There is always danger that the heads of hammers, mallets, and hatchets, if not properly attached, will fly out and seriously injure some one. Loose handles on saws, chisels, and other tools may cause similar trouble.

Other Causes of Shop Accidents

There are certain things that happen again and again in the woodworking shop that might just as easily be avoided. Often when driving screws people will run their finger over the head of the screw after the job has been completed. This may result in the person getting a sharp metal splinter from the screw head in the tip of his finger. While the screw is being turned a small "barb" of sharp metal may become loosened from the edge of the slot. This razor-sharp chip of metal is ready to imbed itself into the finger tip.

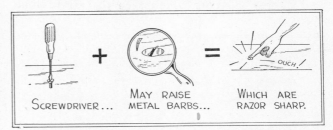

Common wood clamps are sometimes a source of trouble. Work that has been clamped together is extremely bulky and unwieldy while the clamps are fastened on it. Accidents have occurred where people have stumbled into the ends of these protruding clamps, resulting in bodily or facial injury. It is well to put the clamped work away so that people cannot stumble over it.

Beware of all things overhead! How frequently people bang their heads on protruding shelves or parts of construction that extend outward at head level. Plan your shop in such a way as to minimize this danger. Tools and lumber stacked in this manner are sources of danger to every one in the shop.

Fire Prevention as Part of Safety First

Unless it is carefully guarded the shop may become a virtual fire trap. Wood shavings and dry wood provide perfect fuel for a fire. Moreover, the materials used in wood finishing add considerably to the risk.

Kerosene, gasoline, turpentine, and other inflammable finishing solutions, should be kept tightly sealed either in bottles or metal containers. Rags and waste which has been soaked in turpentine, linseed oil, or kerosene may cause spontaneous combustion. They should either be burned after use or stored in covered metal cans. Lighted matches, pipes, or cigarettes, must of course be carefully guarded. As a general thing smoking should be prohibited in the woodworking shop.

If the shop is kept clean and tidy the fire risk will be greatly reduced.

A Healthy Shop is a Safe Shop

The shop should be a pleasant place, where you will enjoy your work. Large manufacturers have learned that shop accidents are greatly reduced when the shop itself is well lighted and well ventilated. The introduction of ventilating and blower systems which free the air of dust and particles of dirt, have gone a long way toward reducing accidents. Good lighting, both natural and artificial, likewise safeguards the worker. Together with the other things that have been mentioned, these features are tremendously important. The healthy shop is the safe shop. After all, the protection of health is the first rule of "Safety First in the Shop."

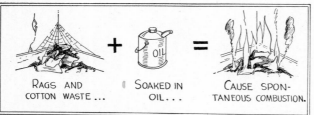

RAGS AND COTTON WASTE... + SOAKED IN OIL... = CAUSE SPONTANEOUS COMBUSTION.

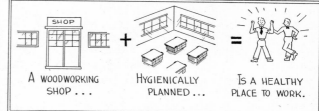

A WOODWORKING SHOP... + HYGIENICALLY PLANNED... = IS A HEALTHY PLACE TO WORK.

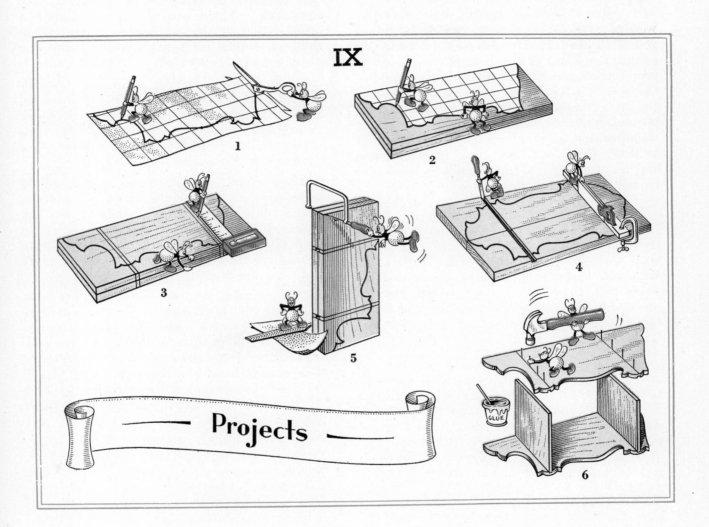

IX

Projects

WITH a practical knowledge of how to do woodworking comes the reward of being able to make useful and attractive wooden articles. The desire to make things yourself is, in fact, the greatest stimulus to this activity. Literally hundreds of thousands of people throughout the country have equipped themselves with home workshops because of the sheer fun and recreation, not to mention the obvious profit, of being able to do their own woodworking. In this way they have been able to bring their own handwork, furniture, and articles of utility into their homes and also save money in home maintenance.

Many home workshop enthusiasts recall their school days when they made projects in the school woodworking shop. In the school shop they first tried their hand with tools. With this background they were able in later years to understand and pursue the practice of woodworking. Perhaps their original training provided the incentive for their later activity.

For the beginner, the amateur, or even the advanced woodworker, it is desirable to employ tool skill only on well designed and nicely chosen projects. Obviously, good workmanship is wasted when it is employed in the construction of something which is poorly designed. The greatest skill in the world will not serve to make anything out of such a project.

On the other hand, a good design is multiplied in value when carefully and skillfully constructed, *by hand*. Thus the skilled woodworker is able to make things that are many times the value of their average commercial counterpart, because of the individuality expressed in hand workmanship.

The designs presented in this chapter were carefully selected, to interest those who use this book. Their construction represents a cross-section of the information contained in the text. Special reference is made in the case of each design, to portions or pages of the text.

These projects are not graduated step-by-step. But some of them are very easy to make. It would be advisable for the beginner to choose these simple projects and then advance according to his ability to those which involve more advanced workmanship.

Every effort has been made to keep all of these projects within the range of average ability. Each item was especially chosen and prepared so as to appear as a good design, in good taste, and to serve in itself as a fitting reward for the effort and skill of the beginner or the advanced craftsman.

Most of these projects were designed especially for this book. Others have appeared in national magazines where they were found to be popular. In presenting the latter, acknowledgment in gratefully made to the editors of those magazines for permission to use drawings and photographs of these designs by John G. Shea, which originally appeared in their pages.

Corner Cupboards, (miniature or full size); Trestle Tables (dining tables or coffee tables); Nautical Screen; Butler's Coffee Table; Nautical Shelves; courtesy, *Woman's Home Companion*. Colonial Wall Shelves; Cornice Boards; courtesy, *House Beautiful*. Colonial End Table; Nautical Lamp; courtesy, *The Home Craftsman*. Scalloped Top Table; Gate Leg Trestle Table; Refreshment Server; courtesy *Popular Homecraft*. Peg-Leg Colonial Lamp; courtesy *Popular Mechanics*.

PLATE 1

A Handy Place to Hang Neckties Is An important male convenience. Indeed, women too may find a use for this article. So it is necessary that a simple and efficient type of necktie rack be presented. A glance at the drawing will show you that this rack is extremely easy to make. Moreover, it is quite attractive and will hold a quantity of neckties. Holes should be drilled in the back of the rack and covered with a couple of small circular key plates to serve as hangers. Otherwise small screw eyes can be used on the top edge, or small holes may be drilled through the back of the rack near the top corners.

REFERENCE TO BASIC PROCESSES IN TEXT

Squaring ....Page 48.
Edge Shaping .... " 51.
Dowel Joints .... " 77.

Tie Rack

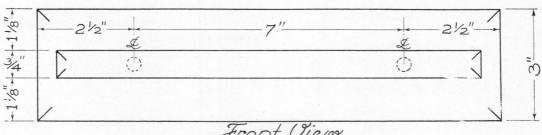

Front View

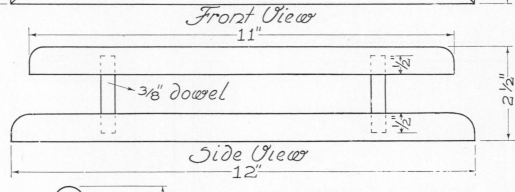

Side View

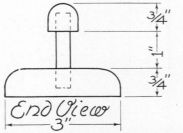

End View

MATERIAL:
1 back — ¾" × 3" × 12"
1 rod — ¾" × ¾" × 11"
2 — ⅜" dowels @ 2" long.

PLATE 2

EVEN THE SIMPLEST DESIGNS ARE EX-
tremely attractive, if well made. This
bookrack involves nothing very difficult in
the way of construction. It can be easily
made by the beginner. However, care should
be taken to see that all parts are cut perfectly square at the edges and that the
top rounding, of the ends, is uniformly
made. It will be noted that the butt-screw
fastening of ends and bottom are reinforced with anchor dowels. Butt joints,
which connect into end grain, are extremely
strong and lasting when made with anchor
dowels.

REFERENCE TO BASIC PROCESSES IN TEXT

Squaring ....Page 48.
Edge Shaping .... " 51.
Counter Boring and Plugging... " 73.
Anchor Dowel Fastenings .... " 73.

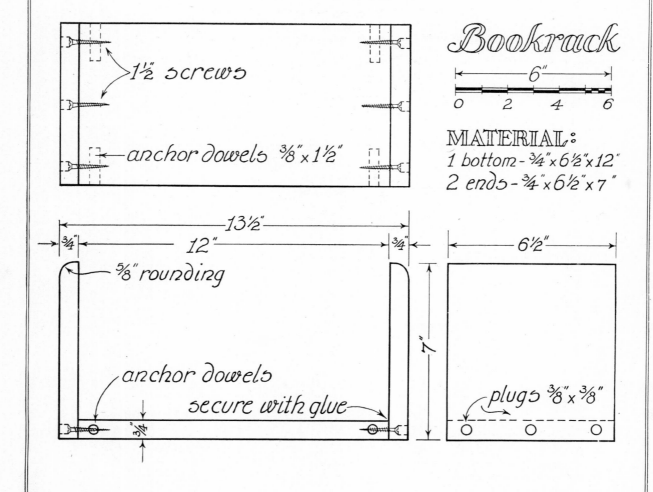

1½" screws

anchor dowels ⅜" x 1½"

Bookrack

6"

0   2   4   6

MATERIAL:
1 bottom - ¾" x 6½" x 12"
2 ends - ¾" x 6½" x 7"

13½"
¾"   12"   ¾"
⅝" rounding

anchor dowels
secure with glue

¾"

7"

6½"

plugs ⅜" x ⅜"

PLATE 3

THESE LITTLE SINGLE SHELVES LEND A QUAINT touch to the Colonial room. Originally they were used to hold tallow candles. The design illustrated is quite typical of those made in New England during the latter part of the seventeenth century.

As indicated in the illustration, the little wall shelf is well adapted for holding potted plants or trailing ivy. It may likewise be used for decorative objects or hobby collections. Obviously, this design is extremely easy to follow, even for the beginning woodworker.

REFERENCE TO BASIC PROCESSES IN TEXT

Use of Templates ....*Page 52.*
Cutting Curves and Scrolls............ " 52
Dado Joints .... " 81.

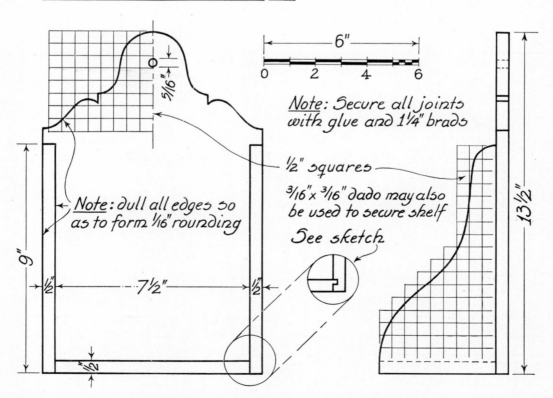

MATERIAL:
1 back – ½"x 8½"x 13½"
2 sides – ½"x 4½"x 9"
1 shelf – ½"x 4½"x 7½"

½"
4½"

Wall Shelf

6"

0   2   4   6

Note: Secure all joints with glue and 1¼" brads

½" squares

³⁄₁₆"x ³⁄₁₆" dado may also be used to secure shelf

See sketch

Note: dull all edges so as to form ¹⁄₁₆" rounding

5/16"

9"

½"   7½"   ½"

½"

13½"

PLATE 4

HERE IS A NICE LITTLE PROJECT FOR the beginning woodworker. Indeed, it is sufficiently attractive to capture the attention of even the most advanced student. The design is Colonial, and while the project was used originally as a container for long-stemmed clay pipes, it is every bit as useful for holding letters and loose papers.

The parts are first squared to size and are then shaped in the manner explained for cutting curves. All pieces are nailed together, the nails being set beneath the surface, their heads concealed with plastic wood or putty filler. Be sure to sand all parts thoroughly before applying the finish.

REFERENCE TO BASIC PROCESSES IN TEXT

Squaring ....Page 48.
Boring Holes .... " 52.
Use of Templates .... " 52.
Glue and Brads .... 68, 75.
Cutting Curves and Scrolls.. " 52.

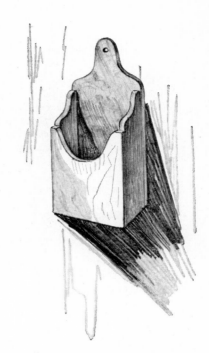

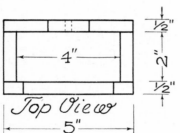

Top View

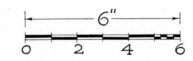

Wall Box

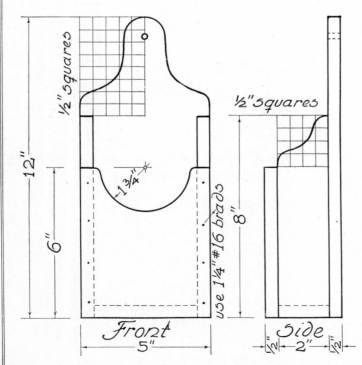

Front

Side

MATERIAL:
1 back - ½" × 5" × 12"
2 sides - ½" × 2" × 8"
1 front - ½" × 5" × 6"
1 bottom - ½" × 2" × 4"

use 1¼ #16 brads

PLATE 5

THIS ATTRACTIVE AND EASILY MADE cutting board will serve as another welcome addition to your kitchen. It is a splendid beginning project because its construction introduces a variety of simple woodworking processes with an extreme economy of materials. These boards have been made of maple with a contrasting center piece of walnut. While hardwoods are preferable, the beginning craftsman may desire to use softwoods of contrasting color. The finished job should be planed flush on both surfaces, sanded thoroughly, and given a coat or two of shellac or lacquer.

REFERENCE TO BASIC PROCESSES IN TEXT

Squaring .... Page 48.
Edge Shaping .... " 50.
Rounding Corners .... " 51.
Dowel Joints .... " 77.
Gluing and Clamping .... " 75.

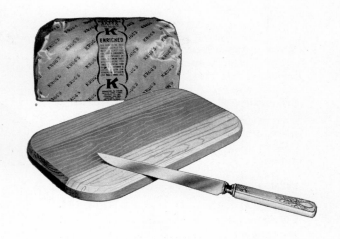

Cutting Board

MATERIAL:
1 center strip – ¾" × 3" × 12"
2 side strips – ¾" × 2" × 12"

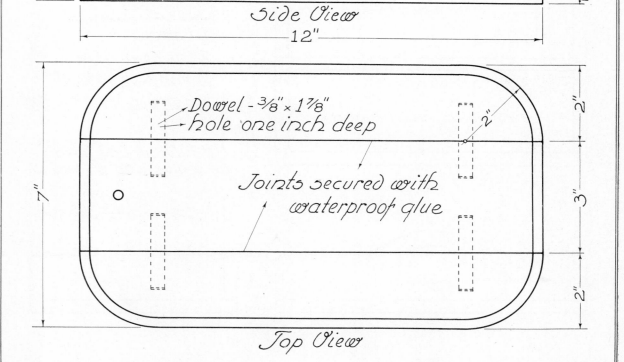

Side View

Dowel – ⅜" × 1⅞"
hole one inch deep

Joints secured with waterproof glue

Top View

PLATE 6

THERE SHOULD BE AT LEAST ONE OF THESE utility boxes in every home. As the name indicates, this carefully designed little box can be used for a variety of purposes, principally, of course, for holding cutlery.

Here is another one of these easy-to-make articles that should offer little difficulty in construction, even for the be ginner.

REFERENCE TO BASIC PROCESSES IN TEXT

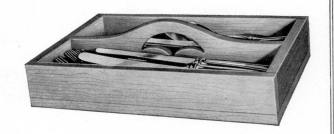

Utility Box

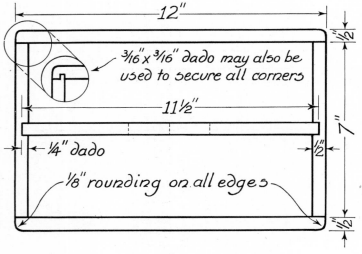

3/16" x 3/16" dado may also be used to secure all corners

12"

1/2"

11 1/2"

7"

1/4" dado

1/2"

1/8" rounding on all edges

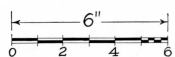

6"

0   2   4   6

MATERIAL:
1 bottom—1/2" x 8" x 12"
2 sides—1/2" x 1 3/4" x 12"
2 ends—1/2" x 1 3/4" x 7"
1 handle—1/2" x 2 3/4" x 11 1/2"

Note: Secure all joints with glue and 1 1/4" brads

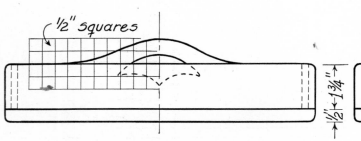

1/2" squares

1/2" 1 3/4"

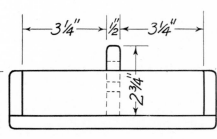

3 1/4"   1/2"   3 1/4"

2 3/4"

PLATE 7

INSPIRED BY AN ANTIQUE SEVENTEENTH CENTURY WALL sconce, this quaint design suggests itself for a variety of modern uses. It can be wired to serve as a light bracket or used with tallow candles for an effect of originality. However, it is most decorative when holding a potted plant or ivy.

Why not make a pair of these sconces and place them on each side of your fireplace or inside doorway? The sconce is easy to make. The conical tin roof comes from sheet metal, a discarded tin can, or even stiff cardboard which is later enameled. The tin roof can be peened for hand-wrought effect. A mirror may be introduced at the back to reflect the plant, if you wish.

REFERENCE TO BASIC PROCESSES IN TEXT

Use of Templates .... Page 52.
Edge Shaping .... " 51.
Butt Fastenings .... 73, 74.

Candle Sconce

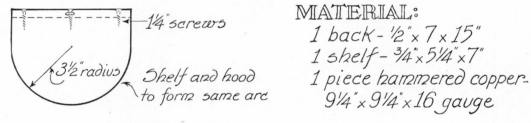

1¼″ screws

3½″ radius

Shelf and hood to form same arc

MATERIAL:
1 back - ½″ x 7 x 15″
1 shelf - ¾″ x 5¼″ x 7″
1 piece hammered copper - 9¼″ x 9¼″ x 16 gauge

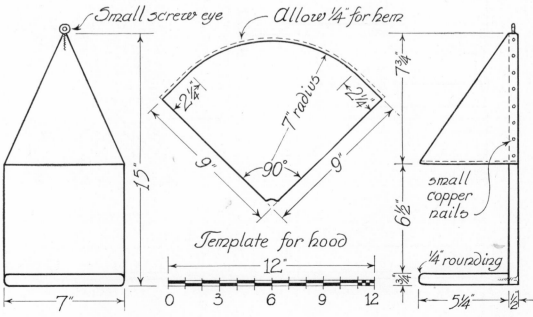

Small screw eye

Allow ¼″ for hem

15″

7″

2½″   7″ radius   2¼″

9″   90°   9″

Template for hood

12″

0   3   6   9   12

7¾″

6½″

¾″

small copper nails

¼″ rounding

5¼″   ½″

PLATE 8

THE BIRDS IN YOUR NEIGHBORHOOD will be eager to wing their way at mealtimes to this very practical feeder. You can mount it on a wire and connect it from your window to a nearby tree. Use a rope and pulley line to draw it to the window sill.

Pine, ½" thick, serves well for all the construction. The parts should be carefully made and assembled with flathead wood screws. The finished article is painted. We are told that the birds themselves prefer a drab color paint; so don't be tempted to use bright or contrasting colors.

REFERENCE TO BASIC PROCESSES IN TEXT

Squaring .... Page 48.
Screw Fastening .... " 72.
Butt Joints .... " 69.

Bird Feeder

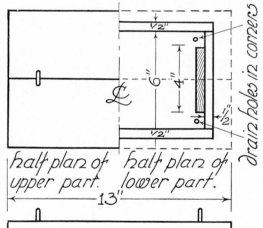

half plan of upper part. half plan of lower part.

Drain holes in corners

MATERIAL:
1 bottom — ½" × 7" × 11"
2 sides — ½" × 1½" × 11"
2 ends — ½" × 1½" × 6"
2 uprights — ½" × 4" × 9"
1 roof board — ½" × 6" × 13"
1   "   " — ½" × 5½" × 13"
2 rafters — ½" × 1" × 5"
2   " — ½" × 1" × 4"

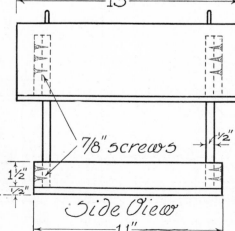

7/8" screws

Side View
11"

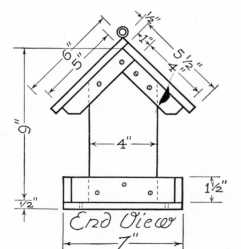

End View
7"

PLATE 9

BIRDS OF NUMEROUS DESCRIPTIONS WILL be delighted to make themselves at home in this attractive little house. It is very easy to make and while not very startling in design, it will serve its purpose ideally.

The House should be carefully made and painted. The craftsman may wish to introduce a simple hinged bottom for cleaning. This improvement can be made by attaching the bottom with two hinges at the back and a couple of hook-and-eye catches in the front.

REFERENCE TO BASIC PROCESSES IN TEXT

Squaring ....Page 48.
Butt Fastenings .... " 69.
Cutting Bevels .... " 50.
Boring Holes .... " 51.

Bird House

MATERIAL:
1 bottom - ½" × 5" × 9"
2 sides - ½" × 3" × 7"
2 ends - ¾" × 4" × 5"
1 roof board - ½" × 4½" × 9"
1   "   "   - ½" × 4" × 9"
1 - ⅜" dowel 2" long

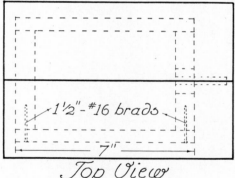

Top View

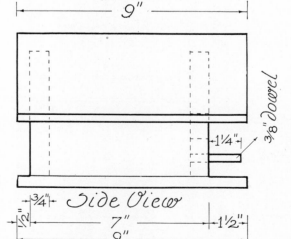

Side View

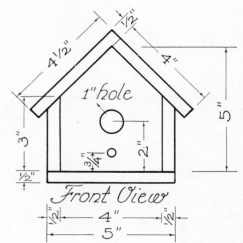

Front View

PLATE 10

HERE IS A HIGH FLYER THAT WILL zoom, loop the loop, do all manner of aerial tricks, and then glide in for a perfect landing. The glider is catapulted from an elastic sling board. The length of the flight is thus determined by the amount of spring given at the start. Make this plane of balsa and be careful to follow the exact proportions given in the working drawing. In order to obtain perfect balance, it may be necessary to shift or counterbalance your parts before gluing them into place.

REFERENCE TO BASIC PROCESSES IN TEXT

Use of Templates............Page 52.
Incised Cutting .... " 54.
Cutting Curves and Scrolls .... " 52.

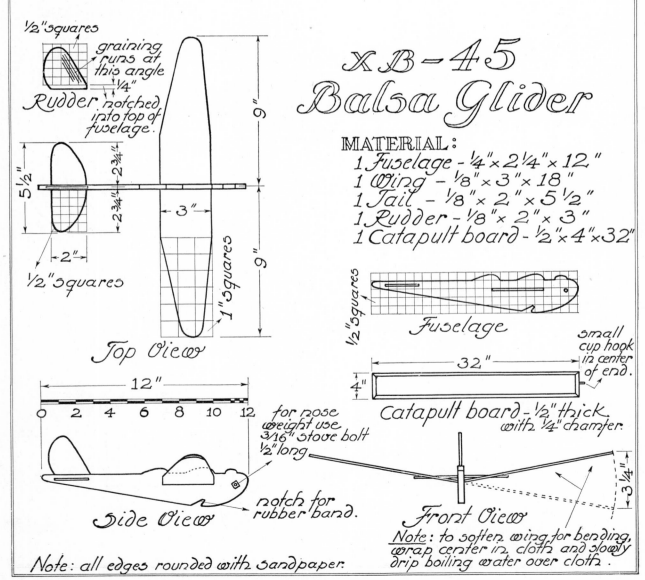

XB-45 Balsa Glider

MATERIAL:

1 Fuselage – 1/4" × 2 1/4" × 12"
1 Wing – 1/8" × 3" × 18"
1 Tail – 1/8" × 2" × 5 1/2"
1 Rudder – 1/8" × 2" × 3"
1 Catapult board – 1/2" × 4" × 32"

1/2" squares
graining runs at this angle
1/4"
Rudder notched into top of fuselage.

5 1/2"
2 3/4"
2 3/4"
2 3/4"
2"
1/2" squares

9"
9"
3"
1" squares

Top View

1/2" squares
Fuselage

small cup hook in center of end.

32"
4"
Catapult board – 1/2" thick with 1/4" chamfer.

12"
0 2 4 6 8 10 12

for nose weight use 3/16" stove bolt 1/2" long

notch for rubber band.

Side View

3 1/4"
Front View

Note: to soften wing for bending, wrap center in cloth and slowly drip boiling water over cloth.

Note: all edges rounded with sandpaper.

PLATE 11

Any Housewife Will Appreciate This Simple Device whereby she may safely keep her utility knives together. Slots are cut in the block for knife blades of varying lengths. The block is hung on the wall within easy reach and there is no possibility of the children coming in contact with sharp blades.

Obviously this project is extremely easy to make. It requires very little wood and should serve as an excellent job for the beginner.

REFERENCE TO BASIC PROCESSES IN TEXT

Squaring ....Page 48.
Use of Templates .... " 52.
Edge Shaping .... " 50.
Boring Holes .... " 51.

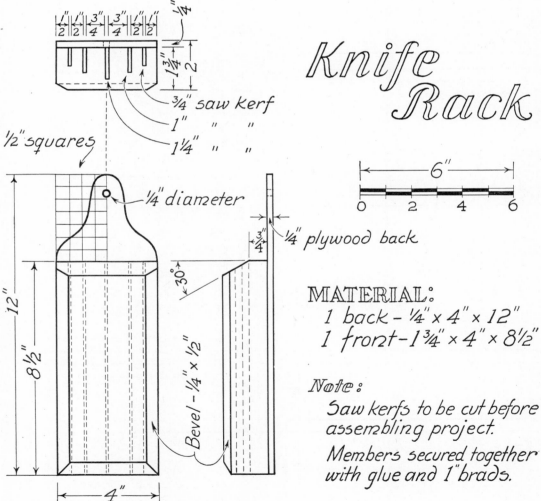

Knife Rack

MATERIAL:
1 back - ¼" x 4" x 12"
1 front - 1¾" x 4" x 8½"

Note:
Saw kerfs to be cut before assembling project.

Members secured together with glue and 1" brads.

PLATE 12

THIS CHARMING LITTLE DESIGN WAS developed as a miniature copy of an early Colonial blanket chest. It will be noted that the construction is extremely simple. The lid is hinged with a cleat and swivel peg which, incidentally, is the exact way that many of the early American chests were constructed.

The making of this project should be quite easy even for the beginning wood-worker. You will be pleased with the result and will find many interesting uses for this little chest in your home.

REFERENCE TO BASIC PROCESSES IN TEXT

Squaring ....*Page 48.*
Edge Shaping .... "   51.
Butt Fastenings .... "   69.

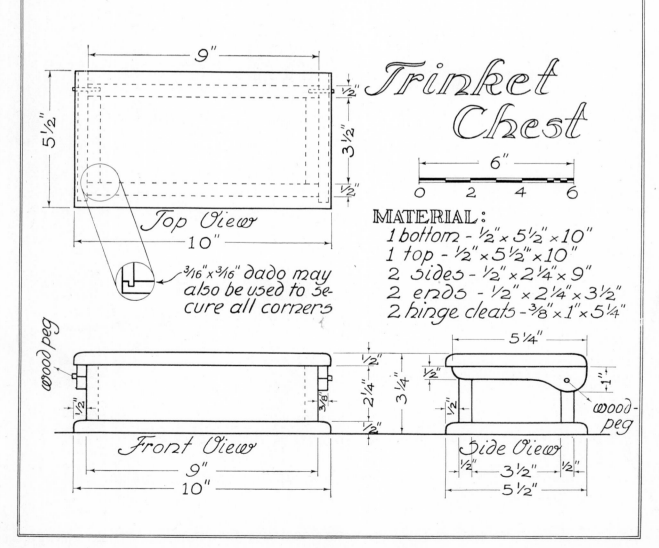

Trinket Chest

Top View

³⁄₁₆" x ³⁄₁₆" dado may also be used to se-cure all corners

Front View

Side View

wood peg

MATERIAL:
1 bottom - ½" x 5½" x 10"
1 top - ½" x 5½" x 10"
2 sides - ½" x 2¼" x 9"
2 ends - ½" x 2¼" x 3½"
2 hinge cleats - ³⁄₈" x 1" x 5¼"

PLATE 13

EVERY BOY SHOULD HAVE A SEA CHEST for the safe keeping of his valuables. Here is the ideal strongbox for baseballs, gloves, tops, bits of fishing tackle, and those many other interesting things which form your prize collection. These items are bound to get lost unless you keep them in a definite place, under lock and key.

The Sea Chest introduces us to the interesting process of dovetailing. The base molding is mitered at the corners. Refer to your text for the edge shaping, and other interesting procedures which the job requires.

REFERENCE TO BASIC PROCESSES IN TEXT

Squaring ....Page 48.
Dovetail Joints ...." 87.
Edge Shaping ...." 51.
Hinge Setting ...." 54.
Miter Joints ...." 82.
Use of Templates ...." 52.
Screw Fastening ...." 72.
Cutting of Curves and Shapes. " 52.

Sea Chest

12"

0 3 6 9 12

MATERIALS:

1 bottom ¾" × 9¼" × 17¾"
1 top   ¾" × 10¼" × 18¾"
2 sides ½" × 7¼" × 17¾"
2 ends   ½" × 7¼" × 9¼"
2 base boards ¾" × 2¼" × 18¾"
2   "   "   ¾" × 2¼" × 10¼"
2 lip moulds ½" × ½" × 18¾"
2   "   "   ½" × ½" × 10¼"
2 handles ¾" × 1¾" × 4"

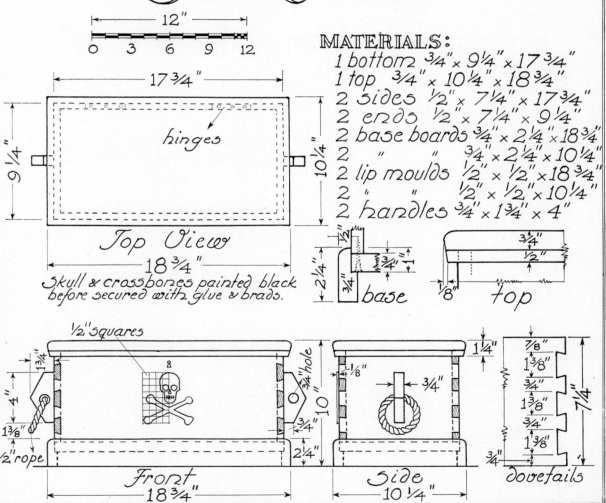

17¾"

9¼"

hinges

10¼"

Top View

18¾"

Skull & crossbones painted black
before secured with glue & brads.

2¼"   ¾   base   ⅛"   top

½"squares

Front
18¾"

Side
10¼"

dovetails

½"rope

7/8"
1⅜"
¾"
1⅜"
¾"
1⅜"
7¼"
¾"

PLATE 14

You Won't Have to Worry About spilling glasses if you make one of these attractive and highly useful trays. Six holes are bored with an expansive bit in the plywood top to hold six average size tumblers. Construction is not difficult and economy of materials is apparent, which makes this project an especially interesting one for the less advanced craftsman.

REFERENCE TO BASIC PROCESSES IN TEXT

Use of Templates ....Page 52.
Incised Cutting .... " 54.
Use of Expansive Bit .... " 52.
Cutting Curve and Scrolls .... " 52.

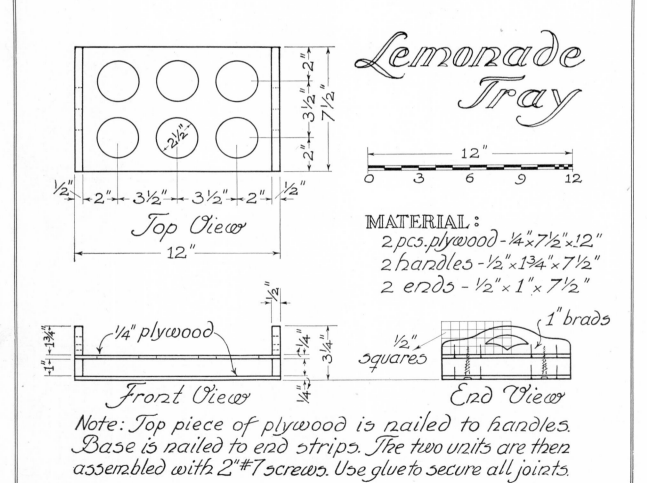

Top View

Lemonade Tray

MATERIAL:
2 pcs. plywood - ¼" x 7½" x 12"
2 handles - ½" x 1¾" x 7½"
2 ends - ½" x 1" x 7½"

¼" plywood

Front View

½" squares

1" brads

End View

Note: Top piece of plywood is nailed to handles. Base is nailed to end strips. The two units are then assembled with 2" #7 screws. Use glue to secure all joints.

PLATE 15

A TRAY OF THIS TYPE IS JUST THE RIGHT size for serving tea or light refreshments. It can also be used as a breakfast tray or for general utility such as holding writing materials or incidentals. The design is pleasant and especially easy to build. This is another one of those beginning projects which may attract the interest of the most advanced craftsman.

REFERENCE TO BASIC PROCESSES IN TEXT

Use of Templates .... Page 52.
Incised Cutting .... " 54.
Butt Joints .... " 69.

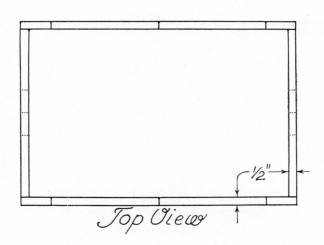

Top View

Serving Tray

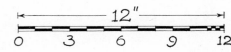

```
0      3      6      9      12
|_____|_____|_____|_____|
        12"
```

MATERIAL:
1 bottom – ½"×11"×16"
2 sides – ½"×1½"×16"
2 ends – ½"×2"×10"

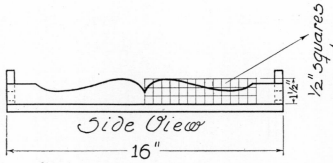

Side View
16"

½" squares

End View
11"

PLATE 16

Here Is Something Different in Table design. It is called a table rather than a shelf because the top is deeper than a conventional shelf and it is mounted on the wall at table height above the floor. This design is especially attractive when used as a console in the hallway or as part of a dressing table group with a mirror above and a bench below. The woodworker will delight in making this project. It calls for good craftsmanship and should encourage the effort of any one who wants to do a good job on a good design. If desired, a simple dado may be substituted for the sliding dovetail.

REFERENCE TO BASIC PROCESSES IN TEXT

Use of Templates ....Page 52.
Edge Shaping .... " 51.
Sliding Dovetail Joints .... " 88.
Rounding Corners .... " 51.

Wall Table

20"

0 2 4 6 8 10   15   20

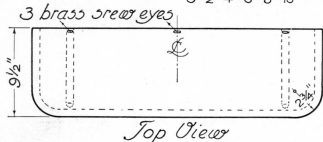

3 brass screw eyes

9½"

2½"

Top View

MATERIAL:
1 shelf — ¾" × 9½" × 30"
2 brackets — ¾" × 8½" × 13"

¾"

¾"

⅜"
⅜"

7⁄8"

Section thru shelf

*Sliding dovetail ends
½" from front of bracket*

¾"

⅜"

¾"

½"

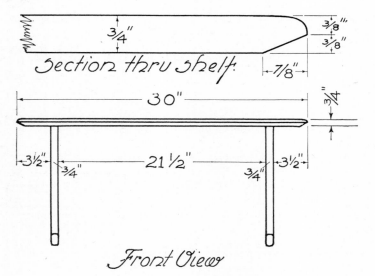

30"

¾"

3½"

¾"

21½"

¾"

3½"

Front View

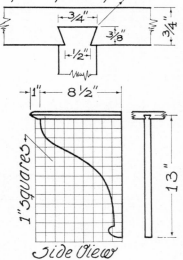

1"   8½"

1" squares

13"

Side View

PLATE 17

THESE HANGING WALL SHELVES ARE BUILT LIKE A ship's ladder, the side supports for the lower shelves hung sailor-fashion with knotted rope. The nautical effect goes well in a boy's room, a hobby or recreation room, or a summer cottage. White pine or Philippine mahogany ⅝" inch thick is used in construction.

Construction involves nothing more difficult than good aim with your coping saw, the art of boring a few holes, and a little careful practice at hammering nails. Use white cotton boat rope, knotted at both ends to link the shelves.

REFERENCE TO BASIC PROCESSES IN TEXT

Use of Templates ....Page 52.
Butt Joints .... " 69.
Dado Joints .... " 81.
Edge Rounding .... " 51.

MATERIAL:

6 sides, ⅝" x 5½" x 9"
3 shelves, ⅝" x 5¼" x 15"

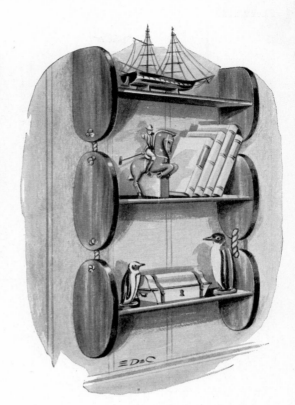

Ship's Ladder Wall Shelf

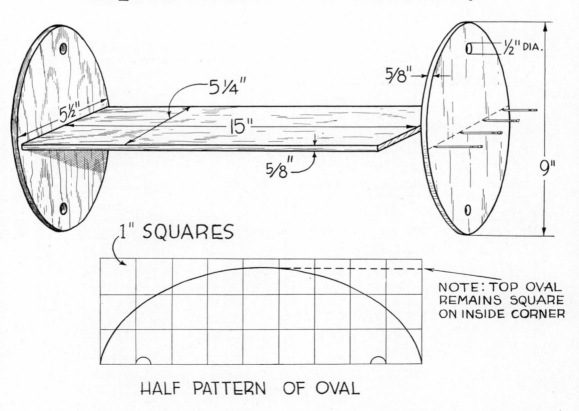

½" DIA.

5/8"

5¼"

5½"

15"

5/8"

9"

1" SQUARES

NOTE: TOP OVAL REMAINS SQUARE ON INSIDE CORNER

HALF PATTERN OF OVAL

PLATE 18

THIS COZY LITTLE ROCKER IS JUST BIG enough to hold yarn, knitting needles, and other stitching and pearling utensils. It snuggles demurely beside your chair and is carried about with the greatest of ease. You can make the knitting cradle yourself. All parts are of soft white pine, sanded and nailed together. Have yourself one—by Christmas.

REFERENCE TO BASIC PROCESSES IN TEXT

Use of Templates ....*Page* 52.
Attaching Hinges .... " 54.
Cutting Curves and Scrolls ...... " 52.
Butt Joints .... " 69.

MATERIAL:

2 ends - ½" x 10¼" x 13¾"
2 sides - ½" x 5¾" x 14"
1 bottom - ½" x 6⅜" x 14"
1 top - ½" x 3" x 14"
2 lids - ½" x 4⅞" x 14"
1 handle - ½" x 2" x 9"

Knitting Cradle

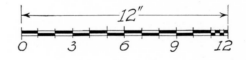

12"

0   3   6   9   12

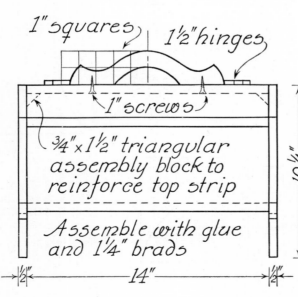

1" squares
1½" hinges
1" screws
¾" x 1½" triangular assembly block to reinforce top strip
Assemble with glue and 1¼" brads
½"   14"   ½"
10¼"

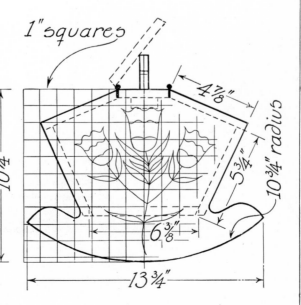

1" squares
4⅞"
5¾"
10¾" radius
6⅜"
13¾"

PLATE 19

CORNICE BOARDS ARE NOT MADE IN STANDARD sizes, so here is an opportunity to make them to order yourself. A little patience and understanding between you and your coping saw, and the job will be mastered.

Look over the designs and pick the ones which seem most appropriate. There is significance to those curves, and each design has its own purpose. The Number 1 design is most elaborate; notice the headpiece and molding jutting out beyond the facing of the front and ends like the top of the old New England cupboard which inspired it.

The second design has a recessed top for shallow containers in which to grow ivy or philodendron. This design strikes a particularly interesting decorative note in the room in which it is used.

Cornice boards should be finished naturally with stain and shellac or painted to suit individual taste. They are guaranteed to head up your windows neatly and add a trim note to the interior decoration of your home.

REFERENCE TO BASIC PROCESSES IN TEXT

Use of Templates ....*Page 52.*
Cutting Curves and Scrolls .... " *52.*
Edge Shaping .... " *51.*

Cornice Boards

REPEAT EACH SIDE OF CENTER LINE →

END PATTERN   CENTER PATTERN

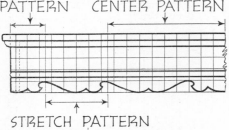

STRETCH PATTERN REPEAT FOR LENGTH

END VIEW

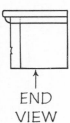

PATTERN

2¾" R
¼" R
1"   4"

REPEAT TO LENGTH

TOP
END

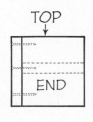

½" ¼-ROUND MOLD
MITRE
½"
6"   4¾"
5"
VARIABLE
½" BEAD

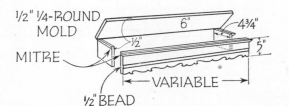

4¾"
6"
½"
VARIABLE

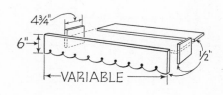

PLATE 20

SAILORS, AND LANDLUBBERS TOO, WILL APPRECIATE the trim lines and nautical fitness of this clever little table lamp. Being easy to make it should challenge the interest of even the very beginner. Note that the light is turned on and off with a twist of the ship's wheel by the simple device of having the socket chain wrapped around a half-spool which revolves at the hub.

Try making this lamp. If you are the least bit handy you will be pleased with your results.

REFERENCE TO BASIC PROCESSES IN TEXT

Edge Shaping ....Page 51.
Stop Chamfer .... " 51.
Incised Cutting .... " 54.

MATERIAL:
1 base, 1⅛" x 6" x 6"
1 post, 1¾" x 1¾" x 7"
1 top, ½" x 3" x 3"
1 wheel, ½" x 6" x 6"
1 wheel block, ⅝" x ¾" x 2¼"
8 dowels, ¼" diameter x 1"
½ spool

Screws, washer, socket, screw eye, connecting pipe, and cord

Nautical Lamp

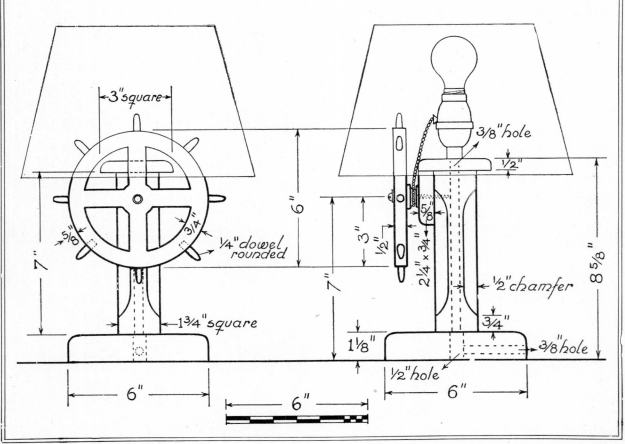

PLATE 21

Trinkets and Playing Cards, As Well as cigarettes, may be conveniently stored in this very attractive little box. It is easy to make and the finished product is something that you will definitely want to own.

The box part is constructed in conventional manner, glue and brads being used to fasten the ends and center partition. The lid and bottom are made of ¼″ plywood. It will be noted that the lid is veined for decoration.

An especially interesting effect is obtained when the side walls of the box are made of white pine and finished with shellac in natural color. The lid and bottom are then stained for contrast.

REFERENCE TO BASIC PROCESSES IN TEXT

Veining (Carving) ....*Page 62.*
Attaching Hinges .... " *72.*
Screw Fastening .... " *72.*

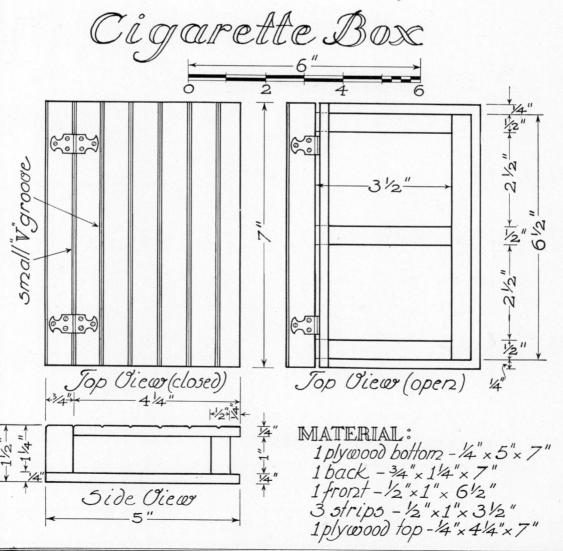

Cigarette Box

Top View (closed)

Top View (open)

Side View

MATERIAL:
1 plywood bottom - ¼″ × 5″ × 7″
1 back - ¾″ × 1¼″ × 7″
1 front - ½″ × 1″ × 6½″
3 strips - ½″ × 1″ × 3½″
1 plywood top - ¼″ × 4¼″ × 7″

PLATE 22

Here Is an Ideal Problem in Face Plate turning. As noted in the illustration, the solution of this problem results in an extremely attractive and useful nut bowl. Inlay is used around the outer edge which, of course, lends an attractive touch. However, the beginner may omit the inlay if he feels that this process is too difficult. In any event the finished job will be just as useful and almost as good looking.

REFERENCE TO BASIC PROCESSES IN TEXT

Face Plate Turning .... *Page 104.*
Inlaying .... " *61.*

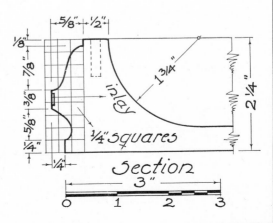

3/16" holes to fit nut picks

4 5/8" 4 3/8"
4" 3 1/2"

Top View

9 1/4"
8"
7"
2 1/4"

Side View
8 3/4"

Nut Bowl

6"
0 2 4 6

MATERIAL:
1 piece - 2 1/4" x 9 1/4" x 9 1/4"
Strip of 1/4" inlay

5/8" 1/2"
1/8" 7/8"
5/8" 3/8"
1/4" 1 3/4"
inlay
2 1/4"
1/4" 1/4" squares

Section
3"
0 1 2 3

PLATE 23

THIS LITTLE DESIGN WAS INSPIRED BY THE work bench used years ago by the old village cobbler. Aside from its own miniature appeal it is useful for holding an ash tray and cigarettes. Moreover, it is easy to make, requires very little material, and is an excellent project for the beginner.

Because the miniature cobbler's bench follows authentically the construction detail of its full-size counterpart, the craftsman may wish to use this plan to make a full-size bench. The full-size design should be scaled to approximately four times the dimensions of this drawing. Square-edged tapered legs may be introduced and the seat shaping scooped out nearer to the end than this drawing indicates. You will be delighted with either the minature or full-sized job.

REFERENCE TO BASIC PROCESSES IN TEXT

Use of Templates .... *Page* 52.
Peg Leg Construction .... " 75.
Use of Expansive Bit .... " 52.
Cutting Rabbets .... " 80.

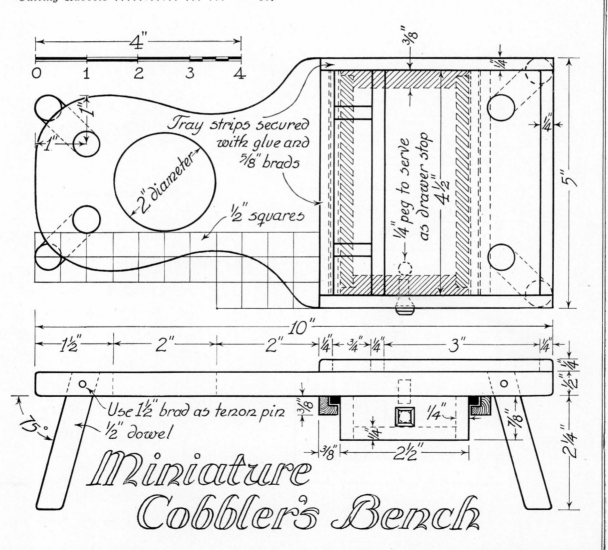

Tray strips secured with glue and 5/8" brads

2" diameter

1/2" squares

3/8"

1/4" peg to serve as drawer stop

4 1/2"

5"

1/4"

1/4"

10"

1 1/2"   2"   2"   1/4"   3/4"   1/4"   3"   1/4"

Use 1 1/2" brad as tenon pin
1/2" dowel

75°

3/8"

1/4"

1/4"

3/8"

2 1/2"

7/8"

2 1/4"

2"   1/2"   1/4"

Miniature Cobbler's Bench

PLATE 24

HERE IS A TIDY WAY TO KEEP YOUR NOTES together, or to bind your collection of stamps and scrapbook material. You will enjoy owning a set of these attractive covers. The materials from which they are made are inexpensive, and the job of making them is extremely simple.

They are cut from plywood. You can find out about plywood on page 17. Because of its alternating grain it must be carefully sawed. The decorative margin lines are veined into the wood. You should check on the boring process, and follow the text for the other information involved.

Of course, you should use your own initials or the initials of the person to whom you intend to give these attractive covers. On a project of this type, the stain is most easily applied with a small rag.

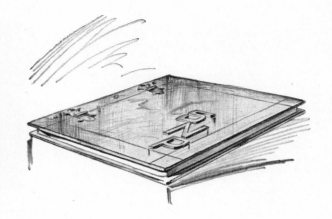

REFERENCE TO BASIC PROCESSES IN TEXT

Squaring ....*Page 48.*
Use of Glue and Brads .... 69, 75.
Boring Holes .... " 51.

Cardboard filler between paper and plywood strip

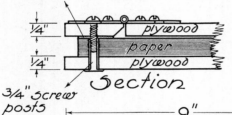

1/4"
1/4"

plywood
paper
plywood

Section

3/4" screw posts

Screw-posts, hinges, and letters painted black before being assembled.

9"

heavy black pencil line

11 1/2"

SNP

Top View

1 1/8"

7 7/8"

Manuscript Covers

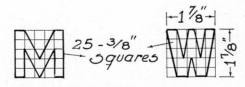

6"
0 2 4 6

MATERIAL:
1 plywood back - 1/4" x 9" x 11 1/2"
1   "   front - 1/4" x 7 7/8" x 11 1/2"
1   "   strip - 1/4" x 1 1/8" x 11 1/2"
3 letters - 1/8" x 1 1/2" x 1 7/8"

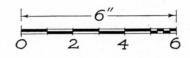

25 - 3/8" squares

1 7/8"
1 7/8"

All other letters designed on squares as shown.

Secure letters with glue and 3/8" brads.

PLATE 25

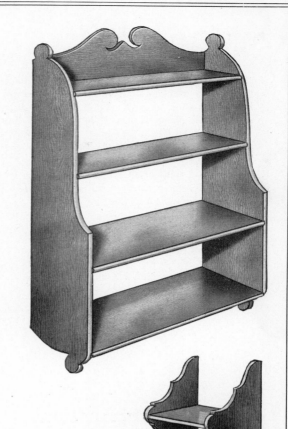

THE EARLY COLONIAL CRAFTSMAN POSSESSED positive genius in the construction of various types of utility shelves. The two designs illustrated were adapted from typical shelf designs of the Colonial era. The larger set of shelves will be useful for holding books, while the smaller design may be used for small volumes, plants, and decorative objects. The beginning craftsman should be able to try his hand at either of these designs.

REFERENCE TO BASIC PROCESSES IN TEXT

Use of Templates ....Page 52.
Cutting Curves and Scrolls .... " 52.
Edge Shaping .... " 51.
Dado Joints .... " 81.
Butt Joints .... " 69.

MATERIAL:

Small Shelves

    2 sides, ½" x 6" x 18"
    2 shelves, ½" x 6" x 7"

Large Shelves

    2 sides, ⅝" x 6½" x 31¼"
    1 top, ⅝" x 5½" x 19"
    1 shelf, ⅝" x 4¾" x 19"
    1 shelf, ⅝" x 5⅜" x 19"
    2 shelves, ⅝" x 6⅝" x 19"

Colonial Wall Shelves

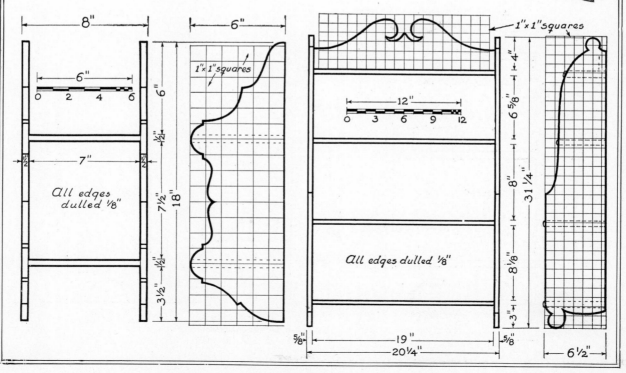

PLATE 26

THIS ATTRACTIVE, COLONIAL INSPIRED BOOKCASE SHOULD serve as a welcome addition to a boy's room. It was especially designed to hold a quantity of books and to occupy a minimum of space. It will be noted that this article fills a common demand; a bookcase is something which nearly everybody enjoys making. This design does not require any great quantity of lumber.

Here is a project that the beginner can easily make. It is only necessary to cut parts square and to be reasonably careful in sawing and shaping curves.

REFERENCE TO BASIC PROCESSES IN TEXT

Use of Templates ....Page 52.
Cutting Curves and Scrolls .... " 52.
Counter Boring and Plugging .... " 73.
Edge Shaping .... " 51.
Use of Anchor Dowel .... " 73.

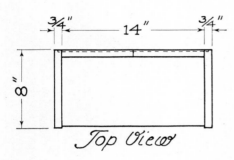

Top View

Bookcase

MATERIAL:
2 sides - 3/4" × 8" × 27 1/2"
3 shelves - 3/4" × 7 5/8" × 14"
1 base piece - 3/4" × 3 3/4" × 14"
1 top piece - 3/4" × 2 3/4" × 14"
1 plyw. back - 1/4" × 14 3/4" × 21 1/4"

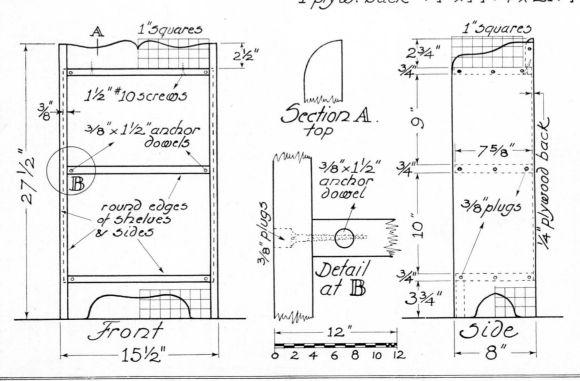

Front
Section A. top
Detail at B
Side

PLATE 27

THE SIMPLE LINES OF EARLY AMERICAN DESIGN ARE BEST displayed in the many small tables, stools, and benches which originated during this era. Such pieces were solid in construction, because they were built for hard service; yet their essential proportions and restrained scrollwork contributed to make them distinctive and very worthy of being copied for homes today.

The table illustrated here possesses all the attributes of solid construction, good proportion, and simple design. Moreover, it is a type of table which the craftsman can make with little difficulty. It is just the right size for use beside your favorite chair; or you may decide to make a pair for both ends of the sofa.

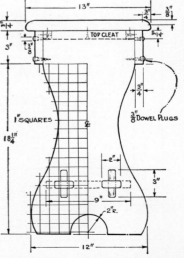

REFERENCE TO BASIC PROCESSES IN TEXT

Edge Shaping .... Page 51.
Rounding Corners .... " 51.
Keyed Mortise and Tenon .... " 84.
Use of Templates .... " 52.
Cutting Curves and Scrolls .... " 52.

MATERIAL:

2 ends, ¾" x 12" x 21¼"
2 aprons, ¾" x 3" x 23"
1 shelf, ¾" x 9" x 22½"

1 top, ¾" x 13" x 26"
4 keys (dowels, ¾" diameter x 3"
4 cleats, ¾" x ¾" x 9"

Colonial End Table

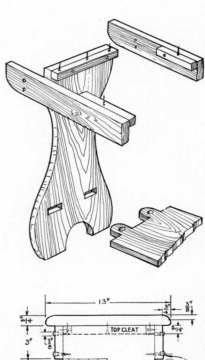

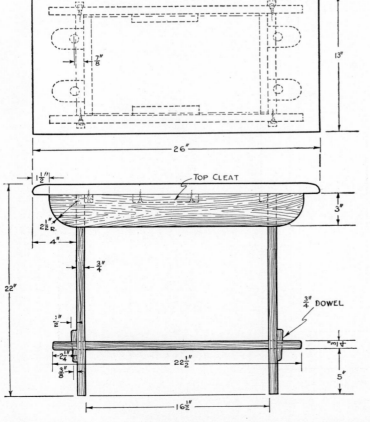

PLATE 28

This Colonial Mirror Frame Fits Nicely In a Boy's Bedroom. The design was inspired by the frames that were used with the first mirrors made in this country. Why not make this frame to replace one of the old mirrors in your home? The job is comparatively easy and if you work carefully you will be pleased with the result.

REFERENCE TO BASIC PROCESSES IN TEXT

Use of Templates ....Page 52.
Cutting Curves and Scrolls .... " 52.
Cutting Rabbets .... " 80.
Cutting Miter Joints (splined miter) .... " 82.

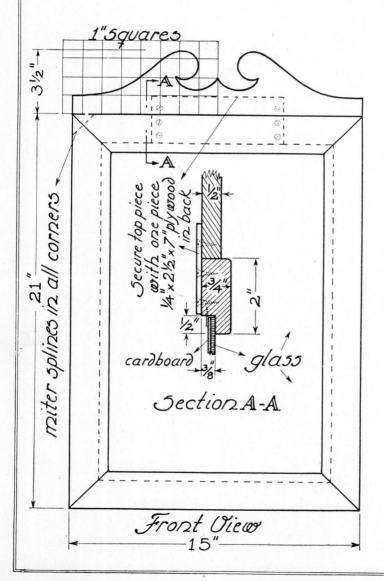

1" squares

3½"

21"

miter splines in all corners

Secure top piece with one piece ¼"×2½"×7" plywood in back

½"

¾"

2"

cardboard

⅜"

glass

Section A-A

Front View

15"

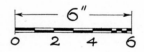

Mirror Frame

6"

0   2   4   6

MATERIAL:
2 sides - ¾"×2"×21"
2 ends - ¾"×2"×15"
1 top piece - ½"×3½"×15"
4 miter splines -
        ⅛"×1"×1¾"
1 piece plyw. ¼"×2½"×7"

PLATE 29

THIS PEG-LEGGED STOOL WAS INSPIRED DIRECTLY by the early fireside stools used so commonly in the early American homes. Nowadays it finds a variety of practical uses both for seating purposes or as a demure end table when placed beside your favorite chair.

This stool introduces the interesting process of peg-legged construction which involves split and wedged tenons. But don't let these terms frighten you. This article is extremely easy to make and can be constructed by the careful beginner.

REFERENCE TO BASIC PROCESSES IN TEXT

Edge Shaping ....*Page 50, 51.*
Peg-Leg Construction .... " 75.

Fireside Stool

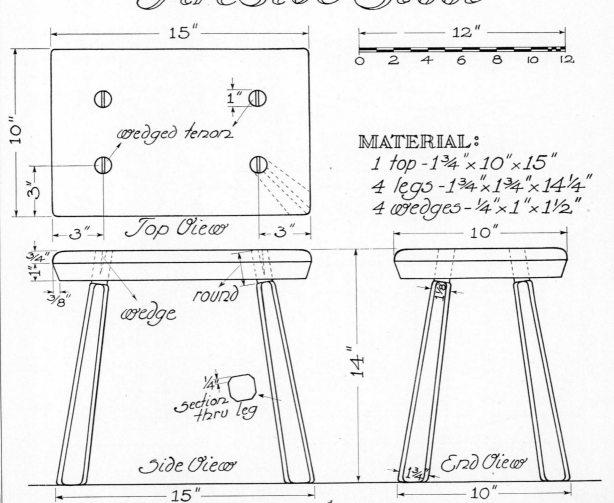

MATERIAL:
1 top - 1¾" × 10" × 15"
4 legs - 1¾" × 1¾" × 14¼"
4 wedges - ¼" × 1" × 1½"

Top View

wedged tenon

Side View

End View

wedge

round

section thru leg

PLATE 30

If You Like Crafty Peg-leg Effects, You Will enjoy making this Colonial Table Lamp. While small in size it embodies in its construction many of the crafty elements which caused the popularity of early Colonial furniture.

The lamp can be made of soft white pine or any fine cabinet wood. It should be well sanded for final polished effect. A pair of these should go very nicely on tables at each end of the sofa.

REFERENCE TO BASIC PROCESSES IN TEXT

Peg-Leg Construction ....*Page* 75.
Stop Chamfers .... "   51.
Edge Shaping .... "   50.

MATERIAL:

4 legs, 1⅛″ x 1⅛″ x 3¾″
1 base, 1⅛″ x 6¾″ x 10″
1 standard, 1⅛″ x 1¼″ x 10¼″
1 cross arm, 1⅛″ x 2″ x 9″
1 dowel peg, ⅜″ x 3″
Electrical equipment: ⅜″ threaded nipples, socket, lamp cord, plug

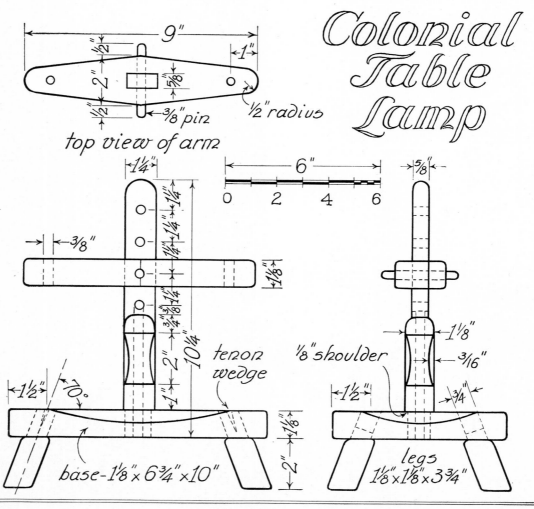

Colonial Table Lamp

top view of arm

tenon wedge

base-1⅛″ x 6¾″ x 10″

⅛″ shoulder

legs 1⅛″ x 1⅛″ x 3¾″

PLATE 31

BACK IN THE COLONIAL DAYS BENCHES WERE USED more frequently than chairs. In fact, during the first period of settlement, chairs were reserved only for the head of the household.

Here is a copy of an early Colonial Bench.

You will notice that the construction is extremely simple, and yet the bench is very sturdy. That is the way furniture was made in the old days.

Through mortise-and-tenon joints hold the rail and uprights. The tenons are then keyed in the typical old-time manner. *Counter boring, rounding of edges,* and the *cutting of templates* are among the processes involved in the building of this bench. All of these processes are explained in your text.

REFERENCE TO BASIC PROCESSES IN TEXT

Squaring . . . . *Page 48.*
Keyed Mortise and Tenon . . . . " 86.
Stop Chamfering . . . . " 51.
Counter Boring and Plugging . . . . " 73.
Anchor Dowel Fastening . . . . " 73.
Cutting Curves and Scrolls . . . . " 52.
Use of Templates . . . . " 52.
Edge Shaping . . . . " 50.

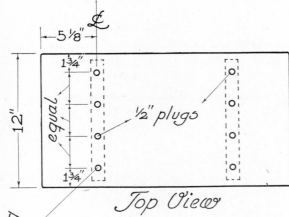

5⅛″

12″

½″ plugs

1¾″

1¾″

equal

Top View

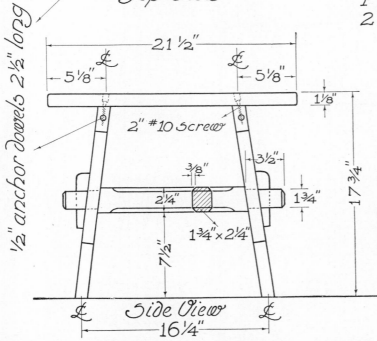

½″ anchor dowels 2½″ long

21½″

5⅛″ 5⅛″

2″ #10 screw

3½″

1⅛″

3⅛″

2¼″

1¾″

1¾″ × 2¼″

17¾″

7½″

Side View

16¼″

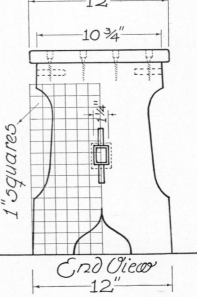

12″

10¾″

¼″

1″ squares

End View

12″

Bench

12″

0 2 4 6 8 10 12

MATERIAL:

1 top — 1⅛″ × 12″ × 21½″
2 legs — 1⅛″ × 12″ × 17″
1 rail — 1¾″ × 2¼″ × 19½″
2 tenon wedges — ½″ × 1¼″ × 5″

PLATE 32

IF YOU ADMIRE GOOD DESIGN IN FURNITURE, HERE IS A TABLE you will certainly want to make. The beautiful stem-turning which this table exhibits is referred to as the classical "ball and vase" design. Turning of this particular type originated in England several centuries ago.

This table should serve as an excellent project for the individual who is interested in becoming acquainted with the woodworking lathe. The top is turned on a face plate. Stem-turning is performed in the manner explained and illustrated in the text.

Unlike many other tables having four legs which must be turned to identical design, this table calls for a single turned stem. For this reason it presents an ideal problem for the student who is not sufficiently advanced to perform duplicate turning.

REFERENCE TO BASIC PROCESSES IN TEXT

Turned Table

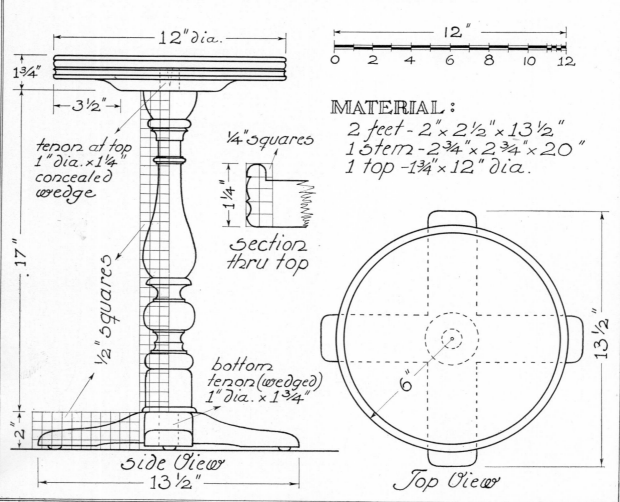

12" dia.

1¾"

3½"

tenon at top
1" dia. × 1¼"
concealed
wedge

¼" squares

1¼"

section
thru top

½" squares

.17"

bottom
tenon (wedged)
1" dia. × 1¾"

2"

Side View
13½"

12"

0 2 4 6 8 10 12

MATERIAL:
2 feet – 2" × 2½" × 13½"
1 stem – 2¾" × 2¾" × 20"
1 top – 1¾" × 12" dia.

13½"

6"

Top View

PLATE 33

FARM GATES HAVE A SPECIAL APPEAL OF THEIR own. They are quaint, picturesque, and sturdy. Moreover, their characteristics have remained unchanged through the centuries. With few variations in design they hang strongly and independently on their long strap hinges with typical cross braces and wooden latches. The homely appeal of these rural gates, which form so picturesque a part of the rural scene, inspires the idea of taking them home in miniature and using them beside our favorite chair or sofa to hold magazines. So, even though these gates are used generally for keeping cows within bounds, they also will serve to keep your magazines attractively contained and lend a bit of additional quaintness to the room in which they are used.

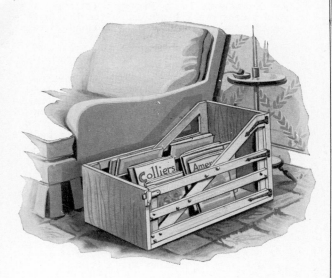

REFERENCE TO BASIC PROCESSES IN TEXT

Use of Templates ....Page 52.
Butt Fastenings .... " 69.
Counter Boring and Plugging .... " 73.
Dowel Joints .... " 77.

MATERIAL:
1 small end—¾"×9"×11"
1 large end—¾"×11"×14"
1 bottom—¾"×11"×16½"
6 rails—½"×1¼"×16½"
2 end rails—½"×1¼"×13¼"
2 end rails—½"×1¼"×8¼"
2 diagonal rail—½"×1¼"×18¾"

Farm Gate
Magazine Basket

12"
0   3   6   9   12

latch block—¾"×¾"×3¼"

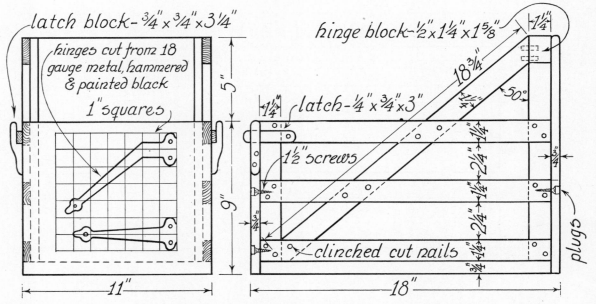

hinges cut from 18 gauge metal, hammered & painted black
1" squares

5"

9"

11"

hinge block—½"×1¼"×1⅝"
1¼"
18¾"
50°
latch—¼"×¾"×3"
1¼"
1½" screws
2¼" 1½" 1¼"
2¼" 1½" 1¼"
¾"
¾"
clinched cut nails
¾" 1¼"
plugs
18"

PLATE 34

As Explained In a Previous Chapter a good sturdy work bench is one of the first requirements of the amateur craftsman. Here is a bench that has all the attributes of lasting strength. Yet it is pleasing in proportion and design and will not take up too much space in the home workshop. Moreover, the work bench illustrated can be easily constructed by the amateur. All parts are cut square to size and bolted together. If the craftsman so desires, he may attach shelf boards above the bottom rails.

This bench combines ideally with the tool board which is illustrated at the head of a previous chapter.

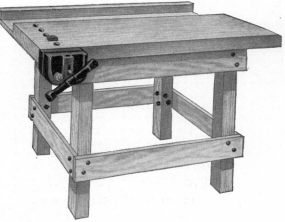

REFERENCE TO BASIC PROCESSES IN TEXT

Squaring Stock to Size ....*Page 48.*
Bolt Fastening .... " *70.*

MATERIAL:
4 legs, 2½" x 2½" x 29¾"
2 bottom rails, 1⅛" x 4" x 35¾"
2 bottom rails, 1⅛" x 4" x 21½"
2 aprons, 1⅛" x 4" x 35¾"
2 aprons, 1⅛" x 4" x 21½"
2 top cleats, 1⅛" x 1⅛" x 24"
2 top cleats, 1⅛" x 1⅛" x 14"

1 vise block, 1" x 4" x 7¼"
1 top, 2¼" x 16" x 50"
1 top (back), ¾" x 9¼" x 50"
1 back strip, ¾" x 2½" x 50"
40 carriage bolts, ¼" x 4"
Nuts and washers
1 vise and bench stop
Flat head screws

Work Bench

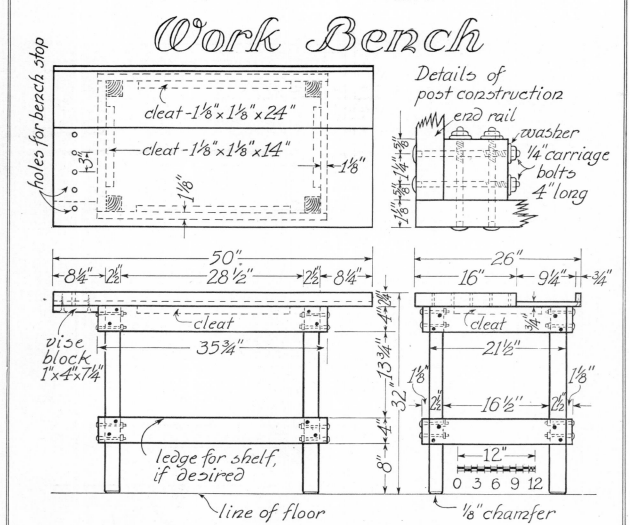

PLATE 35

If You Are Looking for a Gift To Make for a gracious lady (your mother, wife, or best girl), we suggest this tray-table. Made of light but strong half-inch plywood, it is as easy to lift and carry as the ordinary serving tray. Note the four convenient cut-out handholds.

REFERENCE TO BASIC PROCESSES IN TEXT

Use of Templates ....Page 52.
Cutting Curves and Scrolls .... " 52.
Cutting Inside Scrolls .... " 54.
Gluing and Nailing .... 68, 75.

MATERIAL:

1 piece cabinet veneered plywood, ½" x 36" x 60"
2 side cleats, ½" x ½" x 26"
2 end cleats, ½" x ½" x 18"

Butler's Coffee Table

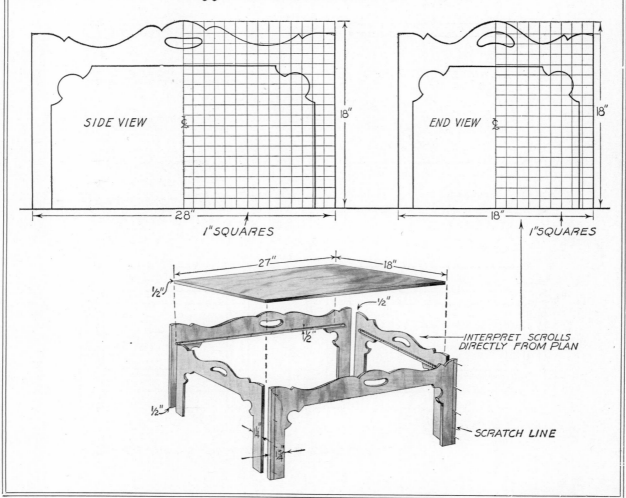

PLATE 36

Seat Weaving of Chairs and Stools Is especially interesting, and while it appears to be a hard thing to do, it is really quite easy. The stool illustrated is nicely adapted to simple weaving. It is an especially attractive and useful design.

It will be noted that the woven-top foot stool follows Colonial construction with chamfered posts, rails, and peg mortise and tenon joints. When assembling the stool it is suggested that the ends be separately put together and top mortises bored *after* these end units have been assembled. In this way it is possible to bore accurately into the ends of the top rails and line up the assembly of top and lower rails.

REFERENCE TO BASIC PROCESSES IN TEXT

Edge Shaping .... *Page* 50.
Mortise-and-Tenon Joints .... " 84.
Use of Draw Bore Pin.......... " 86.
Gluing and Clamping .... " 75.
Seat Weaving .... " 57.

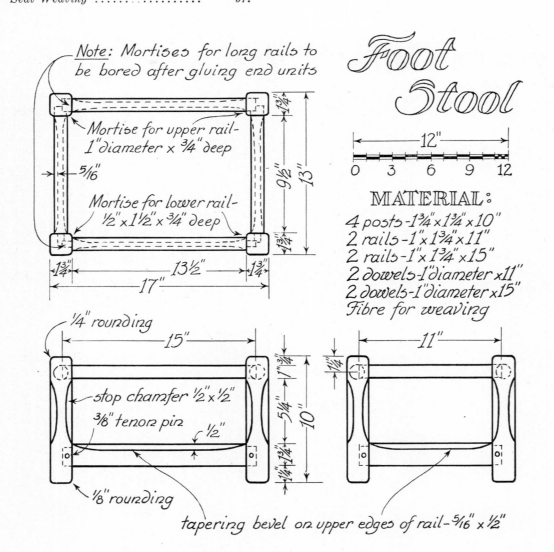

Note: Mortises for long rails to be bored after gluing end units

Mortise for upper rail—1" diameter x ¾" deep

5/16"

Mortise for lower rail—½" x 1½" x ¾" deep

¼"
9½"
13"
1¾"

1¾"   13½"   1¾"
17"

¼" rounding

15"

stop chamfer ½" x ½"
3/8" tenon pin   ½"

1/8" rounding

1¾"
1"
5¼"
10"
1¼" 1¾"

tapering bevel on upper edges of rail—5/16" x ½"

11"

1¼"

Foot Stool

12"
0 3 6 9 12

MATERIAL:
4 posts—1¾" x 1¾" x 10"
2 rails—1" x 1¾" x 11"
2 rails—1" x 1¾" x 15"
2 dowels—1" diameter x 11"
2 dowels—1" diameter x 15"
Fibre for weaving

PLATE 37

THE VILLAGE SMITH USED A BOX SIMILAR to this to hold nails and tools when he was shoeing the old gray mare. It is another one of those reminiscent designs which are always attractive when put to modern use. As indicated in the illustration the blacksmith box not only contains magazines, but can be used as well for holding ash trays, cigarettes, and other articles.

REFERENCE TO BASIC PROCESSES IN TEXT

Magazine Holder

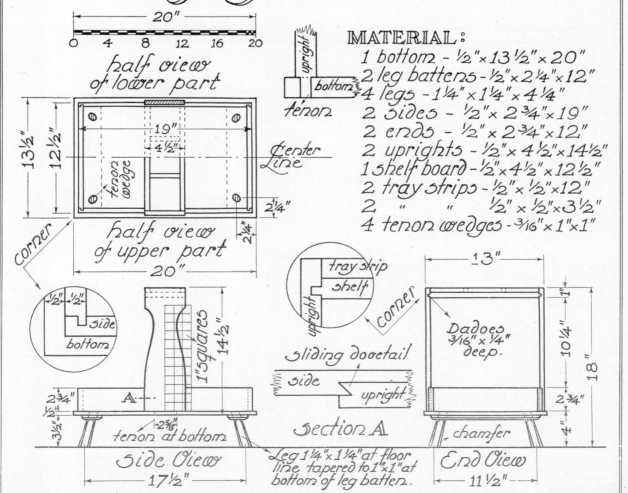

MATERIAL:

1 bottom - ½" × 13½" × 20"
2 leg battens - ½" × 2¼" × 12"
4 legs - 1¼" × 1¼" × 4¼"
2 sides - ½" × 2¾" × 19"
2 ends - ½" × 2¾" × 12"
2 uprights - ½" × 4½" × 14½"
1 shelf board - ½" × 4½" × 12½"
2 tray strips - ½" × ½" × 12"
2 " " ½" × ½" × 3½"
4 tenon wedges - 3/16" × 1" × 1"

half view of lower part

half view of upper part

Side View
17½"

Section A

End View
11½"

169

PLATE 38

DID YOU KNOW THAT THE STRONGEST bows are shaped from staves of wood that have been *split* from the timber? If you saw the staves you are bound to cut *across the grain* somewhere along the length of the piece. Naturally, this weakens your bow and causes it to snap, or to bend unevenly.

The best bows are made from lemonwood, yew, osage orange, lancewood, and hickory. Those woods may be purchased at lumber supply dealers or from dealers in archery supplies.

Why not form an archery club and make your own bows and arrows? Incidentally, every young archer should be cautioned never to draw his bow beyond the length of the arrow. Many good bows have been needlessly broken because this precaution was overlooked.

REFERENCE TO BASIC PROCESSES IN TEXT

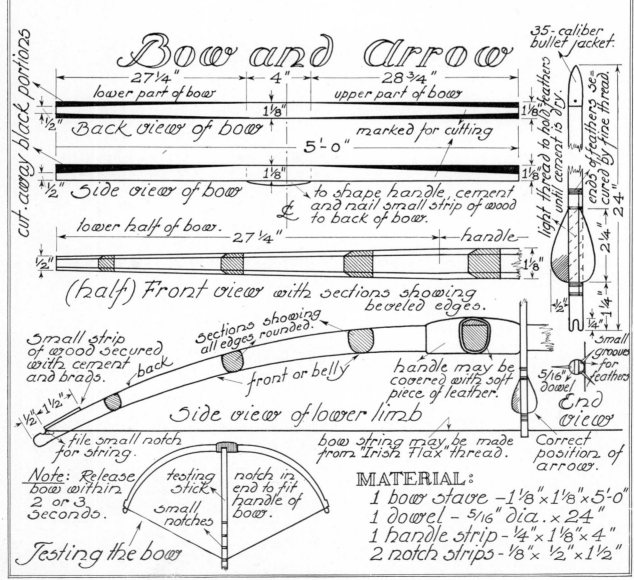

Bow and Arrow

cut away black portions

27¼" lower part of bow — 4" — 28¾" upper part of bow

1⅛"

½" Back view of bow — marked for cutting

1⅛" 1⅛"

5'-0"

1⅛" 1⅛"

½" Side view of bow

to shape handle, cement and nail small strip of wood to back of bow.

lower half of bow.

27¼" — handle

½" 1⅛"

(half) Front view with sections showing beveled edges.

Small strip of wood secured with cement and brads.

sections showing all edges rounded.

back

front or belly

handle may be covered with soft piece of leather.

½" 1½"

Side view of lower limb

file small notch for string.

bow string may be made from "Irish Flax" thread.

35-caliber bullet jacket.

ends of feathers secured by fine thread.

light thread to hold feathers until cement is dry.

24"

2¼"

½"

¼"

5/16" dowel

small grooves for feathers.

End view

Correct position of arrow.

Note: Release bow within 2 or 3 seconds.

testing stick

notch in end to fit handle of bow.

small notches

Testing the bow

MATERIAL:
1 bow stave – 1⅛" × 1⅛" × 5'-0"
1 dowel – 5/16" dia. × 24"
1 handle strip – ¼" × 1⅛" × 4"
2 notch strips – ⅛" × ½" × 1½"

PLATE 39

FRESH AS AN OCEAN BREEZE IS THIS NAUTICAL screen featuring sailcloth panels whipped taut with boat rope and stenciled with yachting class letters, navy insignia, or other marine emblems. Only think what an effect this screen would make in the living room of your seashore or lakeside cottage!

REFERENCE TO BASIC PROCESSES IN TEXT

Dowel Joints ....Page 77.
Edge Rounding ....   "   56.
Attaching Hinges ....   "   54.

MATERIAL:

6 styles, ¾" x 2½" x 64"
3 top rails, ¾" x 4½" x 15"
3 bottom rails, ¾" x 8" x 15"

Nautical Screen

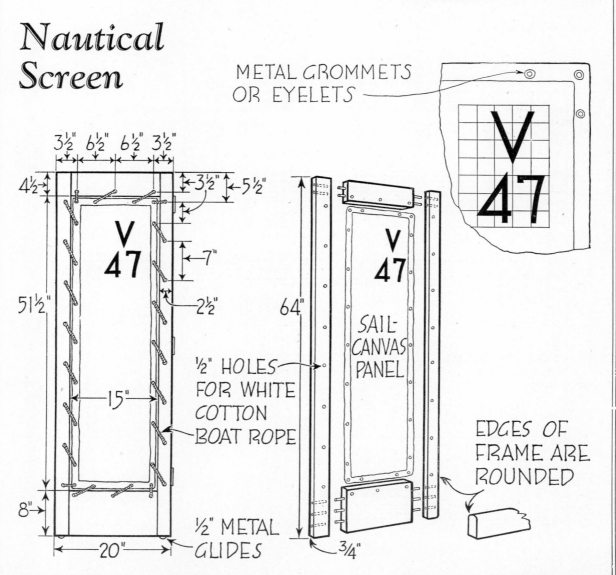

METAL GROMMETS OR EYELETS

V 47

3½" 6½" 6½" 3½"

4½"   3½" 5½"

V 47

7"

2½"

51½"

15"

64"

SAIL-CANVAS PANEL

½" HOLES FOR WHITE COTTON BOAT ROPE

8"

20"

½" METAL GLIDES

¾"

EDGES OF FRAME ARE ROUNDED

PLATE 40

PERHAPS YOU MAY WONDER WHY WE PRESENT a nautical "Yacht Table" as a companion piece to a landlocked, living-room chair. Well, why not? There is something very intriguing about these seafaring tables with their "fiddle-stick" top rigging and trim, sturdy construction. They are in a class by themselves, unhampered by landlubber's concepts of architecture and furniture design.

So why not bring them ashore, work them down to conventional dimensions, and use them as end tables? They are every bit as appealing, and certainly just as practical, when used beside your favorite chair or sofa. More important, however, the little Yacht Table is easy to make. Its counterpart, afloat, is generally made by the ship's carpenter. Construction involves nothing fancy, but plenty of good honest craftsmanship.

REFERENCES TO BASIC PROCESSES IN TEXT

Use of Templates ....Page 52.
Mortise-and-Tenon Joints .... " 84.
Counter Boring and Plugging .... " 73.
Attaching Hinges .... " 54.

MATERIAL:

2 feet, 1½" x 2½" x 10"
1 cross rail (base) 1¼" x 1¾" x 18¾"
2 ends, ¾" x 5" x 19½"
2 aprons, ¾" x 3¾" x 19¼"
1 top, ¾" x 8" x 26"
2 top leaves, ¾" x 8" x 26"
4 top "fiddle sticks," ½" x ¾" x 23"
6 top "fiddle sticks," ½" x ¾" x 5"
6 butt hinges, 3" x ¾"
2 spring leaf supports

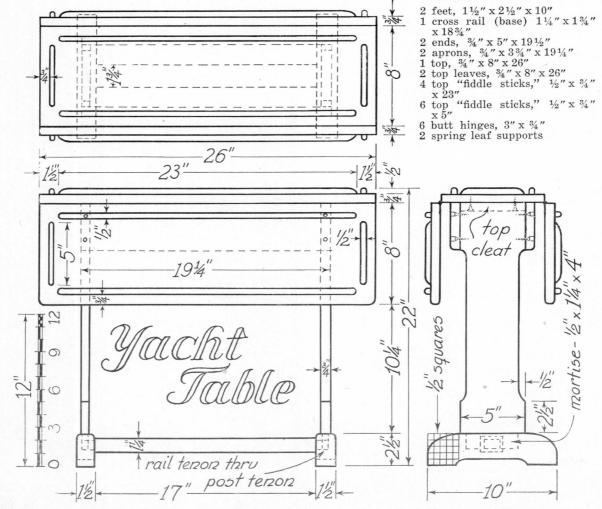

Yacht Table

PLATE 41

When a Number of Hungry Guests Are to be served a hearty repast, there is nothing more handy for the service than a large tray such as the one illustrated. The tray top and glass holders are made as separate units and rest atop a separate X stand. The entire service can be folded up and stored in a closet.

MATERIAL:

"X" Stand
  Legs, 4 pieces, ¾" x 2½" x 37⅛"
  Rungs, 2 pieces (dowel) 1" x 18½"
  Rungs, 3 pieces (dowel) 1" x 20"
  2 yards web strap

Tray
  Bottom, 1 piece, ½" x 21" x 26"
  Sides, 2 pieces, ½" x 6" x 20¼"
  Back, 1 piece, ½" x 6" x 26"

Glass Rack
  2 pieces, ½" x 2" x 18"
  2 pieces, 1" x 4" x 18½"
  2 pieces, ½" x 2" x 14½"
  1 piece, ½" x 2" x 25"
  1 piece, ½" x 4" x 25"
  1 piece, ½" x 2" x 18"
  2 pieces, ½" x 2" x 4"
  2 pieces (miter supports) 1⅛"
    x 2" x 6½"

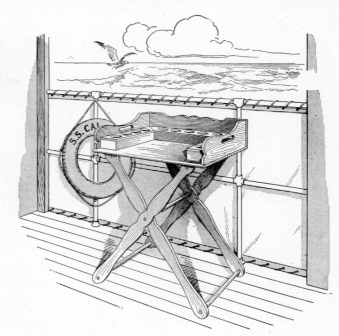

Refreshment Server

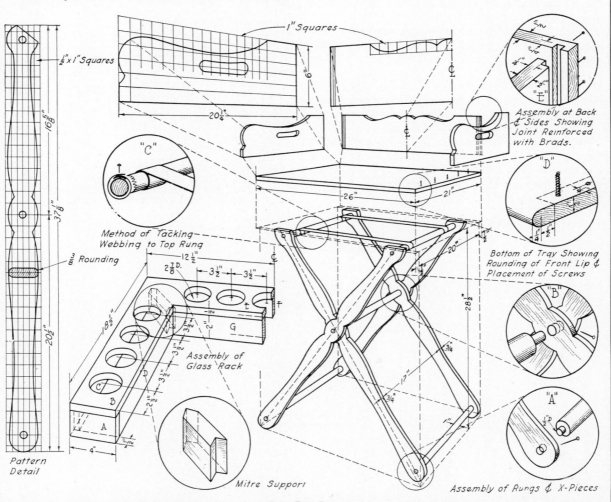

Pattern Detail

Method of Tacking Webbing to Top Rung

Assembly of Glass Rack

Mitre Support

Assembly at Back & Sides Showing Joint Reinforced with Brads.

Bottom of Tray Showing Rounding of Front Lip & Placement of Screws

Assembly of Rungs & X-Pieces

See facing page ————·————→

TABLES OF GATE LEG DESIGN ORIGINATED IN ENGLAND DURING THE SEVENTEENTH CENTURY. Like all other furniture made in that country during the period, they were built rather heavy and it is reasonable to believe that stout gate legs were required to support their broad massive leaves. The gate leg idea was also employed at an early date by our own Colonial craftsmen. In fact, the grace and beauty of Colonial tables of this type seemed at times to exceed that of their English contemporaries.

In America the design of turning that was employed differed from that used on the other side. Likewise, there appeared other features, such as tongue and groove, leaf joints, and peculiarities of construction, which distinguished American gate leg tables from those made elsewhere.

It is believed that the Gate Leg Trestle Table differing structurally, as it does from the conventional gate leg table, is an early American innovation.

Here is an excellent design for the skilled craftsman. Obviously, there is a quantity of turning involved, but the craftsman who undertakes the job has the satisfaction of knowing that he is making something of definite and lasting value.

REFERENCE TO BASIC PROCESSES IN TEXT

MATERIAL:
2 end posts, 1¾" x 1¾" x 26½"
2 gate posts, 1¾" x 1¾" x 28¾"
2 pivot posts, 1¾" x 1¾" x 17¾"
2 gate rungs, 1¾" x 1¾" x 11¾"
2 gate rails, 1¾" x 1¾" x 11¾"
1 lower rail, 1¾" x 1¾" x 34½"
1 apron, ¾" x 5" x 32½"
2 feet, 2½" x 2¼" x 14"
2 top cleats, 1¾" x 1¾" x 12"
1 top, ¾" x 14½" x 46"
2 top leaves, ¾" x 11½" x 46"
6 butt hinges, dowels and flathead screws

PLATE 42

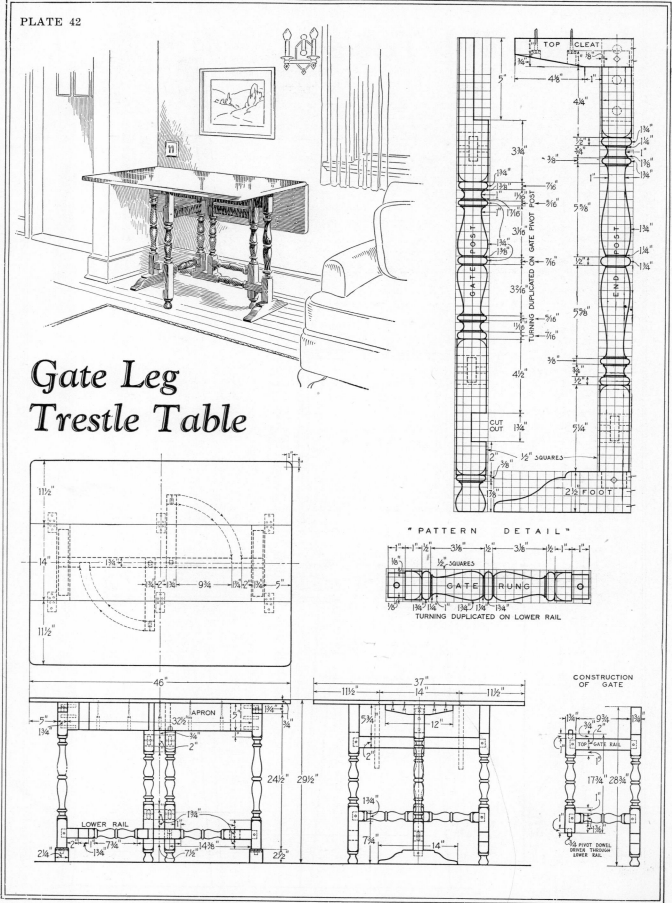

Gate Leg
Trestle Table

"PATTERN DETAIL"

GATE RUNG

TURNING DUPLICATED ON LOWER RAIL

CONSTRUCTION OF GATE

PLATE 43

Scallop Top Table

A NEW FURNITURE DESIGN IS OFTEN PRODUCED BY BLENDING THE elements of one specific design with those of another. Thus, the scrolling which forms a tray effect on the Scallop Top Table was taken from Provincial France where scrolls, possessing this particular line of curving, have been used ever since Louis XV decided he wanted a change. However, the understructure of the table itself comes of good old American stock where originally it was commonly known as a "Pembroke" type.

The clean lines of this table, together with its practical appeal, should recommend it to the craftsman. It can be made of a variety of woods, although it probably looks best when made of walnut.

REFERENCE TO BASIC PROCESSES IN TEXT

MATERIAL:

4 legs, 1⅜ x 1⅜ x 25⅛
3 aprons, ¾ x 4¾ x 8⁵⁄₁₆
1 upper drawer rail, ¾ x 1⅜ x 9¼
1 bottom drawer rail, ¾ x 1⅜ x 9¹³⁄₁₆
1 drawer front, ¾ x 3¼ x 8¼
2 drawer sides, ½ x 3¼ x 10
1 drawer back, ½ x 3¼ x 7¾
1 drawer bottom, ¼ x 7¾ x 7¾
2 drawer slides, ⅝ x 1⅜ x 8⁵⁄₁₆
2 drawer runners, ¾ x ¾ x 8⅞
1 top, ⅝ x 14 x 14
4 sides for tray, ½ x 1¼ x 13½

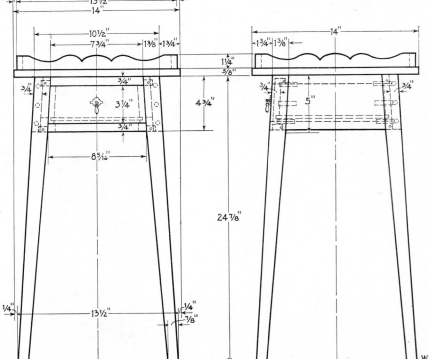

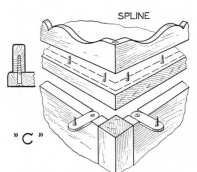

SPLINE

"C"

ASSEMBLY OF SCALLOP EDGE,
TABLE TOP & MITRES

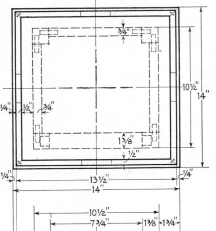

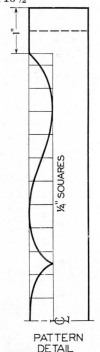

½" SQUARES

PATTERN
DETAIL

W.T.J.

PLATE 44

AREN'T YOU PLEASED WITH THE IDEA of having a small coffee table that's a miniature edition of your big trestle dining table? One day it occurred to the designer that you could build a big table or a little one from the same set of plans.

All you have to do is to scale the dimensions of the full-size design down to half, with just one exception—the thickness of the table top. The full-size tables measure six feet long by thirty-four inches wide; the small ones are therefore three feet long by seventeen inches wide.

Take your choice of two designs—the crossed-leg one shown on the next page or the one with straight supports shown on this page. Build your table of a good quality of soft white pine, thoroughly seasoned—no cracks, twists or warps. Your dealer will help you select boards which will have interesting matched grain.

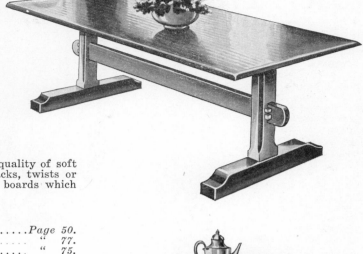

REFERENCE TO BASIC PROCESSES IN TEXT

Edge Shaping	Page	50.
Dowel Joints	"	77.
Gluing and Clamping	"	75.
Counter Boring and Plugging	"	73.
Mortise-and-Tenon Joints	"	84.
Stop Chamfer	"	51.
Use of Templates	"	52.
Cutting Curves and Scrolls	"	52.

MATERIAL:

2 posts, 3" x 4¾" x 27½"
2 feet, 4" x 4" x 28"
2 cleats, 3" x 4" x 28"
1 center rail, 1¾" x 5" x 63½"
1 top, 1⅜" x 34" x 72"

NOTE: For Coffee Table reduce all dimensions *one half* —excepting top which should be ¾" thick.

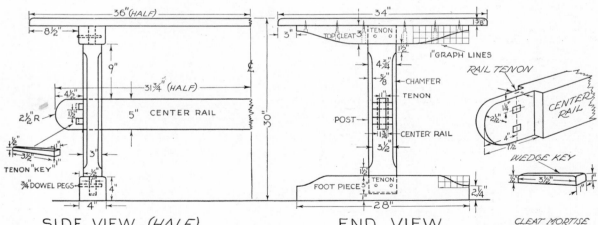

SIDE VIEW (HALF)   END VIEW

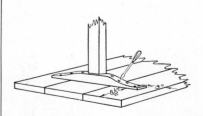

"I" Trestle Table

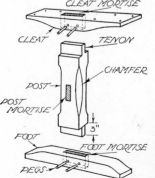

PLATE 45

"X" Trestle Table

REFERENCE TO BASIC PROCESSES IN TEXT

Use of Templates .... Page 52.
Rabbet Joints .... " 80.
Miter Joints .... " 82.
Mortise-and-Tenon Joints .... " 84.
Edge Rounding .... " 56.
Incised Cutting .... " 54.
Use of Expansive Bit .... " 52.

LIKE THE TABLES SHOWN ON THE PRECEDING PAGE, THE X-Trestle design is also of pure early American origin and can be made either full size or as a half dimension coffee table. You will be pleased with either example. The good, old-fashioned craft elements that go into this construction should recommend the job to many.

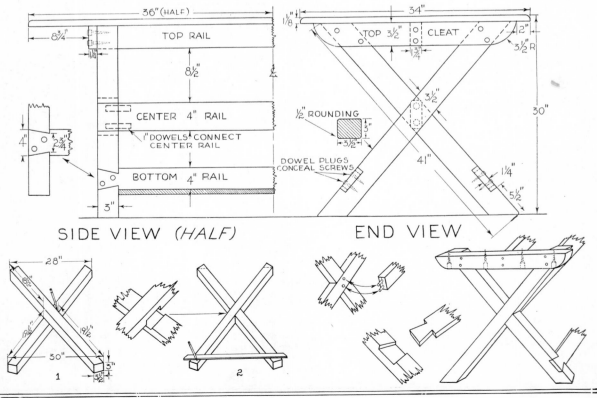

SIDE VIEW (HALF)   END VIEW

PLATE 46

Corner Cupboard

(Miniature or Full Size)

CAN YOU IMAGINE ANYTHING THAT WOULD MAKE A greater hit with your family than a pair of mother-and-daughter corner cabinets, one miniature, the other full size? Plans with two sets of dimensions make this possible. The small cabinet is 24 inches high; by increasing all the measurements (except thickness of back and sides) three times, you get a handsome room-size cupboard six feet high.

You'll find construction simplified because the cabinet is made in two separate units—the back assembly consisting of shelves, sides and back, and the front scrolled facing which is attached in one piece. Use plywood throughout for the miniature cabinet; clear or knotty pine for the full-size job. Line with wallpaper.

REFERENCE TO BASIC PROCESSES IN TEXT

Use of Templates ....Page 52.
Cutting Curves and Scrolls .... " 52.
Counter Boring and Plugging .... " 73.
Gluing and Clamping .... " 75.

MATERIAL:
  2 uprights, ¼" x 3⅜" x 24"
  1 head piece, ¼" x 2" x 9¼"
  1 base piece, ¼" x 1¼" x 7⅜"
  1 door, ¼" x 7⅜" x 8½"

Front Facing:
  1 top cleat, ¼" x 1¼" x 13"
  1 top molding strip, ⅜" x ¾" x 15¼" (shaped)
  1 base molding, ¼" x 1" x 15¼"

Counter strip, ¼" x ½" x 9½"

Back and Shelf Assembly:
  6 shelves, ¼" x 5⅛" x 13⅜"
  2 sides, ¼" x 7⅜" x 24"
  1 back, ¼" x 4" x 24"

NOTE: To make full size cabinet increase all dimensions three times—front of full size cabinet is 72" high and 42⅜" wide; lumber ¾" thick.

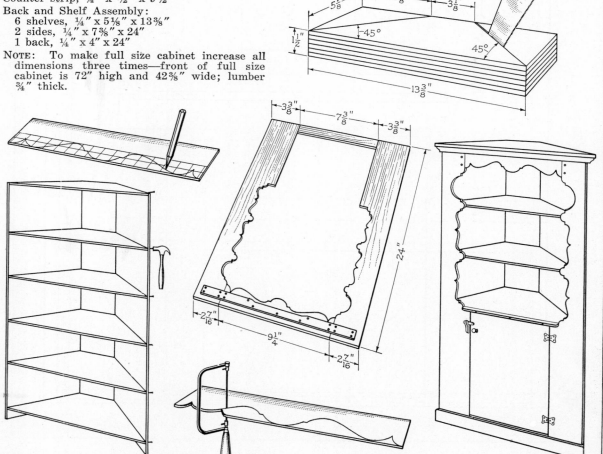

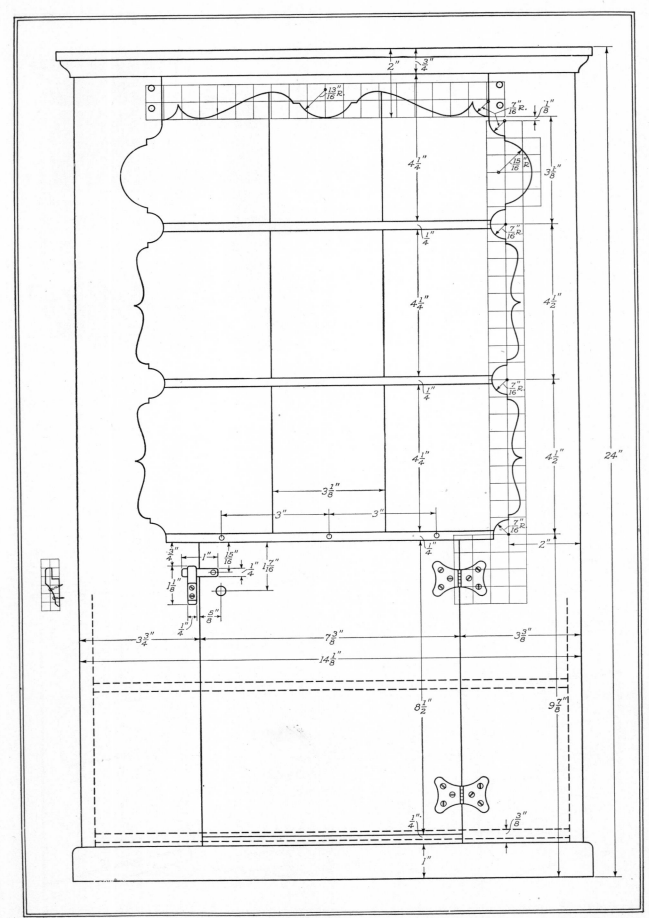

INDEX

PROJECTS